ATLAS OF WORLD CULTURES

ATLAS OF
WORLD CULTURES

A Geographical Guide to
Ethnographic Literature

DAVID H. PRICE

Published in Cooperation with the Human Relations Area Files, Inc.

SAGE PUBLICATIONS
The International Professional Publishers
Newbury Park   London   New Delhi

For information address:

 SAGE Publications, Inc.
2455 Teller Road
Newbury Park, California 91320

SAGE Publications Ltd.
6 Bonhill Street
London EC2A 4PU
United Kingdom

SAGE Publications India Pvt. Ltd.
M-32 Market
Greater Kailash I
New Delhi 110 048 India

Printed in the United States of America

Library of Congress Cataloging-in-Publication Data

Price, David H., 1960–
    Atlas of world cultures.
    "Published in cooperation with the Human Relations Area
Files, Inc."
    Bibliography: p.
    Includes index.
    1. Ethnic groups—Maps. 2. Ethnic groups—Bibliography.
3. Archaeology—Bibliography. 4. Archaeology—Maps.
5. Anthropo-geography—Bibliography. 6. Anthropo-geography—Maps.
I. Human Relations Area Files, inc. II. Title.
G1046.E1P7 1989   912'.13058   88-675683
ISBN 0-8039-3240-5 (cloth)
ISBN 0-8039-4075-0 (paper)

THIRD PRINTING, 1990

CONTENTS

List of Maps

INTRODUCTION

This atlas is designed to direct cross-cultural researchers to key ethnographic works regarding a geographical region of interest, and to help locate groups commonly discussed in the ethnographic literature. This is not a reference book containing information on all known cultures of the world. It is not a definitive sourcebook for settling boundary disputes between cultural groups. It *is* a geographical guide to ethnographic books, articles, reports, archival materials, maps and atlases, and other materials of use to anthropologists. This is the first comprehensive atlas of world cultures that also provides bibliographic background materials so the user can access information about the behavior, habits, beliefs, customs, population size, and changes through time of different cultures around the world.

Past ethnographic atlases either have only covered specific world regions or have only shown the locations of groups without giving any information on the era or habits of the groups represented. Atlases such as the Soviet Institut Etnografii Imeni's *Atlas Narodov Mirea* (540/1102) or Robert Spencer's *Ethno-Atlas* (1035) fall short of their potential usefulness because they fail to direct the user to (a) any body of data that might indicate such basic data as when these groups occupied a given area or (b) to pertinent ethnographies.

TIME

The variable of time has been the greatest problem to overcome in the construction of the atlas. Rather than mapping the locations of all groups represented in the atlas at a single point in time, the atlas locates the region of a cultural group at a period when a specific reference to it was made in the ethnographic literature, and provides a bibliographic reference to the citation. This has been done simply because it would have been impossible to undertake such a project in any other way. If one were to construct a series of maps showing the range and distribution of groups in (for example) East Africa during the last 100 to 200 years, the number of changes occurring in small—10- to 15-year periods—is staggering. To accurately show the dynamic interactions between indigenous groups during this 200-year period would require the construction of 10 to 15 maps for this small region alone. In the earliest drafts of the atlas, maps were created that illustrated some aspects of time-depth for the cultural groups. It became evident very quickly that such an undertaking could easily require thousands of maps. A choice had to be made between locating a few cultural groups' movements on different maps in different time periods, or locating groups on a single map. Having decided on the latter, I still had to resolve the problem of whether the maps should all show the position of groups during a single time period (arbitrarily chosen), or whether the maps would represent groups of different time periods all on the same series of maps. The benefit of the first option is historical consistency but this does not seem as valuable as the second option's ability to direct readers to the widest body of literature. The decision to represent each culture frozen at a single point in space and time was made primarily because I believe the usefulness of this book lies in assisting scholars in locating the groups found throughout the "classic" works of anthropology.

Instead of making a series of maps or mapping, for example, all of Africa as it was in 1830, 1890, 1940, or 1960, I have shown the locations of *specific* groups at *specific* (and different) periods of time. Thus the Nuer and Dinka are shown in the locations that they occupied during Evans-Pritchard's classic study published in 1940 (295). The Tiv are located in the region they occupied in the Bohannans' 1953 (94) study, and the Tallensi are shown in the region that they occupied when Fortes did his 1949 study (349).

The atlas does not purport to show the current locations of the cultural groups shown on the maps. The atlas instead locates the positions of various groups referred to in the sources listed in the bibliography. Because this book is designed with the anthropological reader in mind, certain general decisions concerning the time periods used in each map have been made. The maps of North America are all biased toward the locations of Native American groups before the beginning of the twentieth century. These maps show the locations of well-known indigenous American groups instead of the more current ethnic mosaic of modern Canada, the United States, and Mexico. Most of the locations on the Asian and European maps indicate various nationalities and ethnic groups. Many of the Australian Aboriginal groups shown on maps 29 and 30 no longer exist; others have been moved onto modern reservations, their homelands being the sites of modern cities.

This bias toward showing the traditional rather than modern locations of many of the world's ethnographic groups is also shown in the sources selected for the atlas. Though the bibliography is a mixture of classic and modern studies, I have been biased toward selecting classic works so that users of the atlas can easily access standard works relating to the culture in question.

"CULTURAL" AND "ETHNIC" GROUPS

The "cultural" or "ethnic" groups identified in the atlas are simply some of the groups that have been identified in the extant body of ethnographic data. The atlas does not represent a complete listing of all known ethnographic groups. It is a selected sample taken from some of the available written ethnographic records. This atlas dredges through the problems of "ethnicity" (37), "tribe" (363/478), "cultunit" (816), and "ethnolinguistic units" (428/429) by leaving the decision of the specific units of classification to the authors of the works cited in the bibliography. This has not made the problem disappear, but has only delayed the coping with the problem until the atlas user has need of such specific distinctions. This has been done so that a wide variety of needs may be served by the atlas. Many of the citations refer to groups that are linguistically distinct from surrounding groups, while other citations indicate nonlinguistic differences. The reader must refer to the cited work to determine what criteria have been used in distinguishing particular groups.

Not all groups represented in the atlas necessarily refer to themselves by the names used in the index. The names used in the atlas are the names for groups that were used by the anthropologists or ethnographers who studied the groups. Morton Fried recognized this as a problem of such severity that he concluded there is "little or no evidence showing that any particular 'tribal' name is actually accepted as such by a reasonable portion of those to whom it is applied" (364:32). Because there is such general discrepancy between the names used by a given people for themselves and the names used by others, the problems involved in compiling the atlas would have been compounded if only the names most frequently used by groups themselves were used. In North America alone, the majority of well-known "Tribal Indian" names are distinct from the names these groups use to identify themselves. I question the usefulness in listing such commonly known Native American groups as the Navajo, Ojibwa, Crow, and Mohawk as Tin-neh (1055), Anishinabe (654), Absaroke (654), and Kaniengehaga (654), respectively, as they referred to themselves in their native languages. Other well-known groups include the Nath (Nuer) (295), Zhun/twasi (!Kung) (1002), and Mowach'aht (Nooka) (1105). Had the majority of these names been included in the index as "... see also," the length of the index would have more than doubled, and the production costs would have been prohibitive.

The three most common types of names for the world's cultures can be classified into three typological groups: geographical, Homo exclusive, or pejorative. The name by which a given group is known is often a function of the nature of their contacts with the outside world. The groups that explorers and colonialists first used as guides and interpreters played a large role in determining what became the commonly used names of groups. Even the usage of the term "ethnic" in English originally had the pejorative connotations of "heathen" or "pagan" (252:1). Common translations of "pejorative" cultural group names are "enemy," "cannibal," "non-human," and various derivations on excremental themes. Needless to say, groups known by such pejorative titles did not refer to themselves by such names. These are the names used by other groups at their expense. One can easily imagine missionaries, anthropologists, or explorers trudging through the bush asking a native translator the name of the people living in the next valley, and getting an answer that would translate in English to "enemy."

It would seem that the most common name that groups use for themselves translates simply to "the people." Thus a single group can be known by dozens of names by dozens of outsiders, yet simply refer to itself by the single name of "the people" or the "human beings."

To demonstrate the nature of the problem of choosing which name a group is known by, listed below are only a few examples of different names that some well-known Native American groups are known by:

Common	Trans.	Name Used By Group	Trans.	Cite
Mohawk	"Man Eater"	Kaniengehaga	"People of the Place of Flint"	(654:282)
Apache	"Enemy"	Dine	"the People"	(654:38)
Comanche	"Enemy"	Numinu	"the People"	(654:123)
Dakota	"Enemy"	Oceti Sakowin	"7 council fires"	(654:146)
Flathead	"Flathead"	Se'lic	"the People"	(654:160)
Eskimo	"Flesh Eaters"	Innuit	"the People"	(1036)
Winnebago	"People of Dirty Water"	Hotcangara	"People of Real Speech"	(654:517)
Huron	"Unkept"	Wendat	"Islanders"	(654:167)
Inkalit	"Hair full of Lice"	Innuit	"the People"	(1234:105)
Omaha	"Upstream People"			(787:113)
Cayuse	"People of the Stones"			(654:83)
Nootsack	"Mountain People"	(1092:430)		
Potawatomi	"People of the Place of Fire"	Weshnabek	"the People"	(654:375)
Modoc	"Southerners"	Moklaks	"the People"	(654:277)
Klikitat	"People from Beyond"	Qwulh-hwai-pum	"Prairie People"	(654:226)
Yurok	"Down River People"	Olekwo'l	"Persons"	(654:542)
Miami	"People of the Peninsula"			(654:268)
Inkalit	"People of One Language"			(1234:105)

Common	Trans.	Name Used By Group	Trans.	Cite
Innuit	"People"			(1036)
Haida	"People"			(1092)
Illinois	"People"			(654:191)
Miwok	"People"			(1092:502)
Yokuts	"People"			(1092:523)

This is simply a small sample from the New World; it is easy to imagine how complex this problem becomes when the rest of the world is taken into consideration. There are, of course, many other types of names, ranging from total misunderstandings to indigenous peoples simply answering foreigners with joke answers.

HOW TO USE THE ATLAS

The atlas has bibliographical and geographical information on over 3,500 cultural groups around the world. This information is found in the 40 maps, index, and bibliography. The atlas has three sections: Maps with indexes, Bibliography, and Index by Culture. Each of the maps contains an independent series of numbers from 1 to N, each number represents a cultural group. The atlas may be used in two different ways: cultural groups may be found on maps by finding the given culture in the "Index by Culture" at the back of the atlas, or by looking at an individual map and its index.

The atlas's "Index by Culture" lists all cultural groups represented in the atlas in alphabetical order, and is designed to provide the user with information beyond the mere locality of the group in question. The Index contains the following columns of information: *Cite 1 & Cite 2*: These numbers represent bibliographic entries that provide information on the source materials used to map the cultural group. Citations for the atlas are organized in the bibliography in alphabetical order, with corresponding identification numbers running from 1 to 1237. The numbers that appear in this column correspond to the identification numbers found in the bibliography. *Culture*: This column indicates the name of the cultural group. *Map*: This column indicates the map on which the group is located in the atlas. *No.*: This column indicates the number that is used to identify the cultural group on the specific map referred to in the "Map" column. Most of the numbers on each of the maps are clustered in a progressive numerical order and in most instances a number can be found on a map by scanning for numerically close numbers until the desired number is found. *HRAF*: This column provides the Human Relations Area File code for applicable cultural groups (799). *Murdock's Atlas*: This column indicates whether the group is represented in Murdock's *Ethnographic Atlas* (797/798/33), and provides the identification codes that Murdock used. Below is an example taken from the atlas's "Index by Culture."

Cite 1	Cite 2	Culture	Map	No.	HRAF	Murdock's Atlas
630	581	Kikuyu	21	177	FL10	Ad4

This example provides the following information about the Kikuyu: They are located on map 21 as number 177, background information may be found about them in citations 630 (Lambert, 1956) and 581 (Kenyatta, 1961), the Human Relations Area File has listed them as FL10, and Murdock's Ethnographic Atlas assigned them the code Ad4.

Each map has an index on its preceding facing page. This index lists the cultural groups found on a given map in numerical order so that the user can explore geographical regions without a knowledge of any of the groups' names. This index does not provide any information beyond the map, number and name of group in question. Additional information can be found in the atlas's "Index by Culture."

I have drawn all the maps included in this volume. The maps were intended to assist in the navigation of libraries rather than the navigation of South American rivers or African coastlines. The cartographic accuracy is not exact, but the utility of geographically representing the locations of these cultural groups is served.

ACKNOWLEDGMENTS

I am indebted to Mel Ember and the Human Relations Area File for providing me with the expert services of Timothy O'Leary. Tim did the laborious job of checking the bibliography, map locations, spellings, and codes used. His knowledge of ethnography and ethnographic literature saved the atlas from numerous errors and omissions that crept into the manuscript and maps.

Among the many people who assisted me in the production of the atlas are Mitch Allen, Russ Bernard, Paul Goldsmith, Dan Henk, Ray Jones, Bob Lawless, Daniel McGee, James McKay, Chris McCarty, Mark Papworth, Dana Phillips-McGee, Midge Miller Price, Daniel Reboussin, and Charles Wagley. I am especially grateful to Marvin Harris, who has offered a great deal of encouragement and support, and who allowed me to depose him from his own office so that I might have ample space to spread out thousands of maps and books.

MAPS

Map 1. Circumpolar North

Culture	Number	Culture	Number
Nanoptaim	1	Imaklimuit	66
Pamiagikuk	2	Chukchi	67
Lugsiatsiak	3	Anadyr Eskimo	68
Kangerd	4	Koyukon	69
Anarkat	5	Koyukon	70
Puisortok	6	Kaviagmut	71
Tingamitmiut	7	Kataligamut	72
Ammassalimiut	8	Tanana	73
Julianehaab	9	Ingalik	74
Arsuk	10	Nabesna	75
Ameralik	11	Tanaina	76
Godthiaab	12	Atna	77
Pisigsarfik	13	Chugach	78
Sukkertoppen	14	Agmiut	79
Kangamiut	15	Nahane	80
Holsteins Borg	16	Tutchone	81
Agto	17	Kenai	82
Kangatsiak	18	Eyak	83
Egedesminde	19	Yakutat	84
Jacobshavn	20	Dry Bay	85
Disko	21	Kaska	86
Karajak	22	Kluane	87
Umanak	23	Tareumiut	88
Igidlorssuit	24	Nunatagmiut	89
Poven	25	Unaligmut	90
Upernavik	26	Hare	91
Tasiusak	27	Bear Lake	92
Nugsuak	28	Copper Eskimo	93
Ita Eskimo	29	Lamoot, Eastern	94
Saumingmiut	30	Koryak	95
Padlimiut	31	Chuvanzy	96
Akudnirmiut	32	Koryak	97
Tununirmiut	33	Even-Lamoot	98
Tununirusirmiut	34	Lamoot, Western	99
Arviquurmiut	35	Tungus	100
Netsilik	36	Yokaghir	101
Iglulikmiut	37	Dolgan	102
Kingnaitmiut	38	Yakut	103
Qinguamuit	39	Yesey	104
Killinermiut	40	Evens	105
Kilusiktogmiut	41	Kangalas	106
Asiagmiut	42	Evenki	107
Nagyuktogmiut	43	Tavgi Yakut	108
Puiplirmiut	44	Vadeyev Nganasans	109
Haneragmiut	45	Nganasans	110
Pingangnaktogmiut	46	Samoyed	111
Kogluktogmiut	47	Selkup	112
Noahonirmiut	48	Nenets	113
Akulliakatagimut	49	Yuraks	114
Kanghiryuarmiut	50	Nentsi	115
Kanghiryuatjiagmiut	51	Nentz	116
Wallirmiut	52	Saami	117
Wallirmiut	53	Lapps	118
Kawchottine	54	Komi	119
Kikitarmiut	55	Karelian Izhars	120
Kutchin	56		
Han	57		
Tutchone	58		
Kukparungmiut	59		
Tikeramiut	60		
Malemiut	61		
Kinugumint	62		
Kaviagmut	63		
Yuit	64		
Inguklimiut	65		

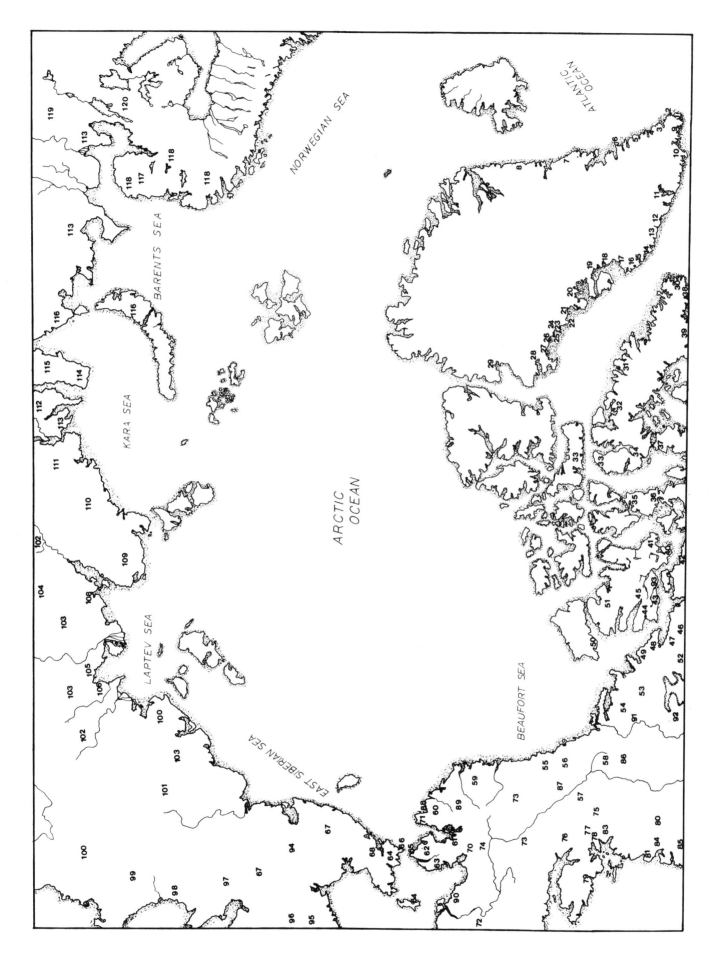

15

Map 2. North America, Northeast

Culture	Number	Culture	Number
Tutelo	1	Nunenumiut	65
Powhatan	2	Airitumiut	66
Nanticoke	3	Netcetumiut	67
Montauk	4	Puthlavamiut	68
Metoac	4	Beothuk	69
Susquehana	5	Pequot	70
Delaware	6		
Erie	7		
Wenrohronon	8		
Wappinger	9		
Niantic	10		
Narraganset	11		
Wampanoag	12		
Massachuset	13		
Nipmuc	14		
Nauset	15		
Iroquois	16		
Seneca	17		
Cayuga	18		
Onondaga	19		
Oneida	20		
Mohawk	21		
Algonkin	22		
Pennacook	23		
Mahican	24		
Abnaki	25		
Penobscot	26		
Malecite	27		
Micmac	28		
Montagnais	29		
Attikamek	30		
Montagnais	31		
Nontagnais	32		
Lake St. John	33		
Chicoutimi	34		
Tadoussac	35		
Escoumains	36		
Bersimis	37		
Papinachos	38		
Oumamiouek	39		
Godbout	40		
Ouchestigouek	41		
Sept-Iles	42		
Shelter Bay	43		
St. Marguerite	44		
Moisie	45		
Mingan	46		
Naskapi	47		
Natashquan	48		
Romaine	49		
St. Augustin	50		
Northwest River	51		
Menihek Lakes	52		
Petitsikapau	53		
Michikamau	54		
Davis Inlet	55		
Cree, Barren Ground	56		
Chimo	57		
Koksoakmiut	58		
Lukshuamiut	59		
Kanithlua	60		
Killtinhunmiut	61		
Qaumauangmiut	62		
Chuckbukmiut	63		
Konith-Lushuamiut	64		

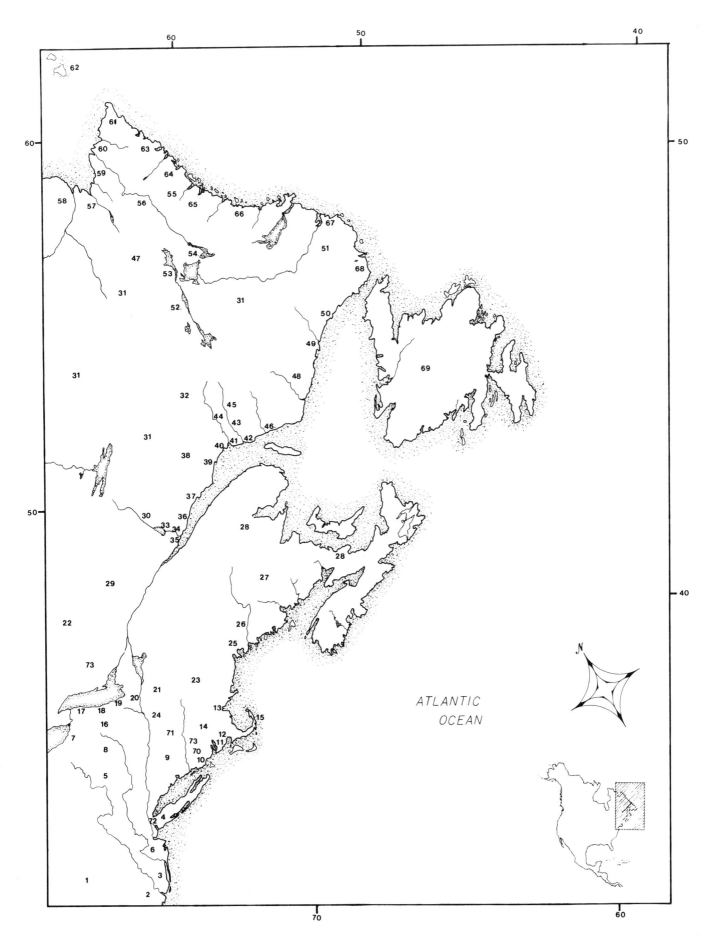

ATLANTIC
OCEAN

17

Map 3. North America, Central North

Culture	Number
Erie	1
Tiononati	2
Huron	3
Ottawa	4
Potawatomi	5
Miami	6
Illinois	7
Kickapoo	8
Winnebago	9
Fox	10
Sauk	11
Menomini	12
Noquet	13
Algonkin	14
Chippewa	15
Cree, Swampy	16
Assiniboin	17
Dakota	18
Iowa	19
Oto	20
Dakota, Santee	21
Omaha	22
Pawnee	23
Ponca	24
Omaha	25
Cheyenne	26
Dakota, Teton	27
Arikara	28
Mandan	29
Hidatsa	30
Crow	31
Arapaho	32
Saulteaux	33
Atsina	34
Cree, Rocky	35
Cree	36
Ahiariut	37
Ojibwa	38
Cree, Barren Ground	39
Pallirmiut	40
Haningayogmiut	41
Caribou Eskimo	42
Harvaqtormiut	43
Tatsanuttine	44
Cree, Springwoods	45
Arviligyuarmiut	46
Qaernermiut	47
Aivillirmiut	48
Netsilik	49
Sagdlirmiut	50
Akuliarmiut	51
Qaumauangmiut	52
Nuvugmiut	53
Tarramiut	54
Itivimiut	55
Kigiktagmiut	56

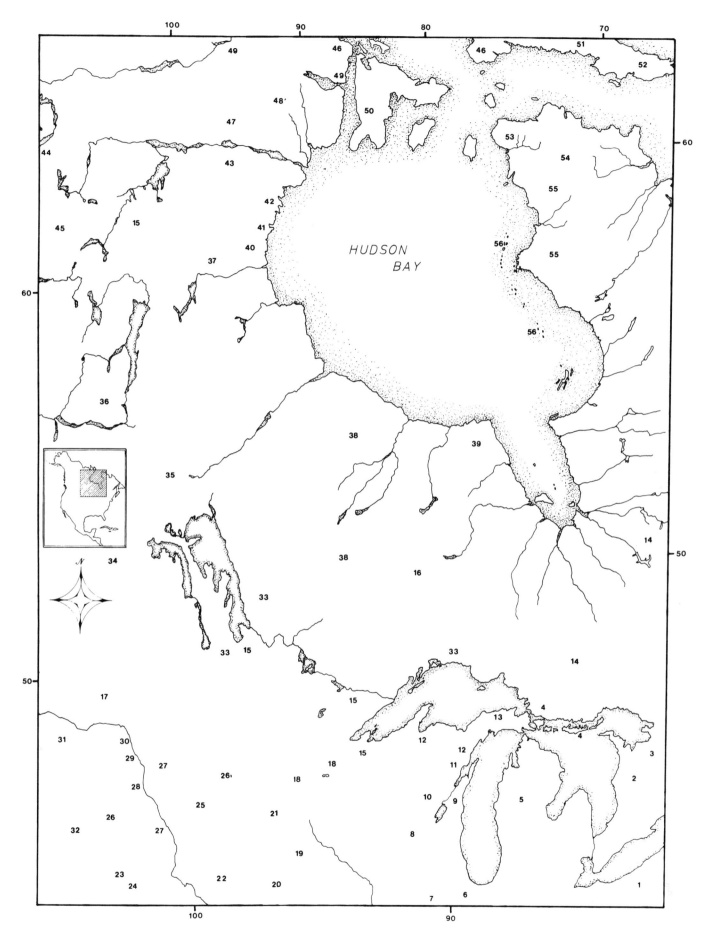

HUDSON
BAY

N

19

Map 4. North America, Northwest

Culture	Number	Culture	Number	Culture	Number
Puntash	0	Chehalis	65	Yellowknife	132
Tolowa	1	Chinook	66	Dogrib	133
Chetco	2	Wynoochee	67	Bear Lake	134
Tututni	3	Humptulips	68	Etchaottine	135
Coquille	4	Copalis	69	Etchaottine	136
Coos	5	Satsup	70	Teglin	137
Umpqua	6	Twana	71	Chilkat	138
Siuslaw	7	Quinault	72	Tagish	139
Long Tom Creek	8	Queets	73	Yakutat	140
Alsea	9	Hoh	74	Ahtna	141
Yaquina	10	Quileute	75	Tutchone	142
Stiletz	11	Ozette	76	Nabesna	143
Tillamook	12	Makah	77		
Clatsop	13	Klallam	78		
Kathlamet	14	Chimakum	79		
Clatskanie	15	Nisqually	80		
Tualatin	16	Puyallup	81		
Yamhill	17	Duwamish	82		
Skilloot	18	Snohomish	83		
Multnomah	19	Skokomish	84		
Pudding River	20	Skagit	85		
Lakmiut	21	Samish	86		
Cascade	22	Nootsak	87		
Clackamas	23	Lummi	88		
Molalla	24	Stalo	89		
Santiam	25	Squamish	90		
Calapuya	26	Seechelt	91		
Yoncalla	27	Lillooet	92		
Tenino	28	Salish	93		
Takelma	29	Songish	94		
Shasta	30	Cowichan	95		
Klamath	31	Nanaimo	96		
Modoc	32	Puntlatsh	97		
Paiute, Northern	33	Comox	98		
Snake	34	Nootka	99		
Bannock	35	Kwakiutl	100		
Hood River	36	Shuswap	101		
Wasco	37	Sarsi	102		
Umatilla	38	Chilcotin	103		
Cayuse	39	Carrier	104		
Nez Perce	40	Bellacoola	105		
Walla Walla	41	Bellabella	106		
Klikitat	42	Tsattine	107		
Shoshoni	43	Beaver	108		
Kiowa	44	Tsimshian	109		
Apache, Kiowa	45	Haida	110		
Crow	46	Kaigani	111		
Assiniboin	47	Niska	112		
Pend d'Oreilles	48	Tongass	113		
Kutenai	49	Tsetsaut	114		
Siksika	50	Stikine	115		
Blackfoot	51	Sekani	116		
Flathead	52	Henya	117		
Kalispel	53	Angoon	118		
Palouse	54	Tlingit	119		
Wanapam	55	Sitka	120		
Spokane	56	Hoonah	123		
Lake Indians	57	Taku	124		
Colville	58	Auk	125		
Okanogan	59	Tahltan	126		
Sanpoil	60	Atlin	127		
Wenatchee	61	Tlingit, Island	128		
Yakima	62	Nahane	129		
Cowlitz	63	Slave	130		
Kwalhiokwa	64	Chipewyan	131		

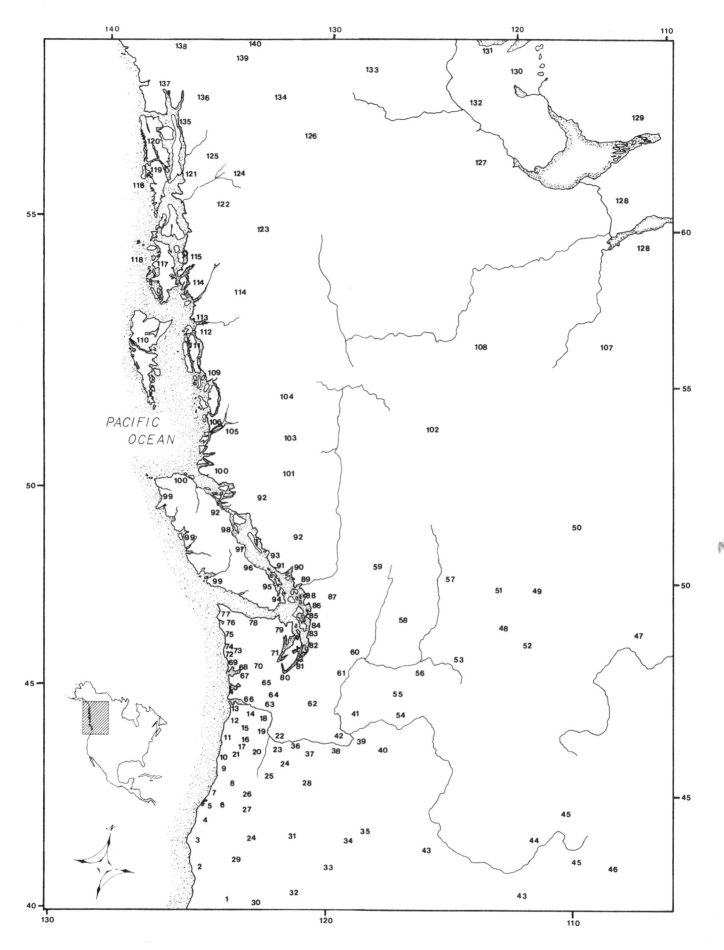

PACIFIC
OCEAN

21

Map 5. North America, Western

Culture	Number	Culture	Number
Seri	1	Pomo	66
Pima, Lower	2	Wailaki	67
Papago	3	Nisenan	68
Qahatika	4	Kato	69
Yavapai	5	Lassik	70
Cocopa	6	Nomlaki	71
Maricopa	7	Konkow	72
Pima	8	Yuki	73
Quechan	9	Wintu	74
Halyikwamai	10	Mattole	75
Cochimi	11	Sinkyone	76
Kohuana	12	Yana	77
Tipai	13	Atsugewi	78
Diegueno	14	Achomawi	79
Kamia	15	Hupa, East	80
Yuma	16	Shasta	81
Luiseno	17	Chimariko	82
Cupeno	18	Hupa	83
Cahuilla	19	Nongatl	84
Serrano	20	Sinkyone	85
Halchidhoma	21	Wiyot	86
Yauapai	22	Chilula	87
Apache, Western	23	Whilkut	88
Havasupai	24	Yurok	89
Zuni	25	Tolowa	90
Navajo	26	Karok	91
Hopi	27	Modoc	92
Paiute, Southern	28		
Walapai	29		
Mohave	30		
Kawaiisu	31		
Gabrielino	32		
Tataviam	33		
Kitanemuk	34		
Shoshoni	35		
Chumash	36		
Salinan	37		
Utechem	38		
Paiute, Owens Valley	39		
Kawaiisu	40		
Yokuts	41		
Esselen	42		
Costano	43		
Tubatulabal	44		
Mono	45		
Monache	46		
Kern	47		
Numic	48		
Pahvant	49		
Paiute, Northern	50		
Timparanutrets	51		
Gosiute	52		
Ute	53		
Washo	54		
Uintah	55		
Ute, Weber	56		
Bannock	57		
Shoshoni	58		
Shoshoni, Western	59		
Maidu	60		
Paiute, Northern	61		
Miwok, Central	62		
Patwin	63		
Wappo	64		
Miwok, Coastal	65		

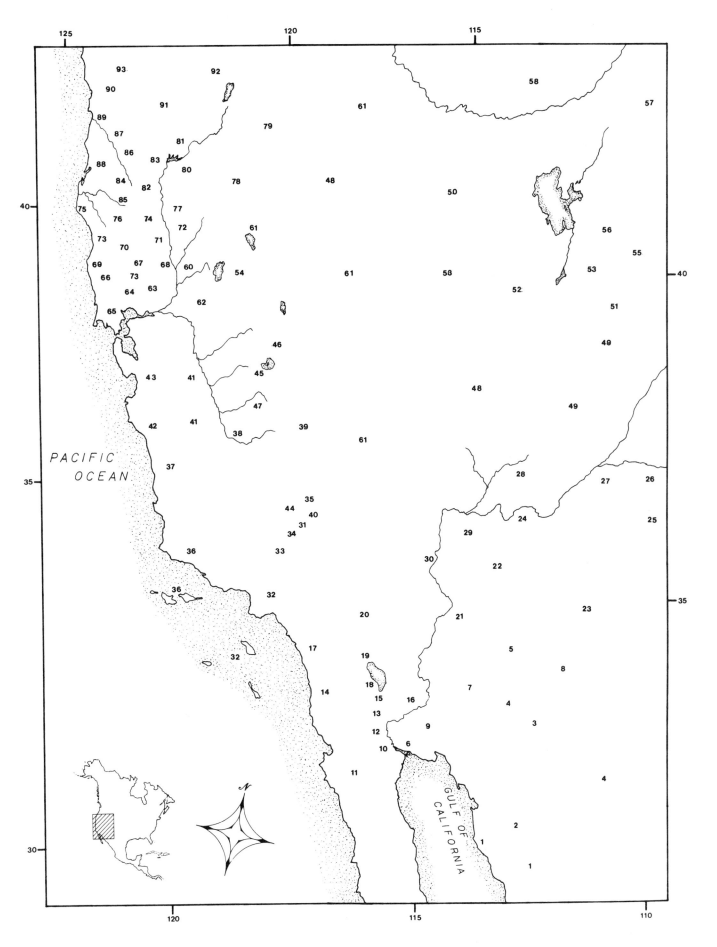

PACIFIC
OCEAN

GULF OF CALIFORNIA

23

Map 6. North America, Central

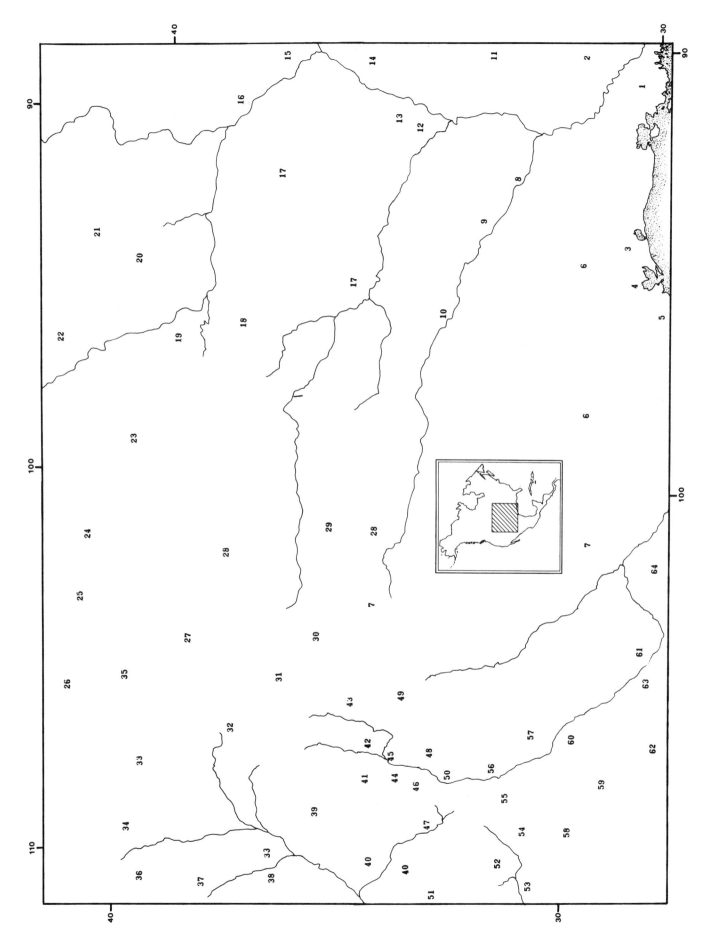

25

Map 7. North America, Eastern

Culture	Number	Culture	Number
Atakapa	1	Guaniguanico	65
Chitimacha	2	Hanamana	65
Biloxi	3	Havana	65
Natchez	4	Macorize	65
Chakchiuma	5	Marien	65
Quapaw	6	Barbacoa	66
Chickasaw	7	Guamahaya	66
Choctaw	8	Jagua	66
Kaskinampo	9	Sabaneque	66
Shawnee	10	Bani	67
Michigamea	11	Boyaca	67
Mosopelea	12	Cayaguayo	67
Moneton	13	Cubanacan	67
Yuchi	14	Guaimaro	67
Tuskegee	15	Ornoray	67
Koasati	16	Aguacadibe	68
Tali	17	Bayamo	68
Muskogee	18	Bayaquitiri	68
Alabama	19	Marisi	68
Mobile	20	Maguan	68
Pensacola	21	Cuciba	68
Muklasa	22	Huereo	69
Creek	23	Ameyao	69
Cherokee	24	Yaguabo	69
Tutelo	25	Ciboney	70
Delaware	26	Bainoa	70
Nanticoke	27	Cahibo	71
Conoy	28	Caizcimu	71
Powhatan	29	Hubabo	71
Weapemeoc	30	Maguana	71
Moratuc	31	Mayaguez	72
Roanoke	32	Utuado	72
Pomouik	33	Caribs	73
Secotan	34	Arawak	74
Neusiok	35	Taino	75
Cape Fear Indians	36	Camaguey	76
Pedee	37		
Waccamaw	38		
Cusabo	39		
Hitchiti	40		
Tamathli	41		
Guale	42		
Yamasee	43		
Tacatacura	44		
Saturiwa	45		
Chatot	46		
Apalachee	47		
Osochi	48		
Yustaga	49		
Potano	50		
Utina	51		
Fresh Water Indians	52		
Acuera	53		
Timucua	54		
Ocale	55		
Ais	56		
Tocobaga	57		
Mococo	58		
Pohoy	59		
Jeaga	60		
Tekesta	61		
Seminole	62		
Calusa	62		
Lucayans	63		
Guanachahibe	64		

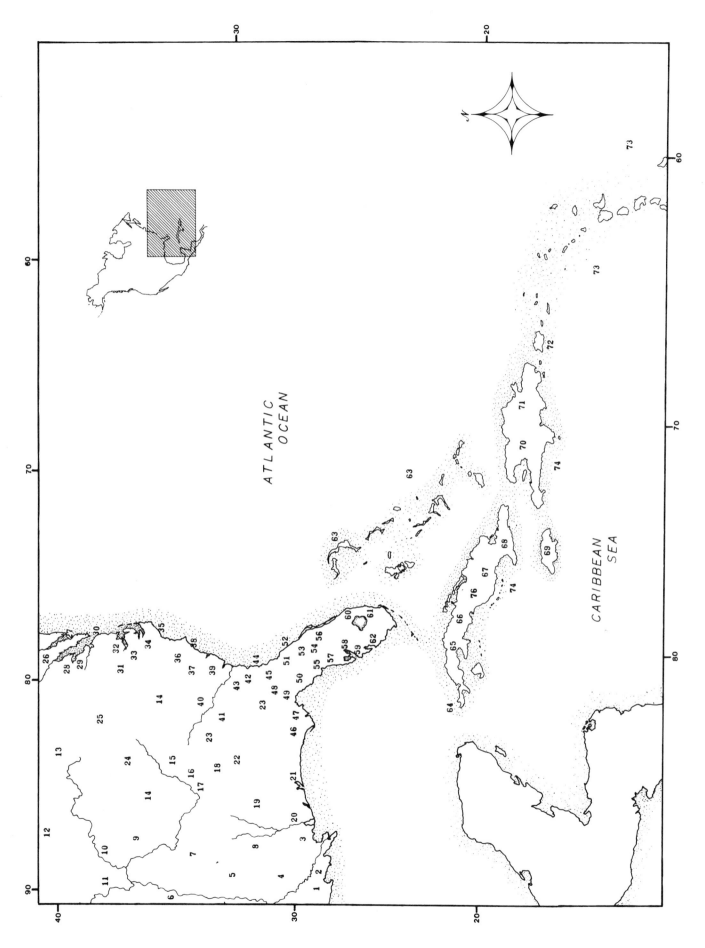

Map 8. North America, Southern

Culture	Number	Culture	Number
Boruca	1	Tarahumara	63
Guaymi	2	Salineros-Cabezas	64
Guetare	3	Concho	65
Quero	4	Apache, Mescalero	66
Voto	5	Jumanos	67
Orotina	6	Suma	68
Rama	7	Pima, Lower	69
Ulua	8	Yaqui	70
Niquiran	9	Pericu	71
Diria	10	Waicuri	72
Yosko	11	Cochimi	73
Matagalpa	12	Seri	74
Sumo	13	Pima	75
Tawahka	14	Eudeve	76
Wanki	15	Opata	77
Cabo	16	Jova	78
Miskito	17	Karankawa	79
Paya	18	Coahuiltecan	80
Kamsa	19	Tonkawa	81
Lenca	19		
Mam	20		
Jicaque	21		
Ulva	22		
Pipil	23		
Maya	24		
Chol	25		
Tzotzil	26		
Tzeltal	27		
Mixe	28		
Chontal	29		
Zoque	30		
Huave	31		
Zapotec	32		
Chatino	33		
Nahuatl	34		
Popoluca	35		
Totonac	36		
Mixtec	37		
Tlapaneco	38		
Azteca	39		
Mextitlaneca	40		
Tepecano	41		
Otomi	42		
Tamaulipeco	43		
Janambre	44		
Pame	45		
Guamar	46		
Cuauhcomeca	47		
Tarascan	48		
Cazcan	49		
Cora	50		
Zacatec	51		
Tepehuanes	52		
Tarahumara	52		
Guachichile	53		
Tobosos	54		
Lagunero	55		
Guayaki	55		
Concho	56		
Xixime	57		
Acaxee	58		
Guasave	59		
Mayo	60		
Tubar	61		
Guarijio	62		

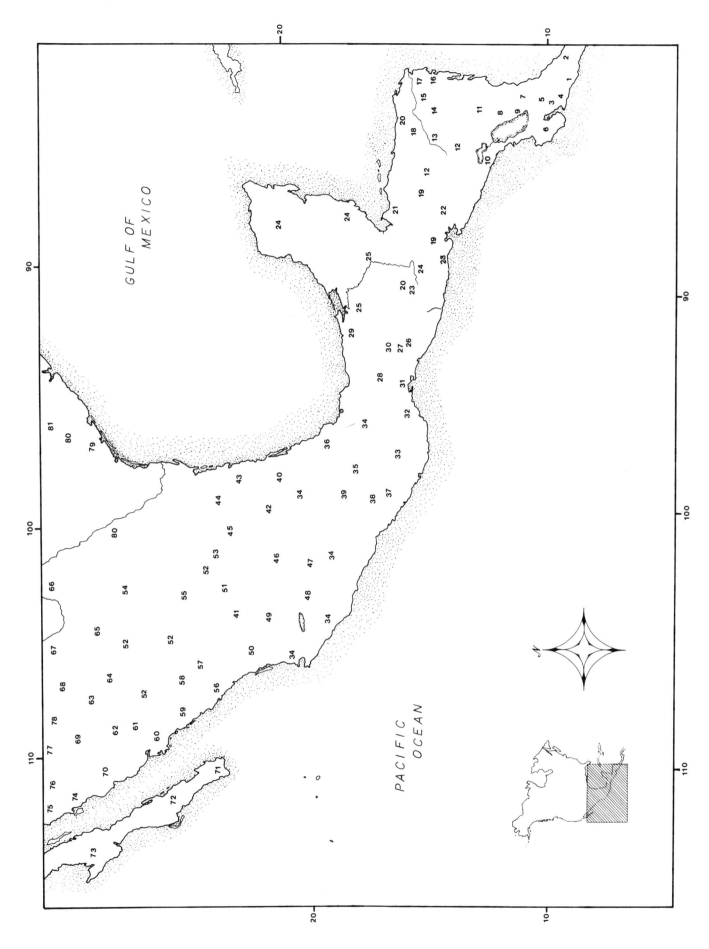

GULF OF MEXICO

PACIFIC OCEAN

29

Map 9. South America, Northwest

Culture	Number	Culture	Number	Culture	Number
Voto	1	Zaparo	66	Guamontey	131
Orotina	2	Boro	67	Jirajara	132
Guetare	3	Witoto	68	Mariusa	133
Boruca	4	Carijona	69	Tacarigua	134
Guaymi	5	Bara	70	Tamanaco	135
Coiba	6	Yagua	71	Saliva	136
Paparo	7	Coto	72	Mayop	137
Tortado	8	Iquito	73	Maco	138
Cuna	9	Yameo	74	Panare	139
Choco	10	Cocamilla	75	Taparito	140
Chibcha	11	Cocama	76	Piaroa	141
Pancenu	12	Mayoruna	77	Tuirimnainai	142
Tairona	13	Omagua	78	Oaycas	143
Cagaba	14	Tikuna	79	Guarequena	144
Guanebucan	15	Wairacu	80	Averiano	145
Caquetio	16	Katukina	81	Yawani	146
Goajiro	17	Kueretu	82	Uaka	147
Yuko	18	Kokama	83	Haue	148
Bari	19	Yuri	84	Schamatairi	149
Kunaguasaya	20	Canamari	85	Schiriana	150
Chibcha	21	Catawishi	86	Uana	151
Mompox	22	Marawa	87	Teque	152
Yemici	23	Yamadi	88	Caraca	153
Aburra	24	Culino	89	Cumanagoto	154
Pantagoro	25	Catukuina	90	Palenque	155
Pozo	26	Catawisi	91	Karina	156
Guamhibo	27	Soliman	92	Warao	157
Panche	28	Mura	93	Caribs	158
Quindio	29	Mundurucu	94	Cumana	159
Quimbaya	30	Maue	95	Akawai	160
Pijao	31	Arauaki	96	Arinagoto	161
Paez	32	Caripuna	97	Arecuna	162
Manipos	33	Manao	98	Patamona	163
Choque	34	Macu	99	Xaruma	164
Guanacoa	35	Ibenama	100	Taulipang	165
Kitsua	36	Aizuare	101	Purigoto	166
Barbacoan	37	Jauapery	102	Makusi	167
Sindagua	38	Waimiri-Atroari	103		
Popayanense	39	Pauishana	104		
Quillacinga	40	Paraitiry	105		
Pasto	41	Paushiana	106		
Cara	42	Wayumara	107		
Cayapa	43	Carahyaby	108		
Yumbo	44	Oremano	109		
Panzaleo	45	Yanomamo	110		
Puruha	46	Bare	111		
Colorado	47	Baniwa	112		
Esmeralda	48	Wakuenai	113		
Manta	49	Ipeka	114		
Huancavilca	50	Araraibos	115		
Canari	51	Cabre	116		
Tumbez	52	Tariana	117		
Palta	53	Uanan	118		
Aguaruna	54	Desana	119		
Tatuyo	55	Wariperidakena	120		
Candoshi	56	Achagua	121		
Cubeo	57	Puinave	122		
Huambisa	58	Guaipuave	123		
Achuara	59	Ouiba	124		
Jivaro	60	Guahibo	125		
Andoa	61	Piapoco	126		
Neva	62	Yaruro	127		
Waorami	63	Otomac	128		
Siona-Secoya	64	Timote	129		
Encabellado	65	Tosto	130		

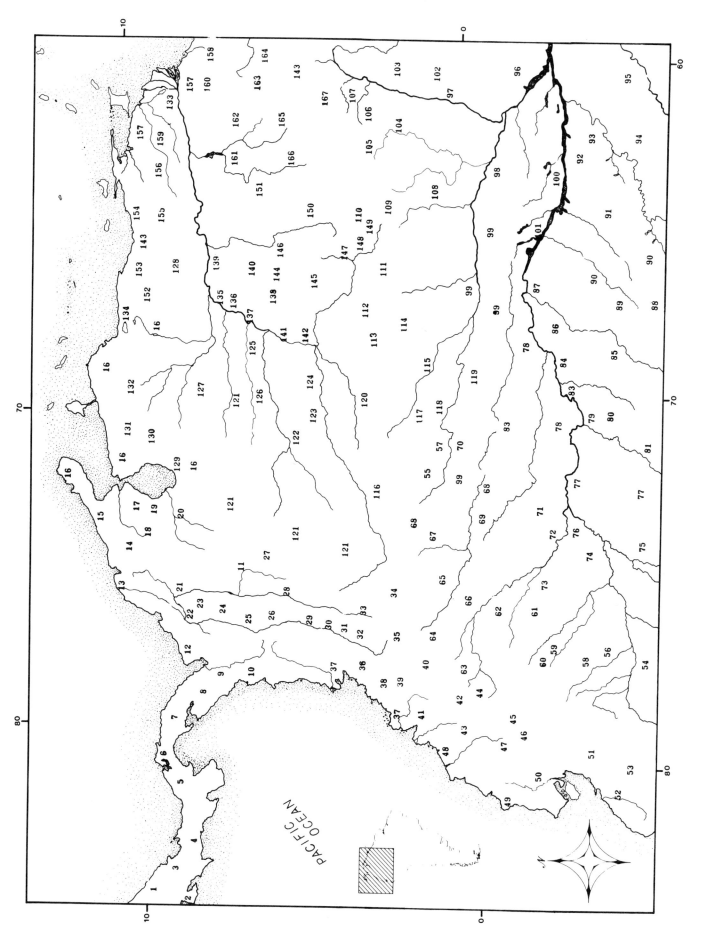

PACIFIC OCEAN

31

Map 10. South America, Northeast

Culture	Number	Culture	Number
Arawak	1	Timbira	66
Warao	2	Tobajara	67
Galibi	3	Teremembe	68
Bush Negro	4	Canella	69
Patamona	5		
Taulipang	6		
Makusi	7		
Wapishana	8		
Atorai	9		
Taruma	10		
Aucaners	11		
Oyana	12		
Wama	13		
Waiyarikule	14		
Waiyana	15		
Palikur	16		
Emerillon	17		
Maye	18		
Norague	19		
Oyampi	20		
Calayua	21		
Pianokoto	22		
Piriou	23		
Coussari	24		
Apalai	25		
Mura	26		
Kasuiana	27		
Cariguano	28		
Mundurucu	29		
Maopityan	30		
Sauiana	31		
Jauapery	32		
Wai-Wai	33		
Terecuma	34		
Maue	35		
Arapium	36		
Kayapo	37		
Kawahiwa	38		
Kuruya	39		
Yuruna	40		
Shipaya	41		
Tapajo	42		
Coani	43		
Arake	44		
Asurini	45		
Arawete	46		
Gorotire	47		
Sambioa	48		
Apinaye	49		
Sherente	50		
Mekranoti	51		
Parakana	52		
Pariri	53		
Arua	54		
Tupinamba	55		
Amanaye	56		
Gavioes	57		
Cariri	58		
Guaya	59		
Tembe	60		
Kabora	61		
Tenetehara	62		
Krene	63		
Potiguara	64		
Ramko-Kamekra	65		

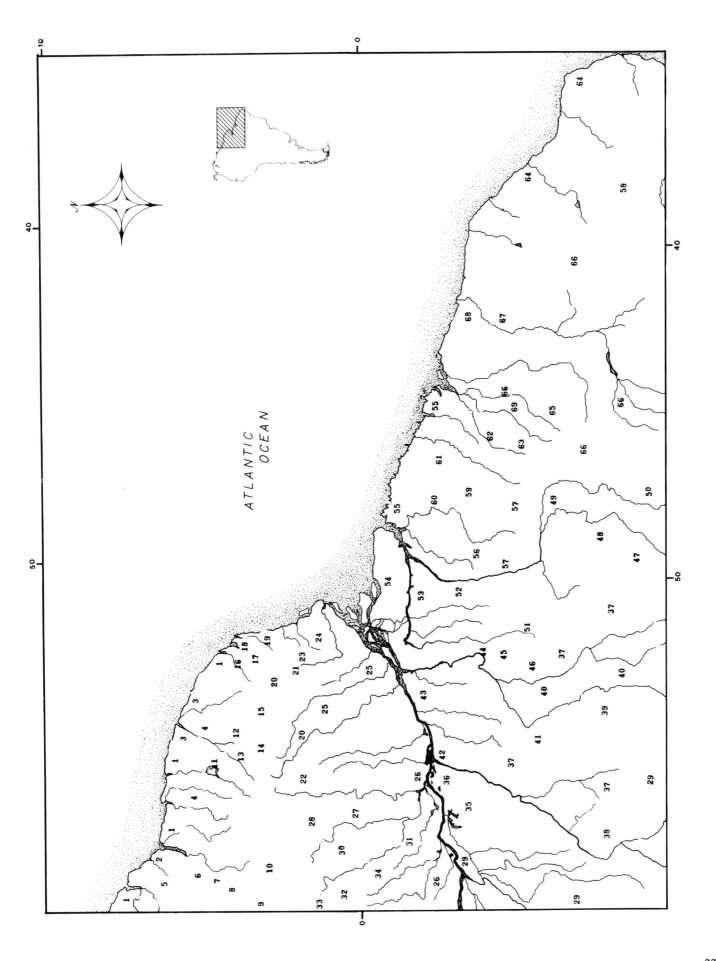

ATLANTIC OCEAN

33

Map 11. South America, West Central

Culture	Number	Culture	Number	Culture	Number
Tallanes	1	Baure	66	Atacama	131
Muchic	2	Itonama	67	Lipe	132
Huambo	3	Bocas Negras	68	Quillaca	133
Chachapoya	4	Caripuna	69	Characa	134
Chayahuita	5	Sinabo	70	Uru	135
Lamisto	6	More	71	Chipaya	136
Hibito	7	Pakaguara	72	Caranga	137
Aguano	8	Toromona	73	Arica	138
Cocamilla	9	Araona	74	Moquegua	139
Shetebo	10	Chama	75	Camana	140
Conchuco	11	Chacobo	76	Cupaca	141
Cholon	12	Cavinena	77	Collagua	143
Huaylas	13	Chapakura	78	Omaguaca	144
Casma	14	Tacana	79		
Chupayachu	15	Mojo	80		
Yaro	16	Movima	81		
Cauatambo	17	Apolista	82		
Chinchacha	18	Leco	83		
Tarma	19	Moseten	84		
Amuesha	20	Chimane	85		
Angara	21	Cochapampa	86		
Yauyo	22	Yuracare	87		
Chincha	23	Siriono	88		
Rucana	24	Yuqui	89		
Quechua	25	Reyesano	90		
Aymara	26	Paikoneka	91		
Cana	27	Guarayo	92		
Canchi	28	Tupari	93		
Caravaya	29	Wayoro	94		
Tiatinagua	30	Koaratira	95		
Tuyuneri	31	Nambicuara	96		
Mashco	32	Apiaca	97		
Machiguenga	33	Cayabi	98		
Campa	34	Iranxe	99		
Piro	35	Paressi	100		
Conibo	36	Umotina	101		
Shipibo	37	Kabishi	102		
Payanso	38	Curuminaca	103		
Remo	39	Pauserna	104		
Mayoruna	40	Bororo	105		
Culino	41	Guato	106		
Darawa	42	Otuke	107		
Wairacu	43	Ayoreo (Moro)	108		
Cuniba	44	Chiquito	109		
Canamari	45	Manasi	110		
Ipurina	46	Chicha	111		
Kapechene	47	Tapiete	112		
Amahuaca	48	Zamuc	113		
Karipuna	49	Chamacoco	114		
Yamamadi	50	Chiriguano	115		
Yuma	51	Ebidoso	116		
Paumari	52	Mbaya	117		
Catukuina	53	Tumereha	118		
Kagwahiv	54	Lengua	119		
Cint Larga	55	Sanapana	120		
Mundurucu	56	Angaite	121		
Kawahib	57	Ashluslay	122		
Arara	58	Maca	123		
Arikemes	59	Toba	124		
Jaru	60	Pilaga	125		
Urupa	61	Lule	126		
Cawahib	62	Choroti	127		
Kepkiriwat	63	Mataco	128		
Tapoaja	64	Chane	129		
Pacaas Novas	65	Vilela	130		

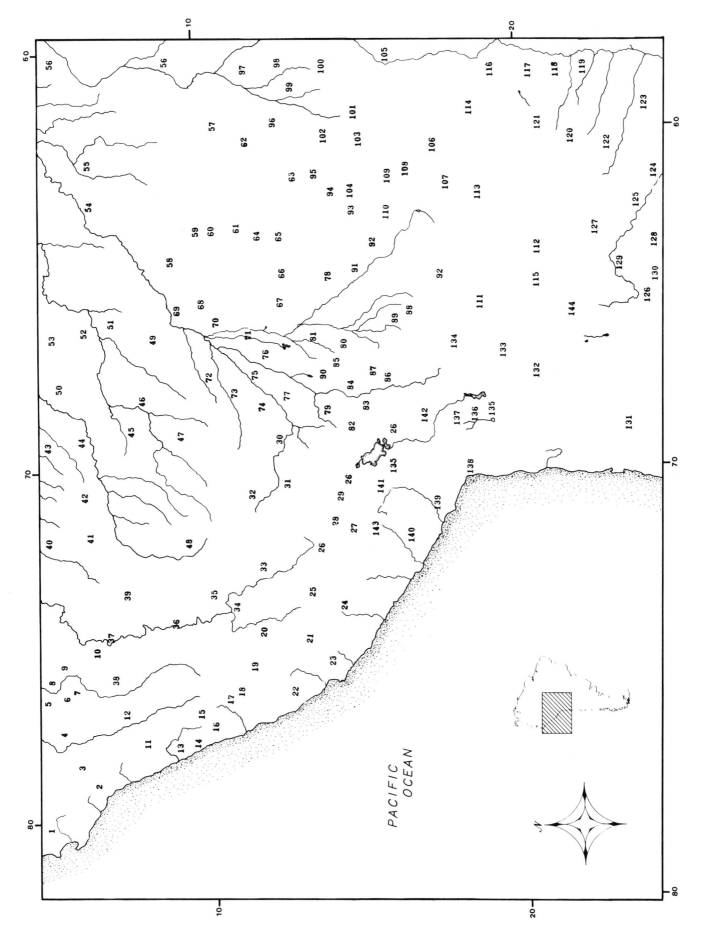

PACIFIC
OCEAN

35

Map 12. South America, East Central

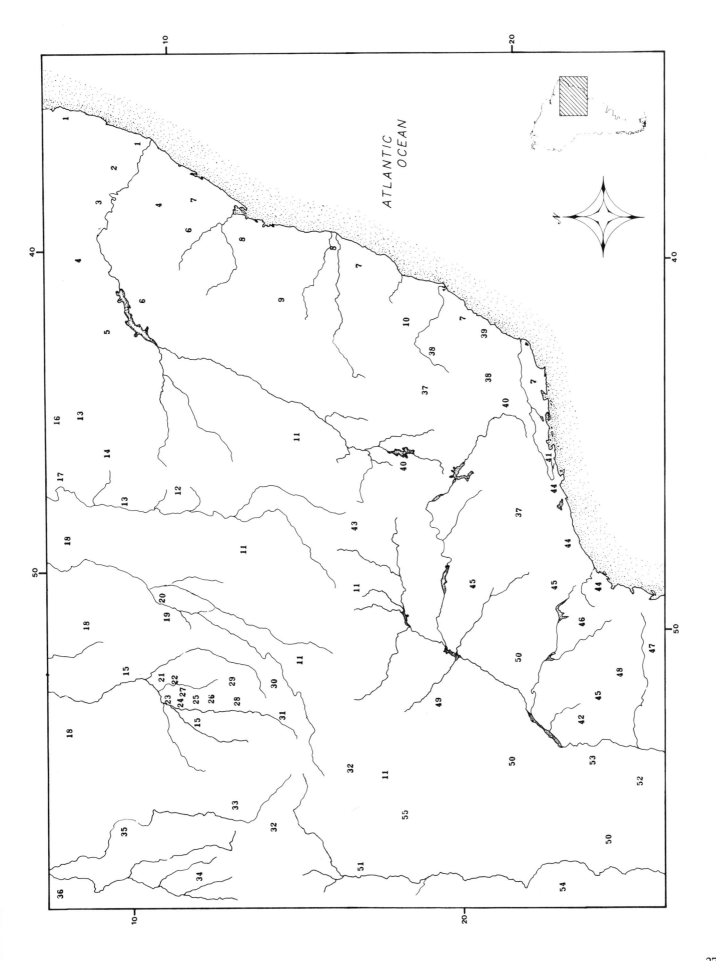

Map 13. South America, South Central

Culture	Number
Chechehet	1
Puelche	2
Pehuenche (Aravcanian)	3
Araucanians	4
Mapuche (Araucanians)	5
Chiquiyami	6
Millcayac	7
Huarpe	8
Allentiac	9
Diaguita	10
Atacama	11
Comechingon	12
Tonocote	13
Abipon	14
Mocovi	15
Mataco	16
Toba	17
Lengua	18
Ache	19
Guarani	20
Timbu	21
Mbegua	22
Minuane	23
Caracara	24
Querandi	25
Chana-Timbu	26
Chana	27
Yaro	28
Bohane	29
Guenoa	30
Charrua	31
Arachane	32
Carijo	33
Botocudo	34
Tape	35
Kaingang (Caingang)	36

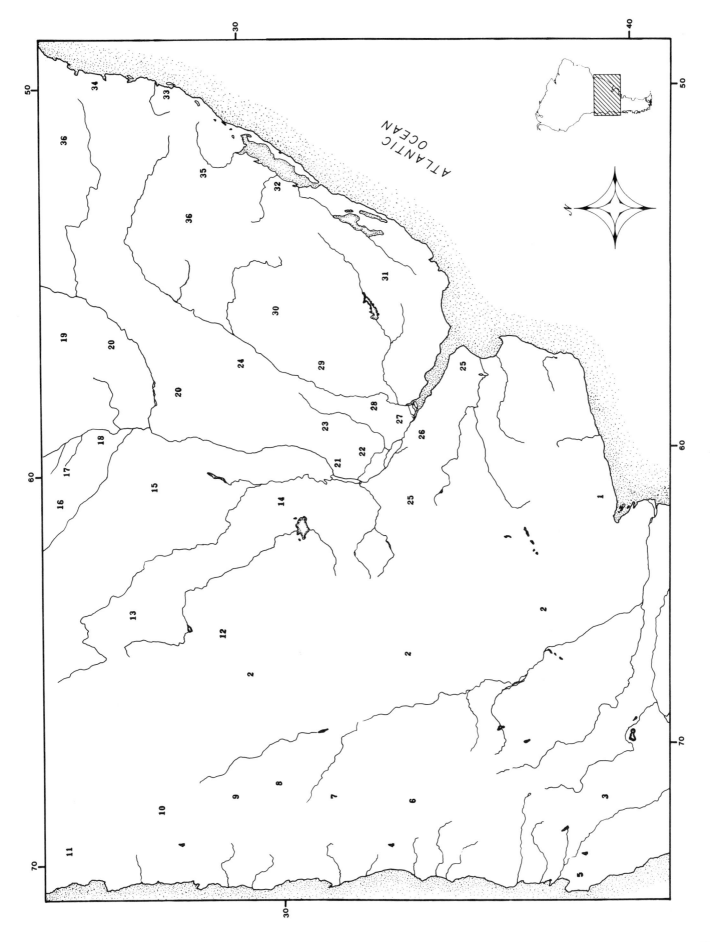

ATLANTIC OCEAN

N

Map 14. South America, Southern

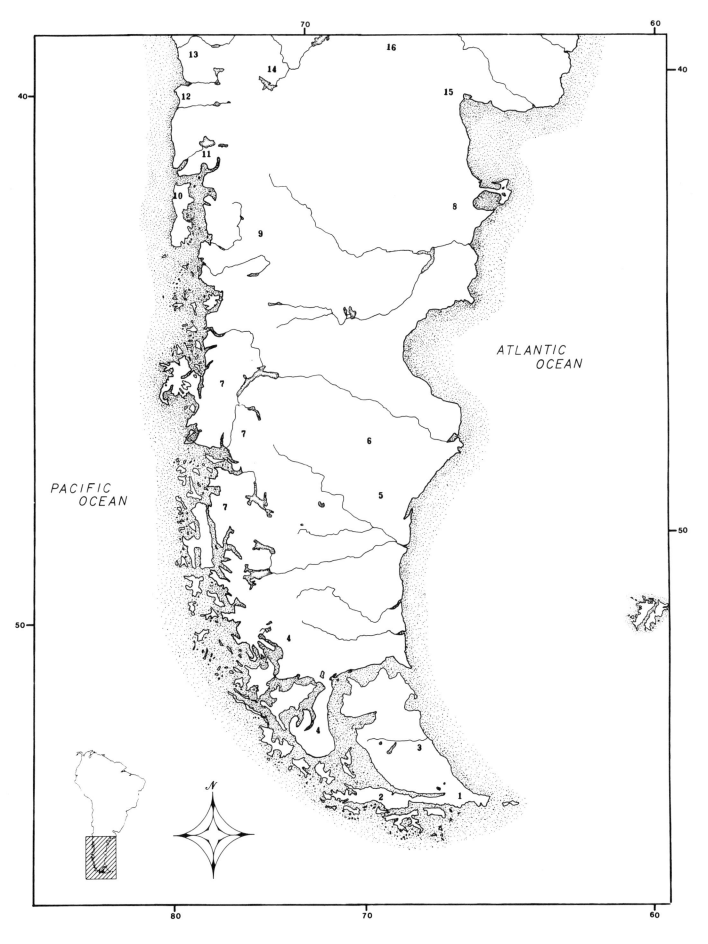

16

13

14

15

12

11

10

8

9

ATLANTIC
OCEAN

7

7

6

5

PACIFIC
OCEAN

7

50

50

4

4

3

N

2

1

80 70 60

Map 15. Africa, West Saharan

Culture	Number
Berber	1
Tuareg	2
Rela	3
Kel Ahaggar, Tuareg	4
Iforas, Tuareg	5
Air, Kel	6
Uraren, Tuareg	7
Nemencha	8
Marazig	9
Kel Ajjer	10
Chaamba	11
Tiris	12
Said Atba	13
Shawiya	14
Kabyle	15
El Arbaa	16
Mzab	17
Ouarsenis	18
Hamiyan	19
Dou Menia	20
Oulad Djerir	21
Ait Idrassen	22
Ait Yafelman	23
Ait Atta	24
Ulad Yihya	25
Nsula	26
Ait Walnzgit	27
Sanhaja	28
Ait Oumalou	29
Ben Guil	30
Beni Amer	31
Rif	32
Zemmur	33
Werigha	34
Zayr	35
Darwa	36
Sraghna	37
Nemadi	38
Shawya	39
Dukkala	40
Shluh	41
Ait Khebache	42
Tekna	43
Moors	44
Imraguen	45
Murd Guachey	46
Regeibat	47

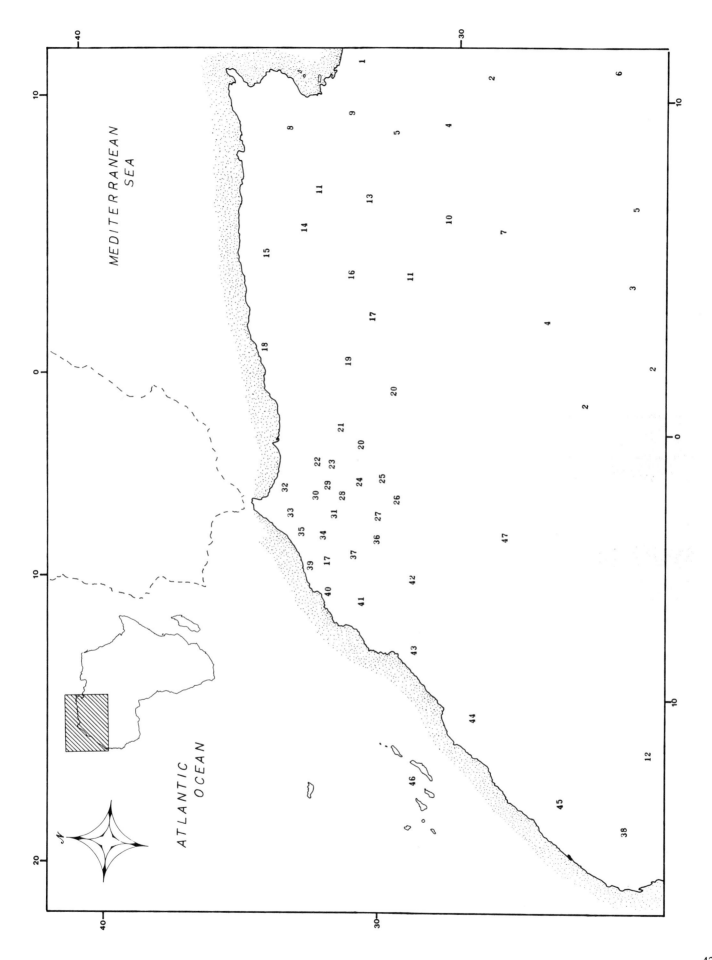

MEDITERRANEAN SEA

ATLANTIC OCEAN

N

43

Map 16. Africa, East Saharan

Culture	Number
Beheria	1
Awlad 'Ali	2
Jawabis	3
Harabi	5
Fawayid	6
Beni Suef	7
Haweitat	8
Ayaida	9
Ma'aza	9
Nubians	10
Baggara Arabs	11
Teda-Tebou	12
Aulad Soliman	13
Sanusi	14
Alamamra	15
Al Haraba	16
Abaydat ('Abaydat)	17
Al Majabra	18
Fawakhir	19
Zuwayah	20
Ajjers	21
Arafah ('Arafah)	22
Dars	23
Awaqir ('Awaqir)	24
Mugharbah	25
Fezzan	26
Megarha	27
Zentan	28

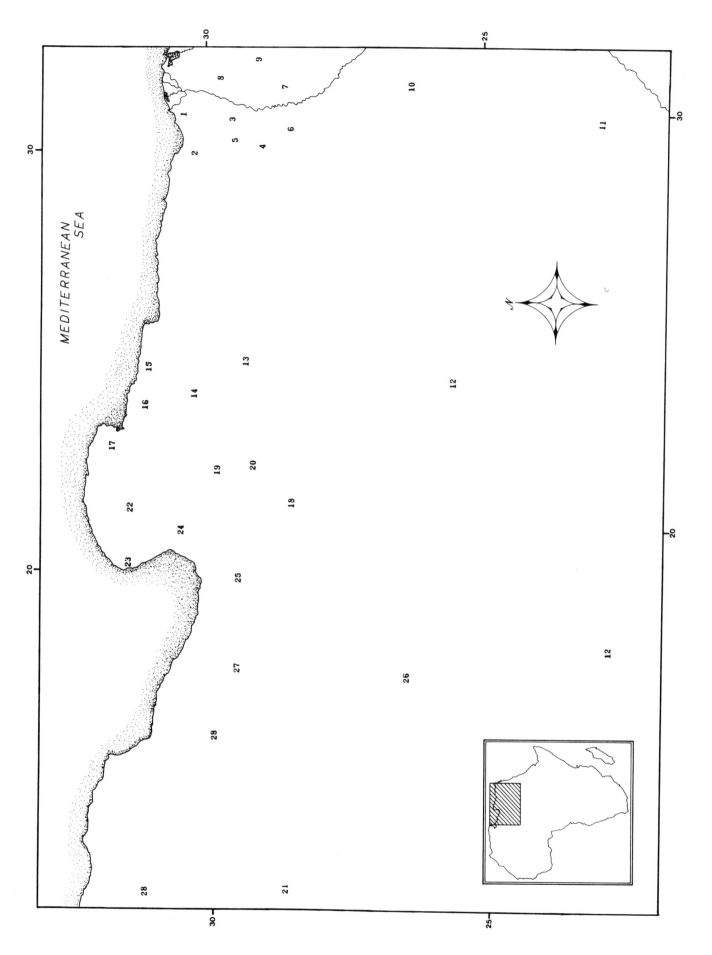

MEDITERRANEAN SEA

45

Map 17. Africa, West

Culture	Number	Culture	Number	Culture	Number
Calabar	1	Grusi	63	Ngere	127
Igbo	2	Gonja	64	Banyua	128
Itsekiri	3	Busansi	65	Senufo	129
Ijo	4	Mossi	66	Dan	130
Berabiche	5	Songhai	67	Tura	131
Oru	5	Djerma	68	Kono	132
Jekri	6	Hausa	69	Toma	133
Bini	7	Nupe	70	Kissi	134
Sobo	8	Gade	71	Gbande	135
Ika	9	Gwandara	72	De	136
Igara	10	Koro	73	Belle	137
Udam	11	Katab	74	Mandingo (Malinke)	138
Tiv	12	Kurama	75	Bassa	139
Igbira	13	Kanuri	76	Gola	140
Upila	14	Tuareg	77	Vai	141
Kukuruku	15	Tuareg, Ferouan	78	Mende	142
Ishan	16	Kel Tamajaq	79	Koranko	143
Edo	17	Aulliminden	80	Kirm	144
Ora	18	Gbari	81	Temne	145
Akoko	19	Arago	82	Sherbro	146
Ife-Ilesha	20	Koromba	83	Lokko	147
Ondo	21	Gourmantche	84	Bullom	148
Ijebu	22	Lowiili	85	Valunka	149
Egba	23	Lodagaba	85	Limba	150
Gu	24	Yadsi	86	Susu	151
Fon	25	Kel Antessar	87	Dialonke	152
Aja	26	Bozo	88	Baga	153
Yoruba	27	Bambara	89	Nalu	154
Mahi	28	Dogon	90	Landuman	155
Fo	29	Bobo	91	Koniagui	156
Aizo	30	Iforas, Tuareg	92	Bassari	157
Dahomey (Fon)	31	Kel Ahaggar, Tuareg	93	Soninke	158
Aizo	31	Kounta	94	Diakhanke	159
Kukuruku	32	Berabiche	95	Bedik	160
Ge	33	Kel Adrar	96	Souninke	161
Watyi	34	Karago	97	Tukylor	162
Anlo	35	Kassonke	98	Wolof	163
Kwahu	36	Hodh	99	Lebou	164
Ewe	37	Malinke	100	Serer	165
Adangme	38	Mau	101	Diola	166
Ga	39	Tene	102	Balante	167
Akyem	40	Kumbu	103	Ballouk	168
Fanti	41	Birifor	104		
Ashanti	42	Wangara	105		
Bono	43	Bumbu	106		
Wala	44	Baule	107		
Kana	45	Agni	108		
Ak Posso	46	Atie	109		
Tem	47	Akan	110		
Nanumba	48	Gagu	111		
Konkomba	49	Bete	112		
Dagomba	50	Guro	113		
Lamba	51	Bakwe	114		
Besorube	52	Abriwi	115		
Gurma	53	Plawi	116		
Anoufo	54	Tewi	117		
Fulani . . . see also Fulbe	55	Padebu	118		
Fulbe	55	Grebo	119		
Mamprusi	56	Kru	120		
Tallensi	57	Sapo	121		
Dagati	58	Sikon	122		
Wa	59	Gien	123		
Bariba	60	Kran	124		
Dagaba	61	Gio	125		
Bona	62	Kpelle	126		

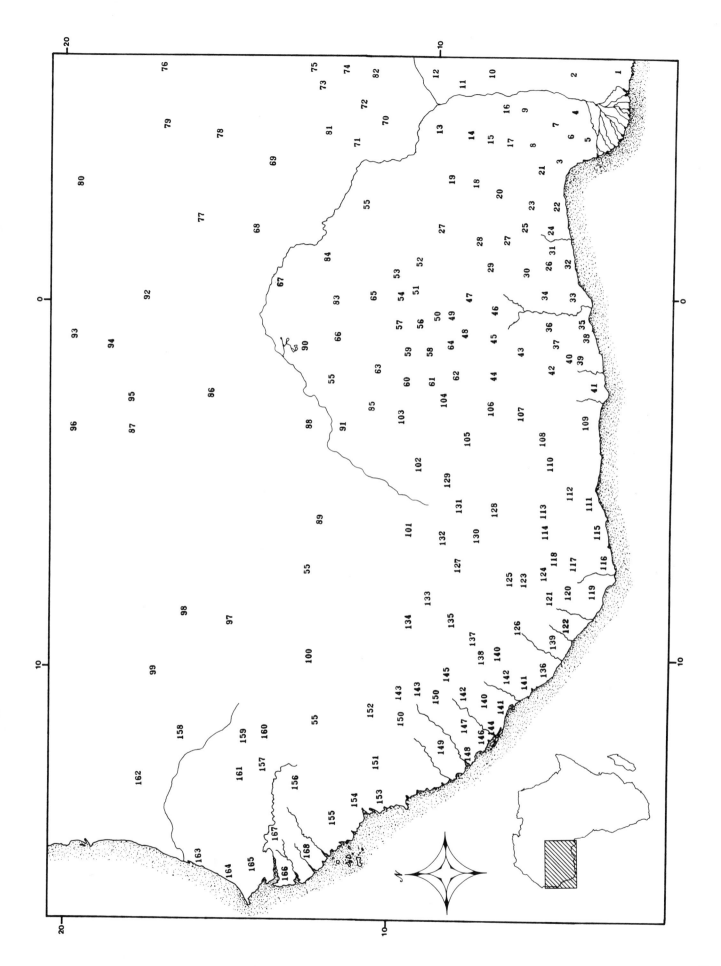

47

Map 18. Africa, Central

Culture	Number	Culture	Number	Culture	Number
Tanga	1	Shuwa	66	Bwaka	131
Fang	2	Chari River Groups	67	Basiri	132
Mako	3	Sara	68	Yakoma	133
Pygmy (Cameroon)	4	Kanembou	69	Bongo	134
Kaka	5	Mandara	70	Bapoto	135
Wute	6	Koto	71	Nzakara	136
Pande	7	Warjawa	72	Biri	137
Yanghere	8	Afawa	73	Gabou	138
Baia	9	Kanuri	74	Kare	139
Eton	10	Buduma	75	Mbo	140
Mbam	11	Afusare	76	Mangbetu	141
Banen	12	Dietko	77	Balese Ndake	142
Mungo	13	Maguzawa	78	Keliko	143
Limba	14	Bambara	79	Azande	144
Basakomo	15	Azzas	80	Pambia	145
Bafia	16	Air	81	Nuer	146
Ndop	17	Damergu	82	Mondari	147
Nso	18	Gounda	83	Avukaya	148
War	19	Braoya	84	Nyangbara	149
Wiya	20	Toubous	85	Logo	150
Mum	21	Teda	86	Dinka	151
Tikar	22	Tomagra	87	Toposa	152
Adamaua	23	Ouria	88	Pojulu	153
Tang	24	Gouroa	89	Kakwa	154
Bum	25	Arna	90	Lotuko	155
Kom	26	Gadoa	91	Ndu Lendu	156
Bali	27	Kecherda	92	Kuku	157
Ibibio	28	Dogorda	93		
Duala	29	Kokorda	94		
Pongo	30	Ounie	95		
Mungo	31	Mourdia	96		
Kpe	32	Ankaza	97		
Mboko	33	Anakazza	98		
Fugon	34	Djagada	99		
Chamba	35	Daza	100		
Udam	36	Bideyat	101		
Kole	37	Zaghawa	102		
Bamileke	38	Noarma	103		
Agoi	39	Tama	104		
Yako, (Ekoi)	40	Wadai	105		
Igbo	41	Kreda	106		
Idoma	42	Fur	107		
Jukun	43	Karranga	108		
Tiv	44	Soungor	109		
Kirdi	45	Gimr	110		
Fali	46	Midob	111		
Ninzam	47	Kababish (Baggara)	112		
Awe	48	Hawawir	113		
Gwandara	49	Batahin	114		
Mada	50	Kawahla	115		
Yeskwa	51	Meganin	116		
Hausa	52	Hamar	117		
Koro	53	Shilluk	118		
Afo	54	Kreish	119		
Arago	55	Rizegat	120		
Giliu	56	Nuba	121		
Jerawa	57	Shenabla	122		
Gbari	58	Humr	123		
Chawai	59	Bederiat	124		
Birom	60	Laka	125		
Bolewa	61	Ngapou	126		
Fulani . . . see also Fulbe	62	Mandja	127		
Kanum	63	Ndere	128		
Kapsiki	64	Dakwa	129		
Matakam	65	Banzirti	130		

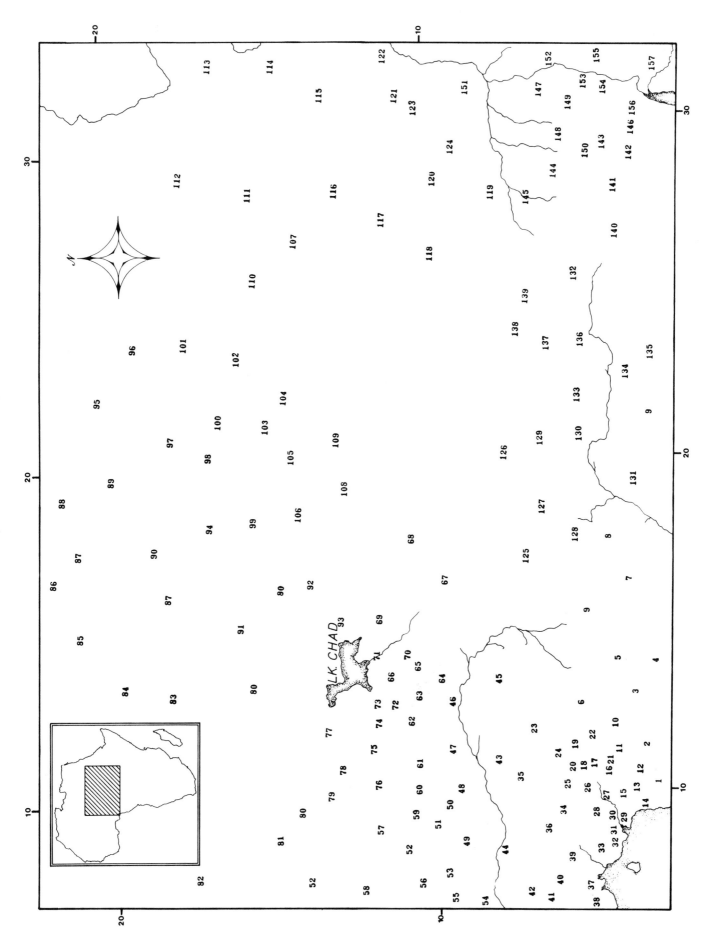

LK. CHAD

49

Map 19. East Africa & Arabian Peninsula

Culture	Number	Culture	Number	Culture	Number
Masa'id	1	Al Murra	66	Gumma	130
Ayaida	2	Bait Imani	67	Begemder	131
Laheiwat (Safaiha)	3	Bait Kathir	68	Agon	132
Haweitat	4	Rashid	69	Tigre	133
Aleiqat	5	Harasis	70	Mansa	134
Qararsha	6	Junuba	71	Beni Amer	135
Muzeina	7	Quda'a	72	Eritrea	136
Suwarka	8	Riyam	73	Halenga	137
Terabin	9	Amr	74	Shamkella	138
Tiyaha	10	Tayy	75	Besharin	139
Ma'aza	11	Kinda	76	Hadendowa	140
Billi	12	Yhamad	77	Atbara	141
Beni Sakhr Bedu	13	Huddan	78	Gabail Ukhra	142
Ruwallah	14	Ali Bin Morrah	79	Amarar	143
Shararat	15	Daru	80	Nubians	144
Shammar	16	Bani Kitab	81		
Anizah	17	Awamir	82		
Hutaim	18	Al Hibab	83		
Beni Atiyah	19	Bani Hajir	84		
Juhainah	20	Al Muraikhat	85		
Harb	21	Beni Hajar	86		
Mutair	22	Bahar-Lu	87		
Pusht-I-Kuh	23	Basseri	88		
Utaibah	24	Qashqai	89		
Gasim	25	Vaisi	90		
Bariyah	26	Mamassani	91		
Awazim	27	Kuh-Giluye	92		
Bani Khalid	28	Bakhtiari	93		
Hasa	29	Inan-lu	94		
Sibea	30	Kamse	95		
Ojman	31	Nafar	96		
Suhul	32	Duzdgah	97		
Duwasir	33	Darazi	98		
Qahtan	34	Safari	99		
Baalasmar	35	Jani Khan	100		
Shamran	36	Mazidi	101		
Baqum	37	Mehni	102		
Ghamid	38	Darab Khani	103		
Thaqif	39	Avil	104		
Hozayl	40	Damani	105		
Baalahmah	41	Rais	106		
Al Shalawah	42	Lashari Baluch	107		
Balgarn	43	Khitar	108		
Bani Shahr	44	Baranzai	109		
Bani Hilal	45	Ashan	110		
Juddah	46	Dehwar	111		
Rijal Al Ma	47	Dorazai	112		
Hashid	48	Hot Baluch	113		
Ibn Amir	49	Darusar	114		
Bakil	50	Jangizai Maid	115		
Zaraniq	51	Jadgal	116		
Khawlan Al-Akiya	52	Birdi	117		
Madhhij	53	Maid	118		
Bani Yam	54	Baluchi	119		
Dahm	55	Somali	120		
Jauf	56	Afar	121		
Abida	57	Danakil (Afar)	121		
Al Hawaashib	58	Galla	122		
Yafi	59	Koma	123		
Nahd	60	Berta	124		
Saar	61	Ingassana	125		
Shanafir	62	Uduk	126		
Humum	63	Burun	127		
Mahra	64	Meban	128		
Karabi	65	Amhara	129		

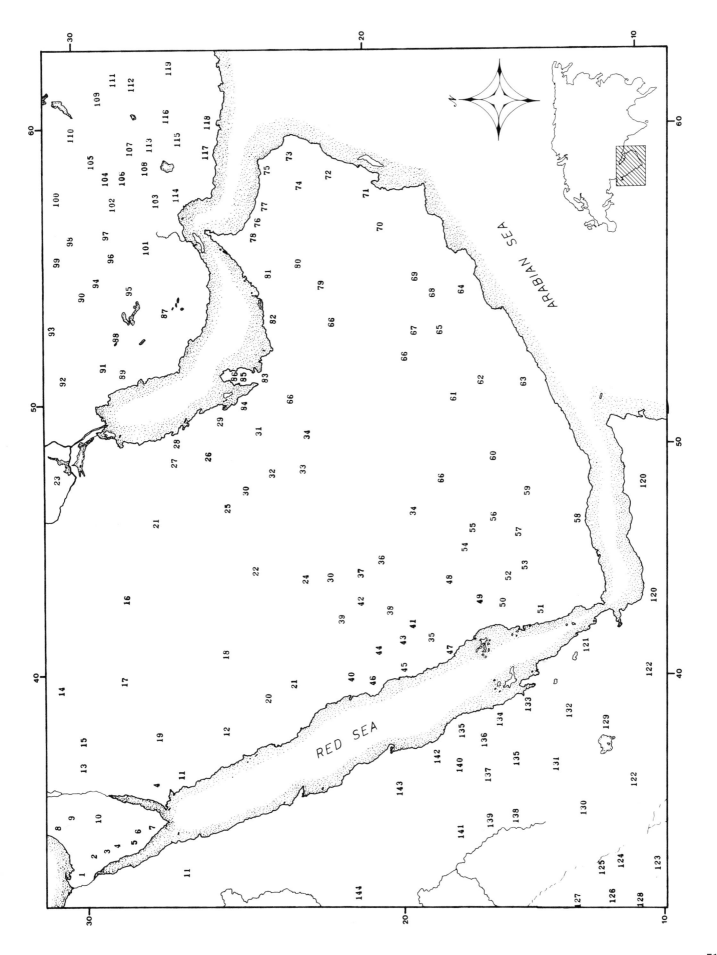

51

Map 20. Africa, West Central

Culture	Number	Culture	Number
Kpe	1	Bashilange	66
Mungo	2	Teke	67
Duala	3	Mbochi	68
Limba	4	Achikouya	69
Makka	5	Kongo	70
Fang	6	Vili	71
Kombe	7	Bakamba	72
Tanga	8	Yombe	73
Yasa	9	Dondo	74
Bosyeba	10	Balali	75
Mpongwe	11	Ndibu	76
Adyumba	12	Fumbu	77
Bakele	13	Sise	78
Nkomi	14	Bali	79
Mapounou	15	Mbata	80
Punu	16	Sorongo	81
Bayaka	17	Cisama	82
Mberenzabi	18	Ovimbundu	83
Bakere	19	Ndongo	84
Shake	20	Bangala	85
Kota	21	Zombo	86
Kele	22	Bayaka	87
Makaa	23	Songo	88
Baya	24	Yanzi	89
Sanga	25	Mbala	90
Bandza	26	Chokwe	91
Pande	27	Songo	92
Kaka	28	Ovimbundu	93
Pomo	29	Maxinje	94
Binga	30	Lunda	95
Bwaka	31	Pinde	96
Bangala	32	Bayaka	97
Baya	33	Balua	98
Bali	34	Kwango River Groups	99
Bongo	35	Bunda	100
Bapoto	36	Lulua	101
Mabinza	37	Tukkongo	102
Ngbandi	38	Bashilele	103
Azande	39	Bunda	104
Mbudja	40	Wongo	105
Doko	41	Yeke	106
Bombesa	42	Kasai River Groups	107
Mongo	43	Lomami	108
Baloulou (Mongo)	44	Tumbwe	109
Nbombe	45	Holoholo	110
Tswa	46	Bemba	111
Ngbaka	47	Luapula	112
Kom	48	Kuba	113
Ekonda	49	Moer	114
Mbuti	50	Lungu	115
Twa	51	Bwile	116
Mba	52	Unga	117
Nande	53	Bisa	118
Nyanga	54	Bemba	119
Batatela	55	Lungu	120
Lendu	56		
Wasongola	57		
Lengola	58		
Wagera	59		
Ohindo	60		
Wazimba	61		
Luba	62		
Ndenges	63		
Kuba	64		
Nkutu	65		

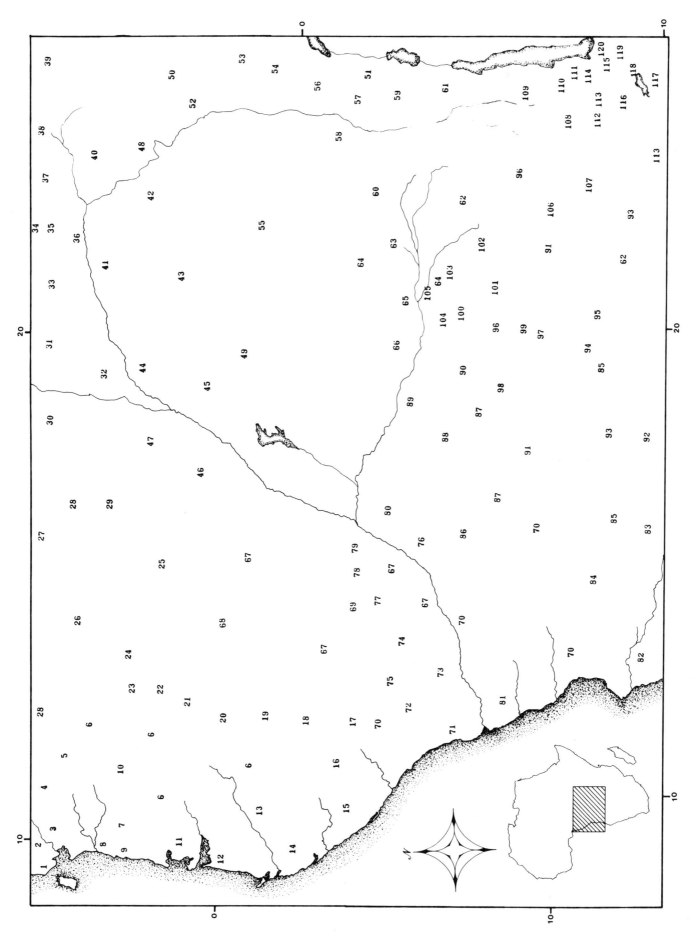

Map 21. Africa, East

Culture	Number	Culture	Number	Culture	Number	Culture	Number
Shilluk	1	Tiriki	66	Marungu	131	Chara	196
Kreish	2	Gusii	67	Bwile	132	Mazhi	197
Dinka	3	Nandi	68	Tabwa	133	Hadya	198
Nuer	4	Tugen	69	Lungu	134	Kaffa	199
Sere	5	Dorobo	70	Fipa	135	Galla	200
Jur	6	Bukuli	71	Nkansi	136	Sidamo	201
Belanda	7	Sese	72	Lyangalile	137	Gofa	202
Thuri	8	Bugusu (Luyia)	73	Mambwe	138	Badutu	203
Atwot, Dinka	9	Buruli	74	Wanda	139	Darasa	204
Luo	10	Ganda	75	Nyiha	140	Gurage	205
Beir	11	Ssingo	76	Safwa	141	Janjero	206
Toposa	12	Nyoro	77	Bungu	142	Nole	207
Didinga	13	Jongn	78	Manda	143	Arusi, Galla	208
Caga	14	Lendu	79	Kimbu	144	Ittu	209
Ik	15	Okebo	80	Sangu	145	Ala	210
Lano	16	Dongo	81	Bena	146	Ania	211
Bari	17	Budu	82	Kinga	147	Argobba	212
Mondari	18	Balese Ndake	83	Hehe	148	Jarso, Galla	213
Pojulu	19	Vonoma	84	Pogoro	149	Harari	214
Kederu	20	Bale	85	Mbunga	150		
Moru	21	Amba	86	Gogo	151		
Mittu	22	Hima	87	Sagara	152		
Abukaya	23	Mbuti	88	Kaguru	153		
Baka	24	Bira	89	Arusha	154		
Mundu	25	Konjo	90	Teita	155		
Nyangbara	26	Toro	91	Ngulu	156		
Azande	27	Koki	92	Guru	157		
Keliko	28	Ankole	93	Kutu	158		
Fajelu	29	Kiga	94	Rufiji	159		
Logo	30	Twa	95	Ndereko	160		
Lugbara	31	Kabula	96	Kwere	161		
Kakwa	32	Haya	97	Zigula	162		
Swahili	33	Nyamb	98	Segeju	163		
Alur	34	Rwanda	99	Digo	164		
Madi	35	Banyanhkole (Ankole)	100	Bondei	165		
Acholi	36	Burundi	101	Sambaa	166		
Lotuko	37	Subi	102	Pare	167		
Napore	38	Zinza	103	Chagga	168		
Dodos	39	Buha	104	Taveta	169		
Turkana	40	Kerewe	105	Kamba	170		
Jie	41	Jita	106	Agiryama	171		
Karamojong	42	Kuria	107	Rabai	172		
Vidunda	43	Kipsigis	108	Chonyi	173		
Tepeth	44	Shashi	109	Jibana	174		
Suk, Hill	45	Sukuma	110	Sanye	175		
Rendille	46	Masai	111	Pokomo	176		
Elmolo	47	Gorowa	112	Kikuyu	177		
Sebei	48	Iraqw	113	Boran	178		
Lango	49	Hadzapi	114	Jopadhola	179		
Pallisa	50	Iramba	115	Samburu	180		
Bunyole	51	Barabaig	116	Nyeri	181		
Teso	52	Irangi	117	Embu	182		
Gishu	53	Burungi	118	Boni	183		
Soga	54	Sandawe	119	Ogadein	184		
Padhola	55	Nyaturu	120	Tharaka	185		
Vugusu	56	Usukuma	121	Meru	186		
Kavirondo	57	Sumbwa	122	Hawiyah	187		
Gwe	58	Vinza	123	Somali	188		
Samia, Gwe	59	Ha	124	Sakuye	189		
Luyia	60	Jiji	125	Gabbra	190		
Nyala	61	Tongwe	126	Gelubba	191		
Isukha	62	Holoholo	127	Konso	192		
Wanga	63	Nyamwezi	128	Wolamo	193		
Kisi	64	Bende	129	Kambatta	194		
Logoli	65	Ukonongo	130	Basketo	195		

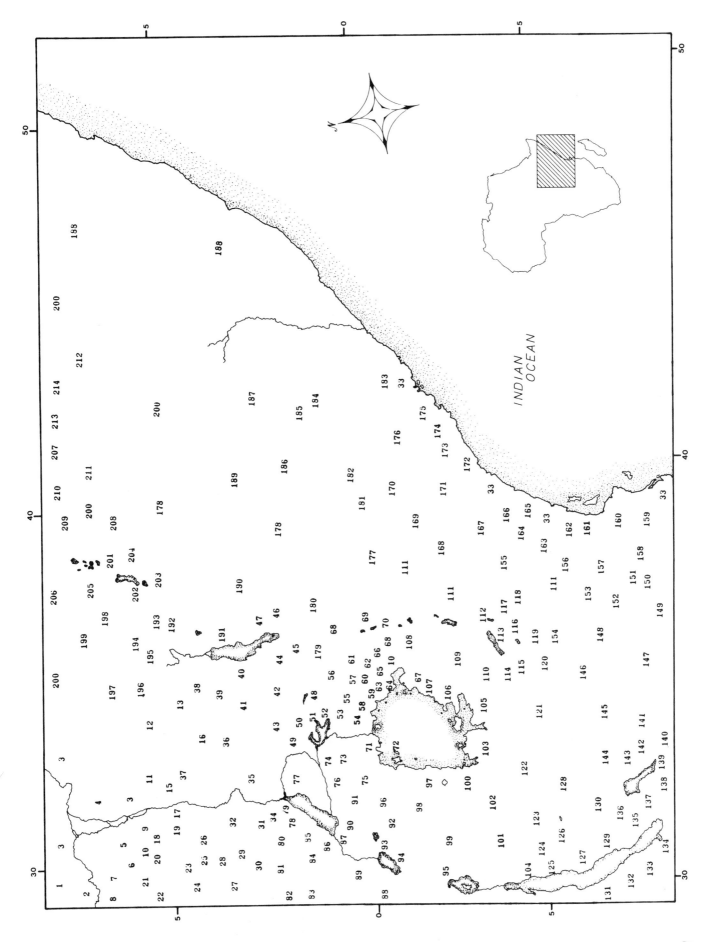

Map 22. Africa, Southwest

Culture	Number	Culture	Number
Chishinga	1	Tswana	65
Luapula	2	Kwena	66
Nukulo	3	Rolong	67
Aushi	4	Kgatla	68
Lamba	5	Huruthse	69
Shila	6	Mekwa	70
Lunda-Ndembu	7	Batlaro	71
Lunda	8	Auen	72
Sewa	9	Khara (!Khara)	73
Temba	10	Bakalahari	74
Luba	11	Naron	75
Swaka	12	Tsaukwe	76
Nyaturu	13	Berseba Hottentots	77
Lala	14	Bethanie Hottentots	78
Luano	15	Witboois	79
Ambo	16	Amraal Hottentots	80
Lenje	17	Hukwe Bushmen	81
Mbwera (Lozi)	18	Kung (!Kung)	82
Nsenga	19	Herero	83
Soli	20	Dama	84
Tonga	21	Bergdama	85
Nkoya (Lozi)	22	Kwangare	86
Ila	23	Ovambo	87
Tonga	23	Kwangali	88
Lumbu	24	Kede	89
Totela	25	Tawana	90
Lushange	26	Himba	91
Kwangwa	27	Kwamatwi	92
Kaonde	28	Tyavikwa	93
Luchazi	29	Vale	94
Akosa	30	Ongona	95
Amahumbu	31	Twa, Southern	96
Luena	32	Kwankhala	97
Chokwe	33	Hakavona	98
Ayisenga	34	Zimba	99
Ishinde	35	Nkumbi	100
Lubale Lozi	36	Nyemba	101
Ambuella	37	Kafima	102
Mbunda (Lozi)	38	Sekele	103
Makoma	39	Tyokwe	104
Nyengo (Lozi)	40	Mbundu	105
Lozi	41	Twilenge-Humbi	106
Ndundulu (Lozi)	42	Ngambwe	107
Simaa (Lozi)	43	Mwila	108
Kwandi	44	Kuvale	109
Kwanyama	45	Kwisi	110
Mbwela	46	Kwepe	111
Ovimbundu	47	Vatwa	112
Ngangela	48	Cisanji	113
Luimbe	49	Ndombe	114
Mwenyi	50	Tyilenge-Muso	115
Mashi (Lozi)	51	Hanya	116
Shanjo	52	Cipungu	117
Subya (Lozi)	53	Esele	118
Mbukushu	54	Mbui	119
Leya	55		
Toka (Lozi)	56		
Ndebele	57		
Hiechware	58		
Mahura	59		
Ngwato	60		
Tserekwe	61		
Ohekwe	62		
Ngwaketse	63		
Kwera	64		

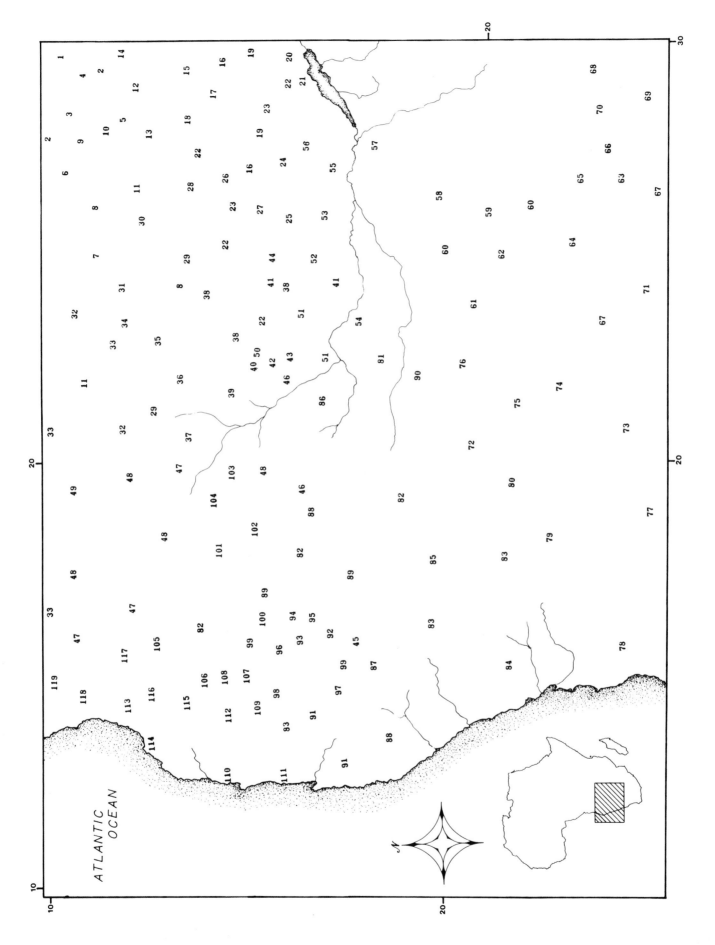

ATLANTIC OCEAN

Map 23. Africa, Southeast

Culture	Number	Culture	Number
Tankarana	1	Teve	66
Sakalava	2	Shona	67
Tsimihety	3	Korekore	68
Betsimisaraka	4	Zezhru	69
Merina	5	Duma	70
Sihanaka	6	Karanga	71
Bezanozano	7	Hlengwe	72
Betsileo	8	Danda	73
Tanala	9	Shangana	74
Taimoro	10	Ndau	75
Tambahoaka	11	Tswa	76
Zafisoro	12	Tonga	77
Taisaka	13	Chopi	78
Timanambondro	14	Venda	79
Mahafaly	15	Hananwa	80
Tandroy	16	Ndebele	81
Bara	17	Thlalerwa	82
Tanosy	18	Kheni	83
Podzo	19	Ndeble	84
Sena	20	Lobedu	85
Swahili	21	Gowa	86
Makua	22	Tsonga	86
Lowwe	23	Pedi	87
Makonde	24	Toka	88
Chuabo	25	Manyika	89
Mwera	26		
Ngindo	27		
Yao	28		
Pogoro	29		
Angoni	30		
Bena	31		
Matengo	32		
Pangwa	33		
Tumbuka	34		
Nyakyusa	35		
Ndali	36		
Ngonde	37		
Lambya	38		
Iwa	39		
Henga	40		
Mba	41		
Tambo	42		
Phoka	43		
Kamanga	44		
Mambwe	45		
Tabwa	46		
Shila	47		
Ushi	48		
Lungu	49		
Ngumbo	50		
Bemba	51		
Senga	52		
Chewa	53		
Bisa	54		
Chikunda	55		
Lala	56		
Lenje (Ila-Tonga)	57		
Ambo	58		
Sala	59		
Nsenga	60		
Gowa	61		
Tonga	62		
Nguni	63		
Zimba	64		
Tawara	65		

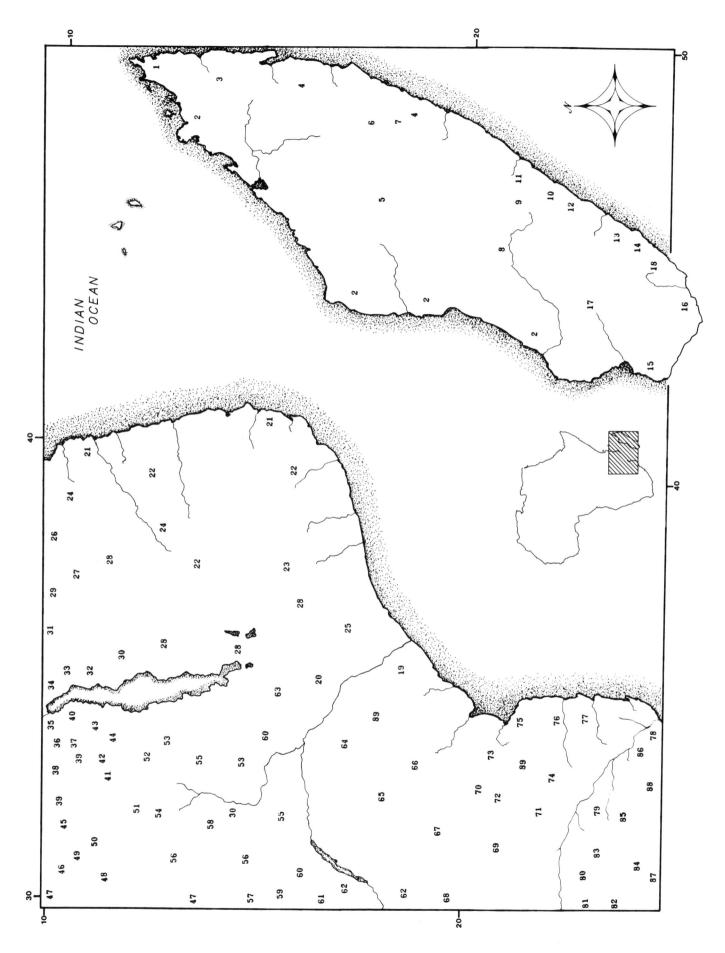

INDIAN OCEAN

59

Map 24. Africa, Southern

Culture	Number
Herero	1
Nama	2
Nama	3
Auen	4
Naron	5
Magon	6
Tswana	7
Kgalagadi	8
Rolong	9
Tlhara	10
Xam	11
Namaqua, Hottentot	12
Chariguriqua, Hottentot	13
Hessequa	14
Inqua, Hottentot	15
Korana	16
Tlhaping	17
Sotho	18
Fingo	19
Ngoika	20
Xhosa	21
Gcoika	22
Bomvana	23
Thembu	24
Mpondomise	25
Bhaca	26
Hlubi	27
Yesibe	28
Nhlangwini	29
Kwena	30
Khuze	31
Makhanya	32
Zulu	33
Tembe Tonga	34
Konde	35
Maputa	36
Swazi	37
Ngomane	38
Nkosi	39
Pai	40
Pedi	41
Ndebele	42
Hwaduba	43
Fokeng	44
Huruthse	45

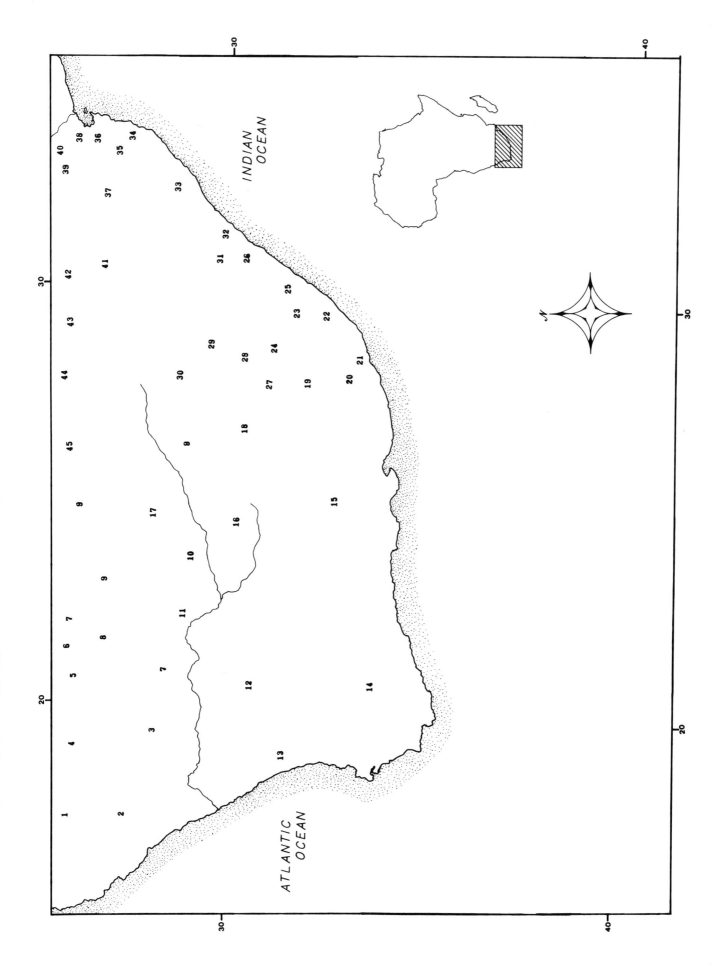

Map 25. India Subcontinent

Culture	Number
Sinhalese	1
Vedda	2
Tamil	3
Malayalam	4
Palivan	5
Nayar	6
Toda	7
Kota	8
Urali	9
Kurumba	10
Koya	11
Yenadis	12
Irular	13
Lambadi	14
Erukala	15
Kannada	16
Naikda	17
Konkan	18
Gond	19
Koli	20
Gond, Maria	21
Dorla Gond	22
Konda Reddis	23
Konda Kapu	24
Bondo	25
Gadaba	26
Dhurwa	27
Kolam	28
Gawari	29
Marathi	30
Varli	31
Bhil	32
Gamta	33
Doubla	34
Gujarati	35
Patelia	36
Mina	37
Grassia	38
Baluchi	39
Sindhi	40
Kachi	41
Ahir	42
Kol	43
Baiga	44
Korwa	45
Oraon	46
Munda	47
Khasi	48
Kharia	49
Juang	50
Santal	51
Garo	52
Karmali	53
Ngalong	54
Nishis	55
Apa tani	56
Naga	57
Konyak	58
Mru	59
Mizo	60
Lakher	61

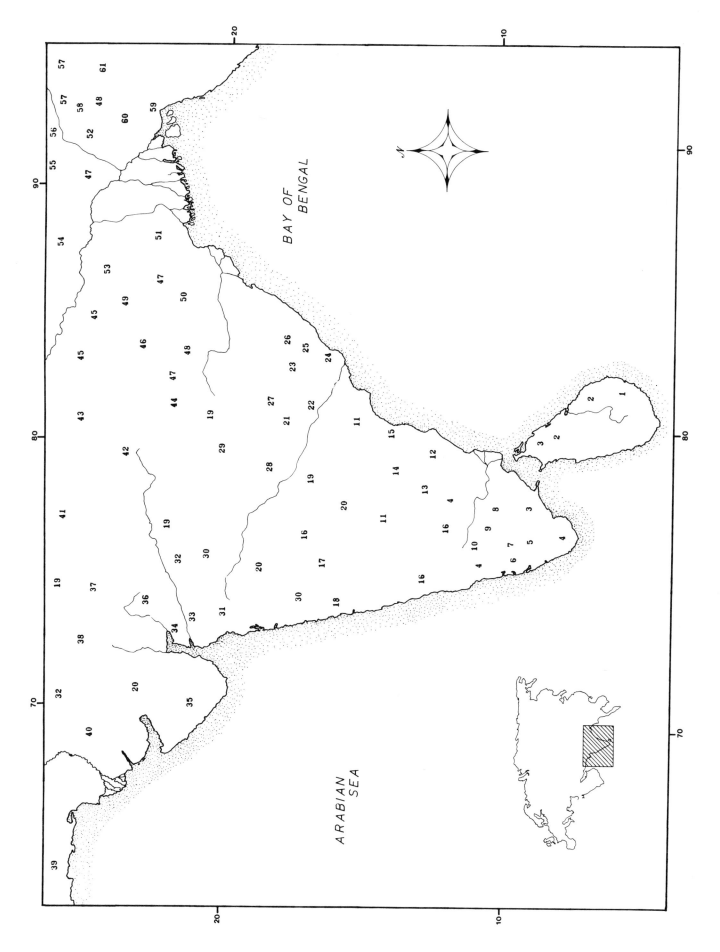

BAY OF BENGAL

ARABIAN SEA

N

63

Map 26. Malay Peninsula

Culture	Number
Orang Laut	1
Orangkanaq	2
Jakun	3
Semelai	4
Temuan	5
Temoq	6
Mahmeri	7
Jan Hut	8
Semoq Beri	9
Belandas	10
Siwang	11
Semang	12
Pangan	13
Batek	14
Semai	15
Temiar	16
Mendrio	17
Jahai	18
Lanoh	19
Kintag	20
Kensiu	21
Siamese	22
Moken	23
Onge	24
Andamanese	25
Karen	26
Mon	27
Miao	28
Lao	29
Yuan	30
Lisu	31
Lua	32
Lahu	33
Mien	34
Hmong	35
Akha	36
Wa	37
Shan	38
Taungthu	39
Yang	40
Palaung	41
Kachin	42
Burman	43
Arakanese	44
Chin	45
Lushai Chin	46
Yunnan	47
Khumi	48
Lakher	49
Assam	50
Samre	51
Aka	52
Khmu	53
Neua	54
Lu	55
Alak	56
Souei	57
Khmer	58
Cham	59
Chong	60
Pear	61
Saoch	62
Biat	63
Vietnamese	64

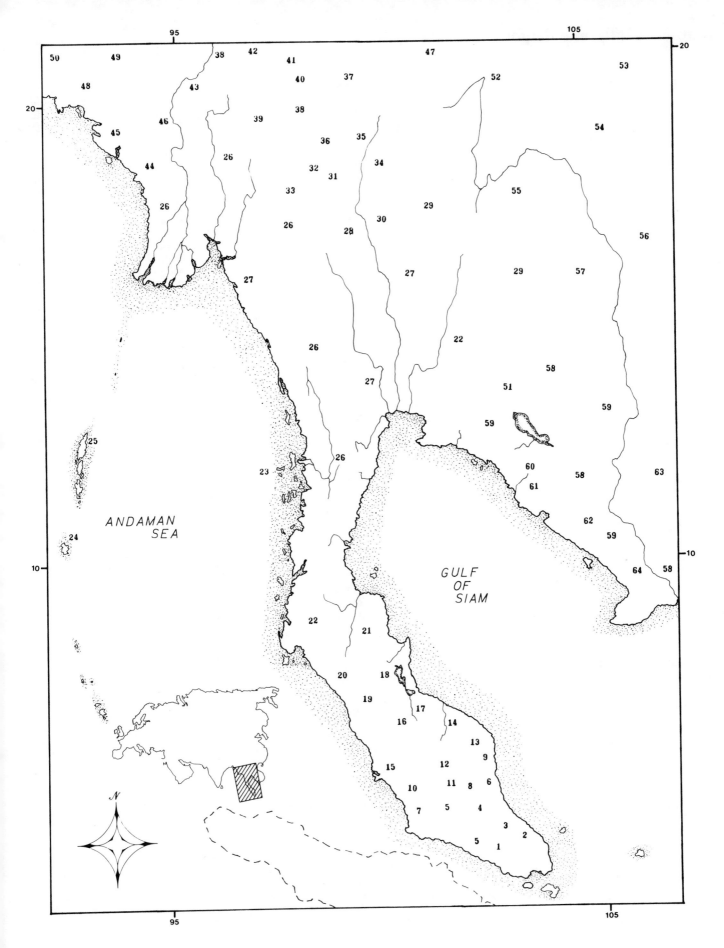

50 49   38   42   41   47   53

    48   40   37
                        38   52
20   46   39   54
       45
         44   36   35
                   26   32 34
                      31   55
                   33   29
                26   30
                      28   29   57   56
                                      27
                 27   22
                                                    58
                          26   51   59
                          27   59
ANDAMAN   60   58   63
SEA   26   61
              25   62
                         23   59
           24   64 58
10   10
                                          GULF
                                          OF
                                          SIAM
                   22
                        21
                   20   18
                        19   17
                        16   14
                   15   13
                                9
                        12
                   10   11 8 6
                   7   5   4
                        5   3 2
                             1

N

95   105

65

Map 27. Philippine Region

Culture	Number	Culture	Number
Samal	1	Li	56
Tausug	2	Hainna	57
Subanun	3	Vietnamese	58
Tiruray	4	Chrau Jro	59
Tagabili	5	Cham	60
Tasaday	6	Koho	61
Bilaan	7	Biat	62
Tagakaolo	8	Mnong	63
Kulaman	9	Chru	64
Bagobo	10	Roglai	65
Moro	11	Rade	66
Ilanon	12	Jarai	67
Maranao	13	Hroy	68
Mandaya	14	Bahnar	69
Agusan	15	Monom	70
Bukidnon	16	Sedang	71
Mamanua	17	Cua	72
Sebuano	18	Duan	73
Hiligaynon	19	Katu	74
Kinaraya	20	Pakoh Hoe	75
Aklanon	21	Red Tai	76
Masbateno	22	Han	77
Samar-Leyte	23	Yao	78
Kenoy	24	Tung	79
Tagbanua	25	Hakka	80
Palawan	26	She	81
Batak	27		
Bisayan	28		
Ratagnon	29		
Hanunodo	30		
Buhid	31		
Ala'ngan	32		
Tadyawan	33		
Bikol	34		
Iraya	35		
Negritos	36		
Visayan	37		
Tagalog	38		
Sambal	39		
Zambales	40		
Ilongot	41		
Nabaloi	42		
Kankanay	43		
Ibaloi	44		
Gaddang	45		
Isinay	46		
Ifugao	47		
Bontoc Igorot	48		
Tingaian	49		
Kalinga	50		
Igorot	51		
Ibanag Ilokano	51		
Apayao	52		
Ryukyu Islands	53		
Naga	54		
Paiwan	54		
Rukai	54		
Hoanya	54		
Siraya	54		
Atayal	55		
Ami	55		
Ketagalan	55		
Kuvalan	55		
Luilang	55		
Toakas	55		

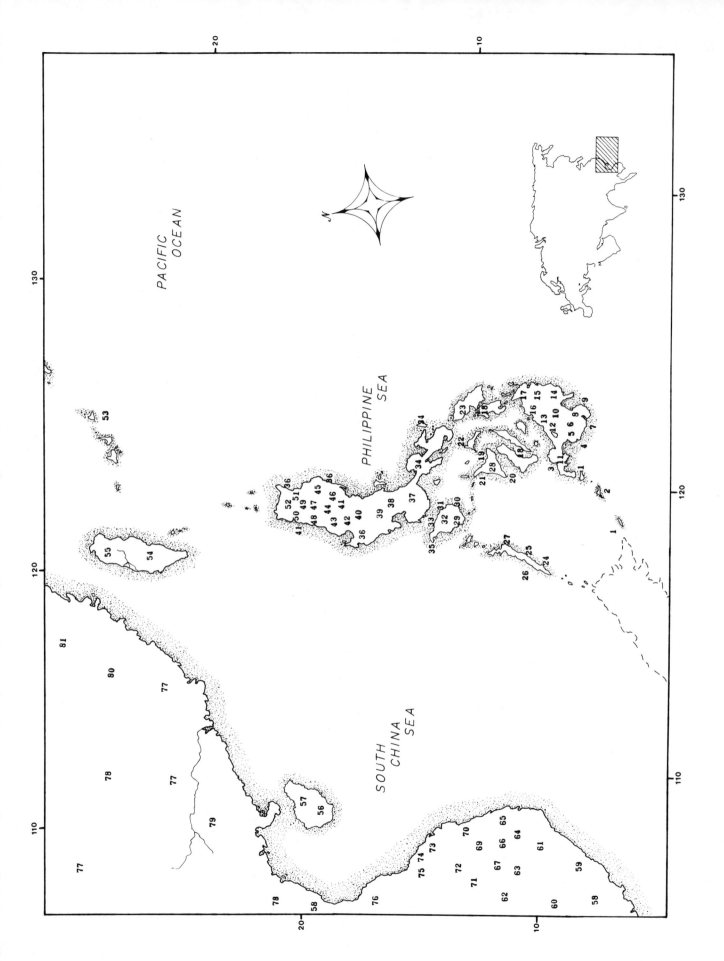

PACIFIC OCEAN

PHILIPPINE SEA

SOUTH CHINA SEA

67

Map 28. Indonesia

Culture	Number	Culture	Number
Kisar	1	Tomini	65
Leti	2	Iban	66
Dagada	3	Gorontalo	66
Wetar	4	Mongondow	67
Tetum	5	Mongondow, Inland	68
Atoni	6	Minahasa	68
Kupangese	7	Loinang	69
Helong	8	Balantak	70
Roti	9	Toradja	71
Savunese	10	Sadang	72
Alor	11	Mori-Laki	73
Solorese	12	Macassarese	74
Larantuka	13	Toala	75
Sikanese	14	Banggai	76
Lionese	15	Salajar	77
Endenese	16	Butung	78
Ngada	17	Wowoni	79
Manggarai	18	Muna	80
Sumba	19	Sula	81
Kodi	20	Buru	82
Bimanese	21	Aloene	83
Sasaks	22	Ceram	84
Balinese	23	Obi	85
Tenggerese	24	Batjan	86
Javanese	25	Sawai	87
Madurese	25	Makianese	88
Sundanese	26	Tidorese	89
Badui	27	Ternatan	90
Abung	28	Tobelorese	91
Redjang	29	Morotai	92
Banka	30		
Engganese	31		
Billiton	32		
Minangkabau	33		
Batak	34		
Alas	35		
Gayo	36		
Atjehnese	37		
Banyak	38		
Niassans	39		
Mentawei	40		
Dayaks	41		
Sambas	42		
Ot-Danom	43		
Ngadju	44		
Maanyan	45		
Kayan	46		
Kenyah	47		
Maloh	48		
Klamantan	49		
Madang	50		
Tidog	51		
Lepu Mauts	52		
Jama	53		
Murut	54		
Limbang	55		
Ranau Dusun	56		
Dusun	57		
Bisayas	58		
Kadayan	59		
Rungus	60		
Brunei	61		
Melanau	62		
Bukitans	63		
Lugats	64		

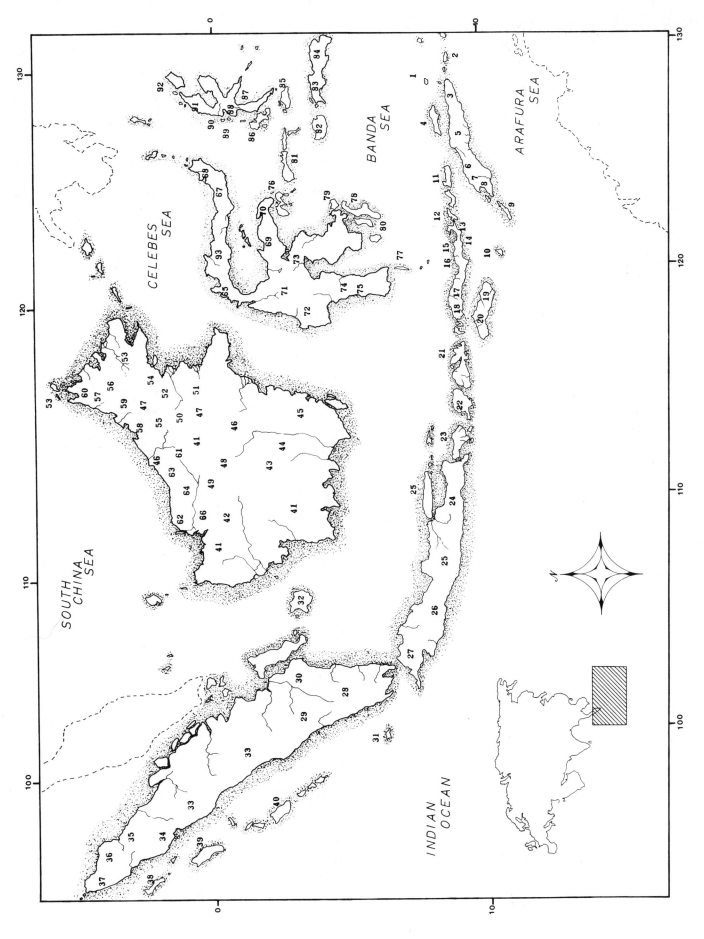

SOUTH CHINA SEA

CELEBES SEA

BANDA SEA

ARAFURA SEA

INDIAN OCEAN

69

Map 29. Australia, Western

Culture	Number	Culture	Number
Tiwi	1	Ndjiband	66
Marlgu	2	Ngaluma	67
Gari	3	Mardudhunera	68
Wurugu	4	Djalendi	69
Amurag	5	Maia	70
Eri	6	Wadjari	71
Gagadju	7	Djiwali	72
Mangaridji	8	Inggada	73
Wuningag	9	Ngugan	74
Ngalakan	10	Nganda	75
Mangarrayi	11	Ngaiawongga	76
Togeman	12	Badimaia	77
Warei	13	Widi	78
Laragia	14	Mandjindja	79
Jawony	15	Janggundjara	80
Wogeman	16	Tangara	81
Yangman	17	Gogada	82
Wadaman	18	Wiranggu	83
Djamadjong	19	Miring	84
Mulluk Mulluk	20	Galago	85
Wogaidj	21	Gelamai	86
Mariwunda	22	Amangu	87
Murinbata	23	Yued	88
Mudbara	24	Balardong	89
Nyining	25	Whadjug	90
Gadjerong	26	Bindjareb	91
Miriwong	27	Wilmen	92
Lungga	28	Nyaginyagi	93
Gwini	29	Wudjari	94
Bagu	30	Goreng	95
Wunambal	31	Ganeang	96
Worora	32	Wadandi	97
Ungarinyin	33	Bibelmen	98
Nimanburu	34	Minung	99
Ugarung	35		
Badi	36		
Yaora	37		
Djara	38		
Njinin	39		
Wandjira	40		
Gorindji	41		
Waneiga	42		
Wailbri	43		
Ngadi	44		
Walmadje	45		
Nyigena	46		
Garadjeri	47		
Nyangamada	48		
Yulbaridja	49		
Mandjildjara	50		
Ngala	51		
Kariera	52		
Nyamal	53		
Nyiabali	54		
Guradjara	55		
Injibandi	56		
Gadudjara	57		
Djargudi	58		
Bindubi	59		
Ngalia	60		
Bidjandjadjara	61		
Nyaanyadjarra	62		
Loridja	63		
Budidjara	64		
Gurama	65		

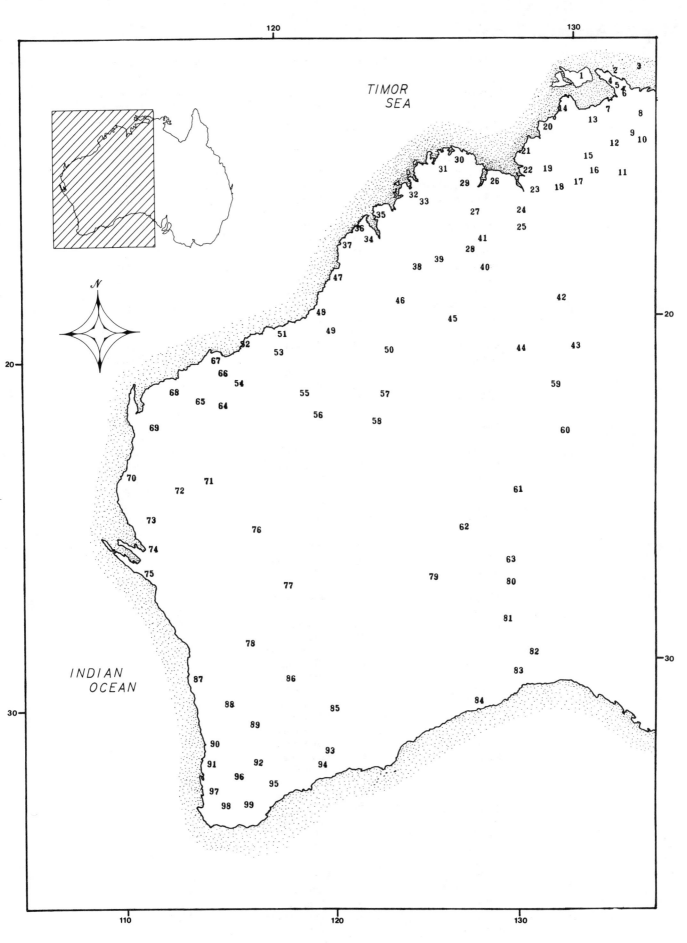

TIMOR
SEA

INDIAN
OCEAN

N

Map 30. Australia, Eastern

Culture	Number	Culture	Number	Culture	Number
Yuin	1	Ungorri	63	Dalleburra	125
Ngarigo	2	Waggumbura	64	Mungoobra	126
Kurnai	3	Thuribura	65	Wagamen	127
Theddora	4	Yarmbura	66	Yir-Yoront	128
Wolgal	5	Emon	67	Gandju	129
Baraba-Baraba	6	Unghi	68	Malnkanidji	130
Wurunjeri	7	Maranao	69	Wikmunkan	131
Bunurong	8	Buntamurra	70	Kanidji	132
Gournditch-Mara	9	Kurnandaburi	71	Tanikutti	133
Mukjarawaint	10	Dirityangura	72	Tjuundji	134
Kulin	11	Yantruwunta	73	Wimmarao	134
Wotjobaluk	12	Dieri	74	Teppathiggi	135
Wathi-Wathi	13	Willara	75	Gammatti	136
Wi-Thai-Ja	14	Lurabunna	76	Lardil	137
Wiradjura	15	Wonkanguru	77	Indjinandi	138
Geawegal	16	Yaurorka	78	Chingali	139
Gringai	17	Ngurawola	79	Jogula	140
Katang-Worimi	18	Ngameni	80	Waderi	141
Kombaingheri	19	Karanguru	81	Alawa	142
Kamilaroi	20	Wonkatyeri	82	Warndarrang	143
Wongaibon	21	Wonkamala	83	Yugul	144
Muthi-Muthi	22	Walibiri	84	Nungabuya	145
Berriait	23	Yelyuyendi	84	Dai	146
Ta-Tathi	24	Pita Pita	85	Boun	147
Wiimbaio	25	Marula	86	Barlamomo	148
Dangani	26	Tilbabura	87	Ritarngo	149
Narrinyeri	27	Auanbura	88	Rainbarngo	150
Jaraldi	28	Orambul	89	Djinba	151
Ramindjeri	29	Tarumbul	90	Nakara	152
Gaurna	30	Konkubura	91	Yandjinung	153
Narunga	31	Gangulu	92	Premingana	154
Ngadjuri	32	Kuke-Bura	93	Tralakumbina	155
Banggala	33	Wakelbura	94	Tebranuykuna	156
Parnkalla	34	Terrabura	95	Puraneters	157
Nauo	35	Kongalu	96	Poyndu	158
Hilleri	36	Bikalbura	97	Teralinak	159
Kuyani	37	Karunbura	98		
Bulalli	38	Warabul	99		
Wilya	39	Tarubura	100		
Nongait	40	Runbubura	101		
Milpulko	41	Ningebul	101		
Barkinji	42	Waranbura	101		
Naualko	43	Ristebura	102		
Paruinji	44	Kuinmurbura	103		
Barunga	45	Yetti-Maralla	104		
Guerno	46	Yankibura	105		
Barrumbinya	47	Dalebura	106		
Wollaroi	48	Mutabura	107		
Yaoro	49	Bombarabua	108		
Badjeri	50	Dorobura	109		
Chepara	51	Munkibura	110		
Kombobura	52	Boanbura	111		
Turrbal	53	Jongga	112		
Munyabora	54	Bingabura	113		
Paringnoga	54	Iningai	114		
Gilambabura	55	Goa	115		
Murubura	55	Wanamara	116		
Olongbura	55	Loritcha	117		
Kiniyen	56	Arunta	118		
Warbaa	57	Iliaura	119		
Yawai	58	Kaitish	120		
Nuku-Nukubura	59	Walpari	121		
Yargo	60	Waagai	122		
Kaiabara	61	Warramunga	123		
Bigambul	62	Workia	124		

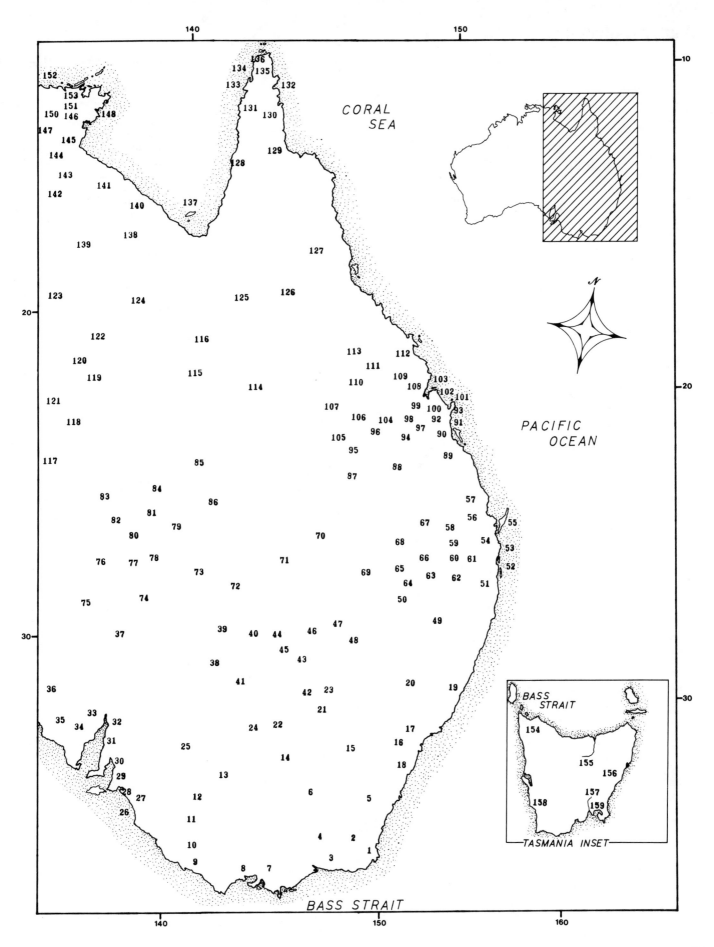

Map 31. Polynesia

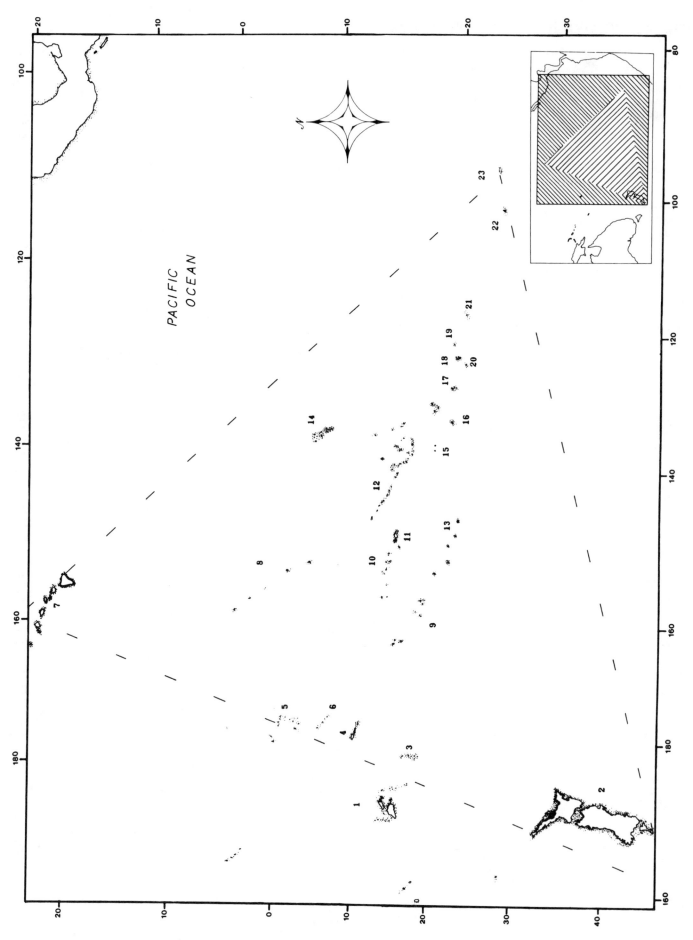

PACIFIC OCEAN

Map 32. Western Melanesia, New Guinea

Culture	Number	Culture	Number	Culture	Number	Culture	Number
Baruya	1	Etoro	70	Dani	134	Gawa	198
Binumarien	2	Augu	71	Awyu	135	Logauleng	199
Lahiwapa	3	Onabasulu	72	Usagek Goliath	135	Kela	200
Gaidemoe	4	Kakoli	73	Ngalik	136	Gaiwa	201
Tiak	5	Wabaga	74	Amyu	137	Weli	202
Langamar	6	Kyaka	75	Asmat	138	Ambo	203
Menya	7	Narak	76	Pranje	139	Toaripi	204
Sambia	8	Maring	77	Kamoro	140	Erema	205
Kai	9	Enga, Kyaka	78	Nduga	141	Roro	206
Wantoat	10	Enga, Raiapu	79	Pisa	142	Maiva	207
Nagarwapuna	11	Laiapo	80	Uhunduni	143	Mekeo	208
Tairora	12	Enga	81	Dern	144	Baba	209
Gadsup	13	Waka	82	Waropen	145	Yemai	210
Akuna	14	Huli	83	Moni	146	Binandere	211
Angu	15	Petamini	84	Simore	147	Aiga	212
Baruya	16	Gebusi	85	Lakahis	148	Nava	213
Awa	17	Honibo	86	Woda	149	Guni	214
Auyana	18	Samo	87	Ekagi	150	Kate	215
Yate	19	Kubor	88	Kapauku	151	Kita	216
Benabena	20	Konai	89	Kiowiai	152	Tauade	217
Sufrai	25	Kora	90	Faur	153	Fuyughe	218
Gimi	26	Duna	91	Arguni	154	Kunimaipa	219
Fore	27	Ipili	92	Fakfak	155	Orokaiva	220
Mbwei	28	Taro	93	Mantions	156	Oriwa	221
Lufa	29	Tombema	94	Manikons	157	Chirma	222
Gende	30	Banaro	95	Mansim	158	Gabadi	223
Hua	31	Mundugumor	96	Samalek	159	Doura	224
Ivori	32	Tchambuli	97	Ayamaro	160	Motu	225
Orokolo	33	Hewa	98	Meyach	161	Koita	226
Koriki	34	Mali	99	Amberbaken	162	Koiari	227
Pawaia	35	Bisis	100	Karen	163	Boli	228
Urama	36	Yeraki	100	Konda	164	Hula	229
Pepeha	37	Yimas	101	Kalabra	165	Seramina	230
Dumu	38	Amarken	102	Salawati	166	Aroma	231
Songu	39	Moando	103	Waigeo	167	Galeva	232
Dom	40	Tanggum	104	Tanimbar	168	Bawaki	233
Kerabi	41	Arapesh	105	Kei Islands	169	Domu	234
Chimbu	42	Kopar	106	Aru Islands	170	Mailu	235
Mingendi	43	Xarirawi	107	Oser	171	Suau	236
Wiru	44	Iatmul	108	Raintana	172	Daiomoni	237
Waiiemi	45	Chambri	109	Yelmek	173	Roboda	238
Saui	46	Yerakai	110	Maklew	174	Dobu	239
Poles	47	Ok	111	Komolom	175	Salakahadi	240
Kibenel	48	Urapmin	112	Yab-Anim	176	Bwaidoga	241
Foll	49	Feramin	113	Makiewahin	177	Trobriand	242
Kewa	50	Eliptamin	114	Boardji	178	Koobe	243
Goroka	51	Awai	115	Yei	179	Bakovi	244
Mendi	52	Abau	116	Moraori	180	Kapore	245
Wola	53	Sawos	117	Kanum-Anim	181	Nakanai	246
Kaimbi	54	Wom	118	Suka	182	Nokon	247
Mbonggu	55	Abelam	119	Zimakani	183	Mandak	248
Kuma	56	Ma	120	Dea	184	Barok	249
Bundi	57	Namie	121	Semariji	185	Tanga Island	250
Boskien	58	Wapei-Paei	122	Kamura	186	Nusu	251
Garia	59	Yeti	123	Gogodara	187	Lavongai	252
Megiar	60	Ormut	124	Bamu	188	Manus	253
Fasu	61	Sutrai	125	Wiram	189	Wogeo Island	254
Siane	62	Tor	126	Sapara	190	Japen	255
Kware	63	Isobei	127	Mikud	191	Biak	256
Kasua	64	Timorini	128	Madiri	192	Numfor	257
Kaluli	65	Saberi	129	Oroimo	193		
Harado	66	Kati	130	Kunini	194		
Kramo	67	Wabo	131	Opau	195		
Dea	68	Tamaya	132	Kapau	196		
Oybae	69	Nngalik	133	Biagai	197		

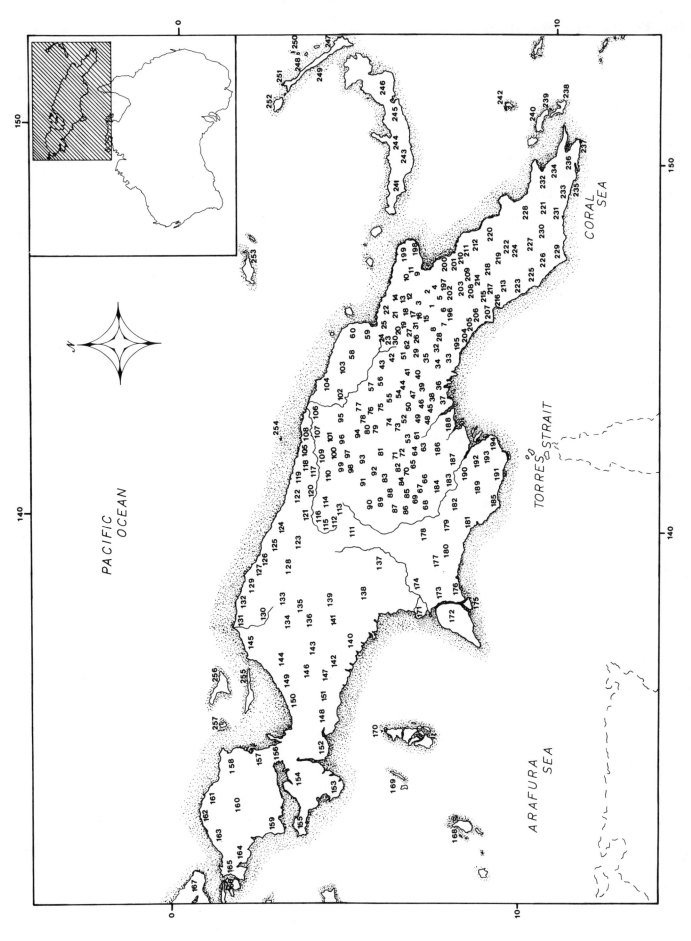

Map 33. Eastern Melanesia

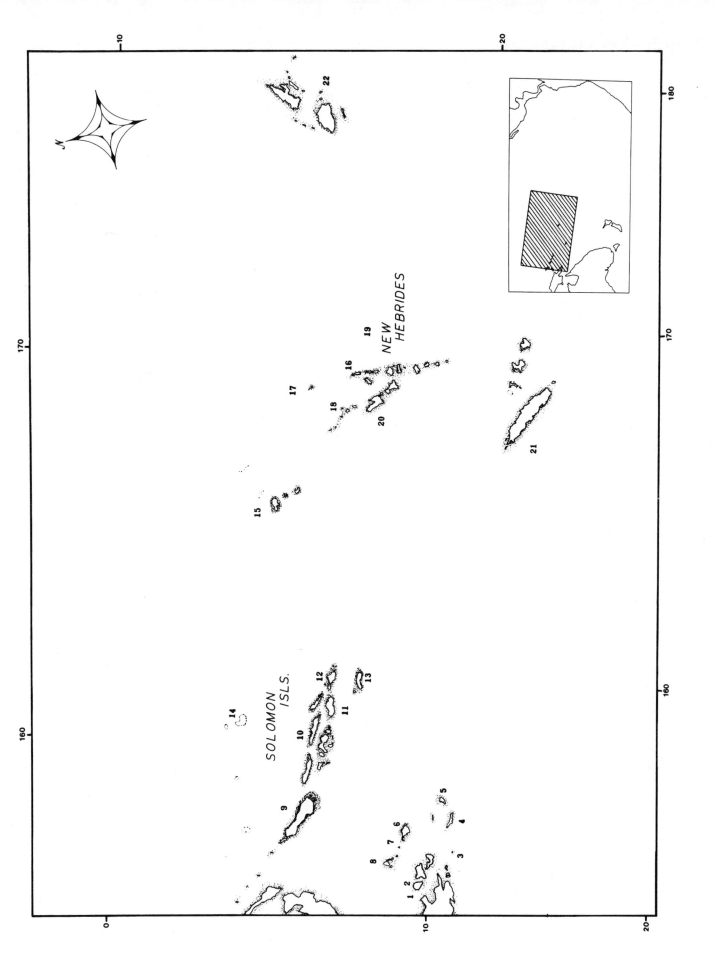

N

SOLOMON ISLS.

NEW
HEBRIDES

22

19
16
17
18
20
21
15

12
13
14
11
10

5
9
6
7
8
1
2
3

Map 34. Micronesia

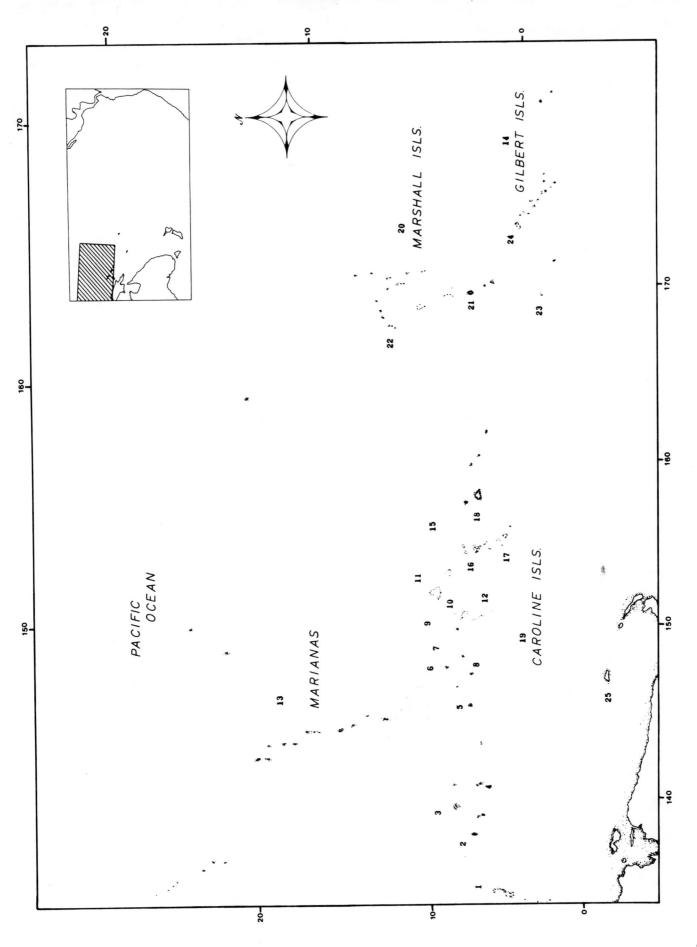

PACIFIC
OCEAN

MARIANAS

CAROLINE ISLS.

MARSHALL ISLS.

GILBERT ISLS.

Map 35. Asian North Pacific

Culture	Number
She	1
Han	2
Hui	3
Manchu	4
Mongol	5
Japanese	6
Ainu	7
Koreans	8
Okinawans	9
Nanaians	10
Russians	11

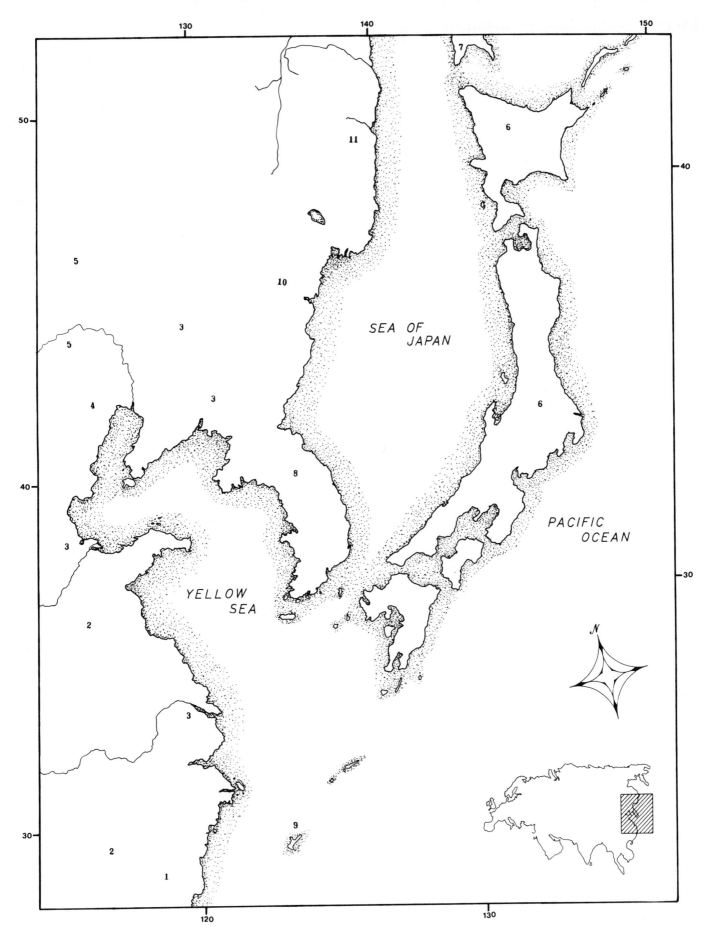

SEA OF JAPAN

PACIFIC OCEAN

YELLOW SEA

N

83

Map 36. Kamchatka Peninsula Region

Culture	Number
Aleut	1
Koryak	2
Even-Lamoot	3
Chuvanzy	4
Chukchi	5
Russians	6
Nivkhi	7
Tungus	8
Evenki	9
Yakut	10
Nanaians	11
Udeghe	12
Orochi	13
Oroks	14
Tartars	15

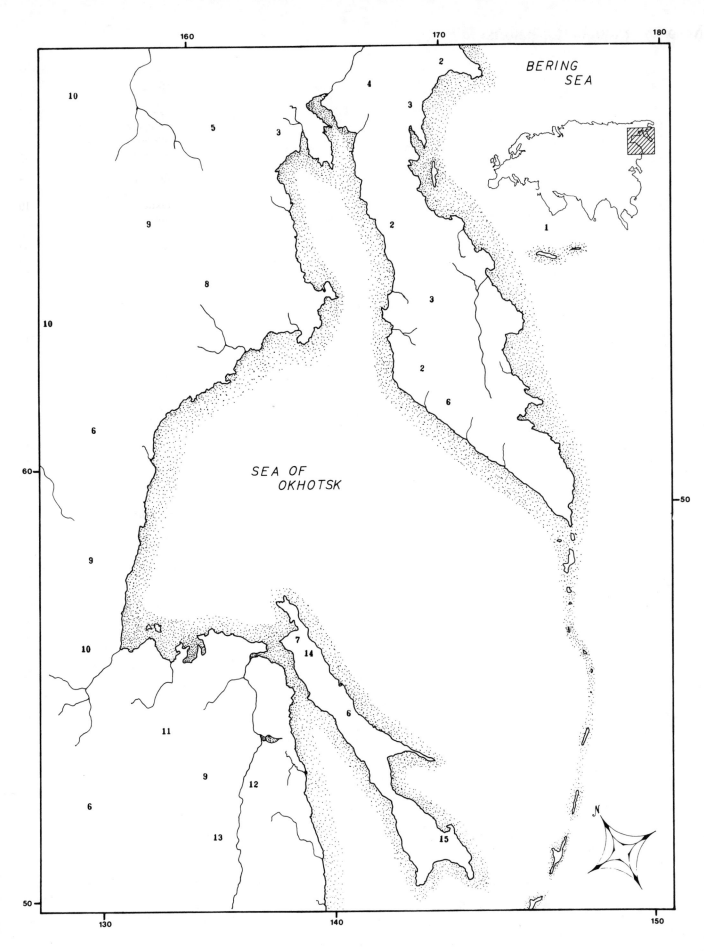

BERING
SEA

SEA OF
OKHOTSK

N

Map 37. Europe, Western

Culture	Number
Greeks	1
Albanians	2
Maltans	3
Sicilians	4
Italians	5
Sardinians	6
Corsicans	7
Montenegrins	8
Yugoslavians	9
Serbians	10
Bulgarians	11
Croats	12
Austrians	13
Tyrolians	14
Jurassians	15
Swiss	16
Corsicans	17
Occitanie	17
Catalonians	18
Basques	19
Spanish	20
Portugese	21
Gallacians	22
French	23
Alsatians	24
Bretons	25
Walloons	26
Flemish	26
Germans	27
Czechs	28
Hungarians	29
Rumanians	30
Russians	31
Poles	32
Danes	33
Lithuanians	34
Estonians	35
Finns	36
Swedish	37
Norwegians	38
Angmagsqlik	39
Lapps, Skolt	39
British	40
Welsh	41
Scottish	42
Isle of Man	43
Irish	44
Icelanders	45

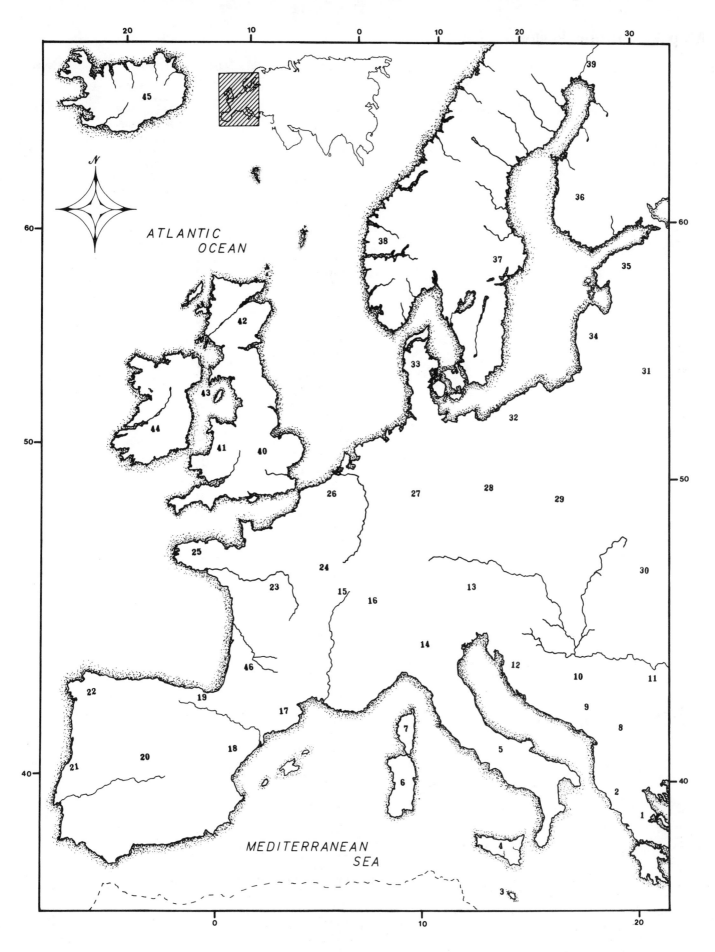

Map 38. Europe, Eastern

Culture	Number	Culture	Number
Howitat	1	Ukrainians	65
Anizah	2	Poles	66
Shammar	3	Moldavians	67
Ruwallah	4	Rumanians	68
Fauara Bedu	5	Bulgarians	69
Sbaa	6	Hungarians	70
Fedaan Bedu	7	Greeks	71
Palestinian	8	Bielorussians	72
Israeli	8	Lithuanians	73
Aqaidat Bedu	9	Latvians	74
Mauali Bedu	10	Estonians	75
Amarat Bedu	11	Russians	76
Hadid	12	Chechen	77
Khorsa Bedu	13		
Susians	14		
Bakhtiari	15		
Lurs	16		
Tajiks	17		
Kuhgalu	18		
Kashkais	19		
Persians	20		
Kajars	21		
Goklen Turkomen	22		
Yomut (Turkmen)	23		
Gurgan Turkoman	24		
Afshar	25		
Azerbaidzhan	26		
Turkomen	27		
Kurds	28		
Atmanika	29		
Armenians	30		
Shaderli	31		
Turks	32		
Laz	33		
Dersimili	34		
Bellikan	35		
Modeki	36		
Jibranli	37		
Hassananli	38		
Talysh	39		
Tat	40		
Lezgian	41		
Aguli	42		
Rutul	43		
Kumyk	44		
Lak	45		
Didi	46		
Avar	47		
Butlikh	48		
Adzhars	49		
Mingrelian	50		
Osset	51		
Georgians	52		
Abkhaz	53		
Karachai	54		
Kabardin	55		
Nogai	56		
Ingushi	57		
Kalmucks (European)	58		
Kazakhs	59		
Choudor Turkomen	60		
Khiva Yomut	61		
Bashkirs	62		
Udmurts	63		
Mordvinians	64		

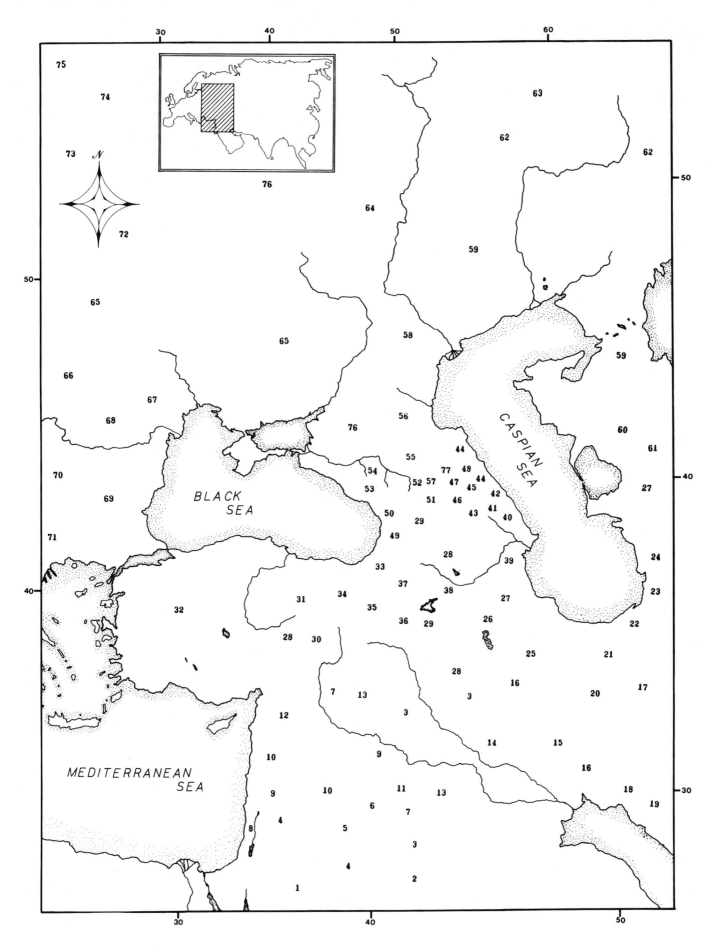

Map 39. Asia, West Central

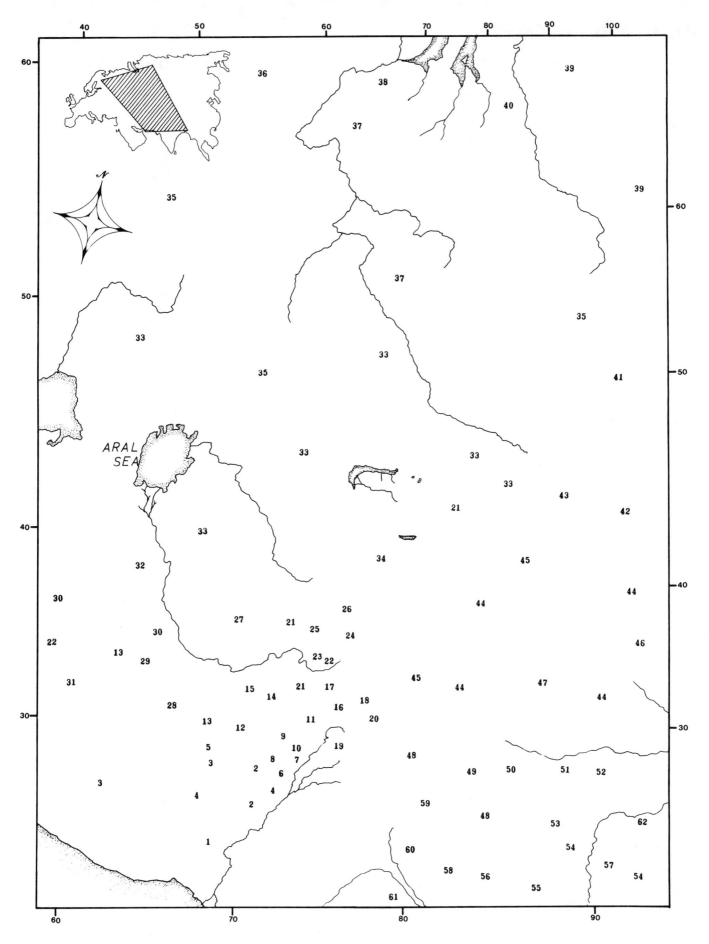

ARAL
SEA

91

Map 40. Asia, East Central

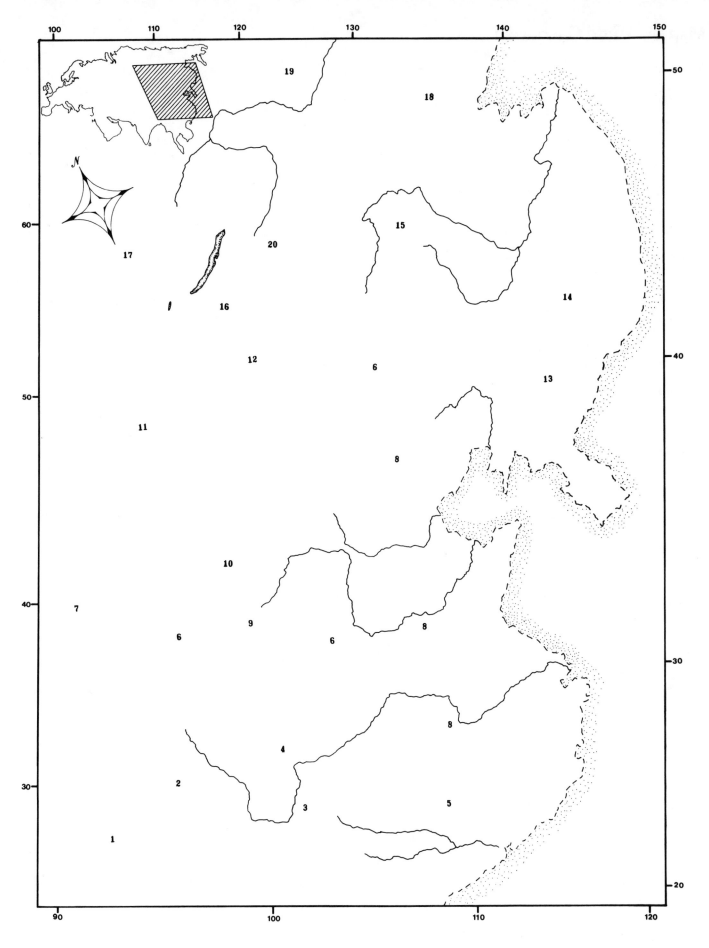

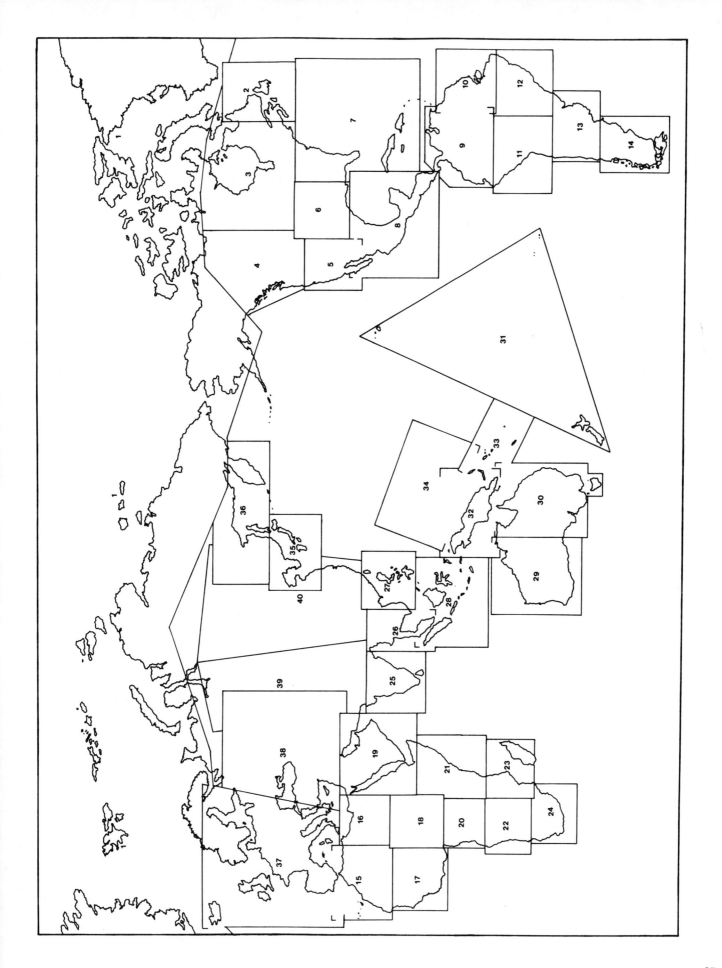

95

BIBLIOGRAPHY

Abbreviations Used

AAAM	American Anthropological Association Memoirs, American Anthropological Association: Washington, DC
ABVMD	Abhandlungen und Berichte des Staatlichen Museums fur Volkerkunde Dresden
AES	American Ethnological Society
AINA	Arctic Institute of North America, Toronto
APAMNH	Anthropological Papers of the American Museum of Natural History
APMAUM	Anthropological Papers of the Museum of Anthropology University of Michigan
ARBAE	Annual Report of the Bureau of American Ethnology, Washington, DC
BAE	Bureau of American Ethnology, Washington, DC
BBAE	Bulletin of the Bureau of American Ethnology, Washington, DC
BAMNH	Bulletin of the American Museum of Natural History
BICU	Bulletin of the International Committee on Urgent Anthropological and Ethnological Research, Wien
CUCA	Columbia University Contributions to Anthropology, New York
ESOA	Ethnographic Survey of Africa, London, International African Institute
HMAI	Handbook of Middle American Indians. Austin: University of Texas Press
HNAI	Handbook of North American Indians, Washington, DC: Smithsonian Institution
HSAI	Handbook of South American Indians. Julian Steward, ed., Washington, DC: Smithsonian Institution [also BBAE, 143, 7 vols.]
ISA	Illinois Studies in Anthropology, Urbana: University of Illinois
JRAI	Journal of the [Royal] Anthropological Institute of Great Britain and Ireland
MSA	London School of Economics Monographs in Social Anthropology
PMP	Papers of the Peabody Museum of American Archaeology and Ethnology, Harvard University, Cambridge, MA
RAI	Royal Anthropological Institute of Great Britain and Ireland, London
RMP	Revista do Museu Paulista. Nova serie, Sao Paulo
RUSNM	Report of the United States National Museum, Washington, DC
UCP	University of California Publications in American Archaeology and Ethnology, Berkeley
UCPA	University of California Publications in Anthropology, Berkeley
UPMAP	University of Pennsylvania, University Museum, Anthropological Papers, Philadelphia
VA	Die Volker Afrikas und ihre traditionellen Kulturens, Wiesbaden, Franz Steiner Verlag
YUPA	Yale University Papers in Anthropology, New Haven, CT

Bibliography

1. Abler, Thomas S. & Elisabeth Tooker, 1978, "Seneca," in B. Trigger, ed., HNAI Vol. 15, pp. 505-517.

2. Abrahams, R. G., 1967, The Peoples of Greater Unyamwezi Tanzania. ESOA, East Central Africa, Pt. 17.

3. Africa Confidential, 1987, Vol. 28(6), March 18):7.

4. Agblemagnon, F. N'sougan, 1969, Sociologie des societes orales d'Afrique Noire. Paris: Mouton.

5. Ahmed, Akbar, 1976, Millennium and Charisma Among Pathans: A Critical Essay in Social Anthropology. London: Routledge & Kegan Paul.

6. Ahmed, Akbar, 1977, Social and Economic Changes in Tribal Areas. London: Oxford University Press.

7. Alba, M. M., 1928, Etnologia y Poblacion Historica de Panama. Panama: Imprenta Nacional.

8. Alexander, Marc, 1982, British Folklore. London: Weidenfeld & Nicolson.

9. Alkire, William H., 1965, Lamotrek Atoll and Inter-Island Socioeconomic Ties. ISA no. 5.

10. Aloshban, Abdulaziz, 1987, "Al Qabila, Inter-Group Relations and the Environmental Context of Bani-Shiher in Southwest Saudi Arabia." Ph.D. Dissertation, Northwestern University.

11. Annandale, Nelson, 1905, The Faroes and Iceland. Oxford: Clarendon.

12. Appell, G. N., 1976, "Introduction," in G. N. Appell, ed., The Societies of Borneo: Explorations in the Theory of Cognatic Social Structure, pp. 1-15. Washington, DC: American Anthropological Association.

13. Ardener, Edwin, 1956, Coastal Bantu of the Cameroons. ESOA, West Africa, Pt. 11.

14. Arensberg, Conrad M. & Sol T. Kimball, 1968, Family and Community in Ireland. Cambridge, MA: Harvard University Press.

15. Arima, Eugene Y., 1984, "Caribou Eskimo," in D. Damas, ed., pp. 447-462.

16. Armstrong, W. E., 1928, Rossell Island. Cambridge: Cambridge University Press.

17. Asch, Michael I., 1981, "Slavey," in J. Helm, ed., pp. 338-349.

18. el Asmar, Fouzi, 1986, Through the Hebrew Looking Glass. London: Zed.

19. Aswad, Barbara, 1971, Property Control and Social Strategies: Settlers on a Middle Eastern Plain. APMAUM no. 44.

20. Baker, Paul T. & M. Little, eds., 1976, Man in the Andes. New York: Hutchinson & Ross.

21. Balandier, George, 1970, The Sociology of Black Africa. New York: Praeger.

22. Balikci, Asen, 1984, "Netsilik," in D. Damas, ed., pp. 415-430.

23. Ball, Ian M., 1973, Pitcairn: Children of Mutiny. Boston: Little, Brown.

24. Bannerman, J. H., 1978, "Towards a History of the Hlengwe People of the South of Rhodesia." NADA 11(5):483-496.

25. Barbour, K. M. et al., 1982, Nigeria in Maps. London: Hodder and Stoughton.

26. Barclay, Harold B., 1964, Buuri al Lamaab. Ithaca: Cornell University Press.

27. Barfield, Thomas J., 1981, The Central Asian Arabs of Afghanistan: Pastoral Nomadism in Transition. Austin: University of Texas Press.

28. Barnett, Homer G., 1955, The Coast Salish of British Columbia. Eugene: University of Oregon Press.

29. Barnett, Homer G., 1959, Being a Palauan. New York: Holt, Rinehart & Winston.

30. Barrett, Richard A., 1972, Benabarre: The Modernization of a Spanish Village. New York: Holt, Rinehart & Winston.

31. Barrett, S. A., 1908, "The Ethno-Geography of the Pomo and Neighboring Indians." UCP 6(1).

32. Barrett, S. A., 1925, "The Cayapa Indians of Ecuador." Indian Notes and Monographs 40, Pts. 1, 2.

33. Barry, Herbert, 1980, "Ethnographic Atlas XXVIIIa&b." Ethnology 19(2-3):245-263, 367-385.

34. Barth, Fredrik, 1953, Principles of Social Organization in Southern Kurdistan, Bulletin no. 7. Oslo: Universitetets Etnografiske Museum.

35. Barth, Fredrik, 1961, Nomads of South Persia. Boston: Little, Brown.

36. Barth, Fredrik, ed., 1963, The Role of the Entrepreneur in Social Change in Northern Norway. Bergen, Norway: Universitetet Arbok.

37. Barth, Fredrik, ed., 1970, Ethnic Groups and Boundaries. London: Allen & Unwin.

38. Barthel, Thomas S., 1978, The Eighth Land: The Polynesian Discovery and Settlement of Easter Island. Honolulu: University Press of Hawaii.

39. Barton, R. F., 1919, "Ifugao Law." UCP 15(1).

40. Barton, R.M.F., 1949, The Kalingas, Their Institutions and Custom Law. Chicago: University of Chicago Press.

41. Bascom, William R., 1969, The Yoruba of Southwestern Nigeria. New York: Holt, Rinehart & Winston.

42. Basden, George, 1966, Niger Ibos. London: Cass.

43. Basso, Ellen B., 1973, The Kalapalo Indians of Central Brazil. New York: Holt, Rinehart & Winston.

44. Basso, Keith H. & Morris E. Opler, 1971, Apachean Culture History and Ethnology, Anthropological Papers no. 21. Tucson: University of Arizona.

45. Bates, Daisy, 1966, The Passing of the Aborigines. London: John Murray.

46. Bateson, Gregory, 1936, Naven. Stanford, CA: Stanford University Press. (1958)

47. Baxter, P. T. W. & Audrey Butt, 1953, The Azande and Related Peoples of the Anglo-Egyptian Sudan and Belgian Congo. ESOA, East Central Africa, Pt. 9.

48. Bay, Edna G., 1985, Asen: Iron Altars of the Fon People of Benin. Atlanta: Emory University, Museum of Art.

49. Bayliss-Smith, Tim P., 1975, "Ontong Java: Depopulation and Repopulation," in V. Carroll, ed., pp. 417-484.

50. Beaglehole, E. & P. Beaglehole, 1938, "Ethnology of Pukapuka." Bulletin of the Bishop Museum 150:1-419.

51. Beals, Ralph L., 1933, "Ethnology of the Nisenan." UCP 3(6).

52. Beals, Ralph L., 1969, "The Tarascans," in E. Vogt, ed., HMAI. Vol. 8: Ethnology, pp. 638-681.

53. Bean, Lowell & Charles Smith, 1978, "Serrano," in Heizer, ed., pp. 570-574.

54. Beattie, John, 1960, Bunyoro: An African Kingdom. New York: Holt, Rinehart & Winston.

55. Beauclair, Inez de, 1970, Tribal Cultures of Southwest China. Taipei: Orient Culture Service.

56. Beck, Lois, 1986, The Qashqa'i of Iran. New Haven, CT: Yale University Press.

57. Becker-Donner, Etta, 1962, "Guapore-Gebiet." BICU no. 5, pp. 146-150.

58. Beckerman, Stephen, 1975, "The Cultural Energetics of the Bari (Motilones Bravos) of Northern Colombia." Ph.D. dissertation, University of New Mexico, Albuquerque.

59. Beckerman, Stephen, 1983, "Carpe Diem: An Optimal Foraging Approach to Bari Fishing and Hunting," in R. Hames & W. Vickers, eds.

60. Behuke, R., 1980, The Herders of Cyrenaica: Ecology, Economy and Kinship Among the Bedouin of Eastern Libya. Urbana: University of Illinois Press.

61. Beidelman, Thomas O., 1967, The Matrilineal Peoples of Eastern Tanzania. ESOA, East Central Africa, Pt. 16.

62. Beidelman, Thomas O., 1971, The Kaguru: A Matrilineal People of East Africa. New York: Holt, Rinehart & Winston.

63. Bejarano, Ramon C., 1980, Indigenas Paraguayos: Epoca Colonial. Asuncion: Editorial Toledo.

64. Bell, Charles, 1928, The People of Tibet. Oxford: Clarendon.

65. Belmonte, Thomas, 1979, The Broken Fountain. New York: Columbia University Press.

66. Benedict, Ruth, 1946, The Chrysanthemum and the Sword. Boston: Houghton Mifflin.

67. Bennett, M. M., 1927, "Notes on the Dalleburra Tribe of Northern Queensland." JRAI 57:399-416.

68. Bennett, Wendell C. & Robert M. Zingg, 1935, The Tarahumara. Chicago: University of Chicago Press.

69. Bernatzik, Hugo Adolf, 1938, Overland with the Nomad Lapps. New York: R. M. McBride.

70. Berndt, Ronald, 1962, Excess and Restraint: Social Control Among a New Guinea Mountain People. Chicago: University of Chicago Press.

71. Berndt, Ronald & Catherine H. Berndt, 1964, The World of the First Australians. Chicago: University of Chicago Press.

72. Berndt, Ronald & Catherine H. Berndt, 1979, Aborigines of the West: Their Past and Their Present. Nedlands: University of Western Australia Press.

73. Berndt, Ronald & Peter Lawrence, eds., 1973, Politics in New Guinea: Traditional and in the Context of Change, Some Anthropological Perspectives. Seattle: University of Washington Press.

74. Berreman, Joel V., 1937, Tribal Distribution in Oregon. AAAM no. 47.

75. Best, Elsdon, 1977, Maori Religion & Mythology. New York: AMS.

76. Bihar Tribal Research Institute, 1960, Tribal Bihar in Maps. Delhi, India: Ranchi.

77. Bindagji, Hussein Hamza, 1978, Atlas of Saudi Arabia. London: Oxford University Press.

78. Biobaku, Saburi O., 1928, The Egba and Their Neighbors, 1842-1872. Oxford: Clarendon.

79. Bird, Junius, 1946, "The Alacaluf." HSAI 1:55-80.

80. Bishop, Charles A., 1976, "The Emergence of the Northern Ojibwa: Social and Economic Consequences." American Ethnologist 3(1):39-54.

81. Blackburn, Thomas C. & Lowell J. Bean, 1978, "Kitanemuk," in Heizer, ed., pp. 564-569.

82. Blackman, William F., 1977, The Making of Hawaii: A Study in Social Evolution. New York: AMS.

83. Blackwood, Beatrice, 1935, Both Sides of Buka Passage. Oxford: Clarendon.

84. Blake, G., J. Dewdney, & J. Mitchell, 1986, The Cambridge Atlas of the Middle East and North Africa. New York: Cambridge University Press.

85. Blau, Harold, J. Campisi, & E. Tooker, 1978, "Onondaga," in B. Trigger, ed., pp. 491-499.

86.   Bliss, Frank & Jurgen Osing, 1986, Kharga and Dakhla Oases. New York: Columbia University Press.

87.   Bloch, Maurice, 1986, From Blessing to Violence: History and Ideology in the Circumcision Ritual of the Merina of Madagascar. New York: Cambridge University Press.

88.   Boas, Franz, 1888, The Central Eskimo. Lincoln: University of Nebraska Press. (republished 1964)

89.   Boas, Franz, 1895, "The Social Organization and the Secret Societies of the Kwakiutl Indians." RUSNM, pp. 311-738.

90.   Boas, Franz, 1934, Geographical Names of the Kwakiutl Indians. New York: Columbia University Press.

91.   Boas, Franz (Helen Codere, ed.), 1966, Kwakiutl Ethnography. Chicago: University of Chicago Press.

92.   Bock, Philip K., 1978, "Micmac," in B. Trigger, ed., pp. 109-122.

93.   Bogoras, Waldemer, 1907, "The Chuckchee," Pt. 2. BAMNH 11:277-733.

94.   Bohannan, Laura & Paul Bohannan, 1953, The Tiv of Central Nigeria. ESOA, Western Africa, Pt. 8.

95.   Boissevain, Jeremy, 1980, Hal-Farrug: A Village in Malta. New York: Holt, Rinehart & Winston.

96.   Bolivar, Coronado R., 1918, La gran Florida. Madrid: Editorial-America.

97.   Borders, Karl, 1927, Village Life Under the Soviets. New York: Vanguard.

98.   Bowen, Thomas, 1983, "Seri," in A. Ortiz, ed., Vol. 10, pp. 230-249.

99.   Bowles, Gordon T., 1977, The Peoples of Asia. New York: Scribner.

100.   Bradbury, R. E. & P. C. Lloyd, 1957, The Benin Kingdom and the Itsekiri. ESOA, Western Africa, Pt. 13.

101.   Brasser, Ted J., 1974, Riding on the Frontier's Crest: Mahican Indian Culture and Culture Change, Mercury Series. Ottawa: National Museum of Man.

102.   Brasser, Ted J., 1978, "Mahican," in B. Trigger, ed., pp. 198-212.

103.   Brewster, A. B., 1922, The Hill Tribes of Fiji. Philadelphia: J. B. Lippincott.

104.   Brigg, Jean L., 1970, Never in Anger: Portrait of an Eskimo Family. Cambridge, MA: Harvard University Press.

105.   Briggs, Lloyd C., 1960, Tribes of the Sahara. Cambridge, MA: Harvard University Press.

106.   British Museum, 1910, Handbook to the Ethnographical Collections. London: Oxford University Press.

107.   Bromley, Myron, 1967, "The Linguistic Relationships of Grand Valley Dani: A Lexico-Statistical Classification." Oceania 37:287-308.

108.   Brookfield, H. C., 1964, "The Ecology of Highland Settlement: Some Suggestions." American Ethnologist 4(2):20-38.

109.   Brookfield, H. C. & Paula Brown, 1963, Struggle for Land: Agriculture and Group Territories Among the Chimbu of the New Guinea Highlands. Melbourne: Oxford University Press.

110.   Brooks, Edwin et al., 1973, Tribes of the Amazon Basin in Brazil 1972. London: Charles Knight.

111.   Brow, James, 1978, Vedda Villages of Anuradhapura: The Historical Anthropology of a Community in Sri Lanka. Seattle: University of Washington Press.

112.   Brown, A. R., 1913, "Three Tribes of Western Australia." JRAI 43:143-194.

113.   Brown, J. Macmillan, 1927, Peoples and Problems of the Pacific. London: Bouverie House.

114.   Brown, Michael F., 1986, Tsewa's Gift: Magic and Meaning in an Amazonian Society. Washington, DC: Smithsonian Institution Press.

115.   Brown, Paula, 1960, "Chimbu Tribes: Political Organization in the Eastern Highlands of New Guinea." Southwestern Journal of Anthropology 16(1):22-35.

116.   Brown, Paula, 1978, Highland Peoples of New Guinea. London: Cambridge University Press.

117.   Brugge, David M., 1983, "Navajo Prehistory and History to 1850," in A. Ortiz, ed., Vol. 10, pp. 489-501.

118.   Brunden, Caroline & Mark Elvin, 1983, Cultural Atlas of China. New York: Facts on File.

119.   Buechler, Ira & Buechler, Judith, 1971, The Bolivian Aymara. New York: Holt, Rinehart & Winston.

120.   Bullock, Charles, 1928, The Mashona. Cape Town: Juta.

121.   Burch, Ernest S., 1984, "Kotzebue Sound Eskimo," in D. Damas, ed., pp. 303-319.

122.   Burrows, Edwin G. & Melford Spiro, 1957, An Atoll Culture. New Haven, CT: HRAF.

123.   Burssens, H., 1958, Les peuplades de L'entre Congo-Ubangi. ESOA, Central Africa Belgian Congo, Pt. 4.

124.   Butt, Audrey, 1952, The Nilotes of the Anglo-Egyptian Sudan and Uganda. ESOA, East Central Africa, Pt. 4.

125.   Butt, Audrey J., 1965, "The Guianas." BICU no. 7, pp. 69-91.

126.   Buxton, L.H. Dudley, 1922, "The Ethnology of Malta and Gozo." JRAI 52:164-211.

127.   Callaway, D., J. Janetski, & O. C. Stewart, 1986, "Ute," in D'Azevedo, ed., pp. 336-367.

128.   Callender, Charles, 1978, "Sauk," in B. Trigger, ed., pp. 648-655.

129.   Callender, Charles, 1978, "Shawnee," in B. Trigger, ed., pp. 622-634.

130.   Callender, Charles, 1978, "Illinois," in B. Trigger, ed., pp. 673-680.

131.   Campbell, T. N., 1983, "Coahuiltecans and Their Neighbors," in A. Ortiz, ed., Vol. 10, pp. 343-358.

132.   Campisi, Jack, 1978, "Oneida," in B. Trigger, ed., pp. 481-490.

133.   Capell, Adrian, 1962, A Linguistic Survey of the Southwestern Pacific, South Pacific Commission Technical Paper no. 136. Noumea: New Caledonia.

134. Carneiro, Robert, 1961, "Slash and Burn Cultivation Among the Kuikuru and Its Implications for Cultural Development in the Amazon Basin." Antropologica Suppl. 2:47-65.

135. Carneiro, Robert, 1962, "The Amahuaca Indians of Eastern Peru." Explorers Journal 40(4):26-37.

136. Carroll, Vern, ed., 1972, Pacific Atoll Populations, Association for Social Anthropology in Oceania Monograph no. 3. Honolulu: University of Hawaii Press.

137. Carte ethnolinguistique de l'Indochine, 1949, Hanoi: l'Ecole Francaise d'Extreme Orient.

138. Caspar, Franz, 1952, Tupari: Unter Indios im Urwald Brasiliens. Braunschweig: F. Vieweg.

139. Catchpole, Brian & I. A. Akinjogbin, 1984, A History of West Africa in Maps and Diagrams. London: Collins Educational.

140. Cawte, John, 1978, "Gross Stress in Small Islands," in C. D. Laughlin & I. A. Brady, eds., pp. 93-121.

141. Central Intelligence Agency, 1968, Gabon, Ethnolinguistic Group Map. Washington, DC: Government Printing Office.

142. Central Intelligence Agency, 1969, Chad, Ethnolinguistic Group Map. Washington, DC: Government Printing Office.

143. Central Intelligence Agency, 1970, Angola, Ethnolinguistic Group Map. Washington, DC: Government Printing Office.

144. Central Intelligence Agency, 1971, Algeria, Ethnolinguistic Group Map. Washington, DC: Government Printing Office.

145. Central Intelligence Agency, 1973, Guinea, Ethnolinguistic Group Map. Washington, DC: Government Printing Office.

146. Central Intelligence Agency, 1973, Mozambique, Ethnolinguistic Group Map. Washington, DC: Government Printing Office.

147. Central Intelligence Agency, 1974, Libya, Ethnolinguistic Group Map. Washington, DC: Government Printing Office.

148. Central Intelligence Agency, 1976, Indian Ocean Atlas. Washington, DC: Government Printing Office.

149. Cerulli, Ernesta, 1956, Peoples of Southwest Ethiopia and Its Borderlands. ESOA, North-Eastern Africa, Pt. 3.

150. Chagnon, Napoleon A., 1974, Studying the Yanomamo. New York: Holt, Rinehart & Winston.

151. Chagnon, Napoleon A., 1977, Yanomamo: The Fierce People. New York: Holt, Rinehart & Winston.

152. Chai, Chen Kang, 1967, Taiwan Aborigines. Cambridge, MA: Harvard University Press.

153. Champion, Arthur M., 1967, The Agiryama of Kenya, RAI Occasional Paper no. 25.

154. Chapelle, Jean, 1957, Nomades noirs du Sahara. Paris: Librairie Plon.

155. Chelhod, Joseph, 1984, L'arabie du sud histoire et civilisation. Paris: G. P. Maisonneuve et Larose.

156. Chiapuris, John, 1979, The Ait Ayash of the High Moulouya Plain: Rural Social Organization in Morocco. APMAUM no. 69.

157. Chinas, Beverly, 1973, The Isthmus Zapotecs: Women's Roles in Cultural Context. New York: Holt, Rinehart & Winston.

158. Chiva, Isac, 1963, "Social Organization, Traditional Economy, and Customary Law in Corsica," in J. Pitt-Rivers, ed., Mediterranean Countrymen, pp. 97-112. Paris: Mouton.

159. Chowning, Ann & Ward H. Goodenough, 1973, "Lakalai Political Organization," in Ronald Berndt et al., eds., pp. 113-174. Seattle: University of Washington Press.

160. Chowning, Ann, 1983, "Wealth and Exchange Among the Molima of Fergusson Island," in J. Leach & E. Leach, eds., pp. 411-427.

161. Christian, Kaufmann, 1972, Das Topferhandwerk der Kwoma in Nord-Neuguinea, Band 12. Basel: Basler Beitrage zur Ethnologie.

162. Clark, A. McFadyen, 1981, "Koyukon," in J. Helm, ed., pp. 582-601.

163. Clark, Annette M., 1974, Koyukuk River Culture. Ottawa: National Museum of Canada.

164. Clark, D. W., 1984, "Pacific Eskimo: Historical Ethnography," in D. Damas, ed., pp. 185-197.

165. Clark, Robert P., 1980, "Euzkadi: Basque Nationalism in Spain, Since the Civil War," in C. R. Foster, ed., pp. 75-100.

166. Clarke, J., S. Nelson, & K. Swindell, 1966, Sierra Leone in Maps. London: University of London Press.

167. Clay, Brenda Johnson, 1986, Mandak Realities: Person and Power in Central New Ireland. New Brunswick: Rutgers University Press.

168. Clifford, Edward Winslow, 1918, "Clans and Moieties in Southern California." UCP 15(2).

169. Cline, Walter, R. Commons et al., 1938, "The Sinkaietk or Southern Okanagon of Washington," in L. Spier, ed., General Series in Anthropology 6:1-262.

170. Clough, Ethlyn T., ed., 1909, Norwegian Life. Detroit: Bay View Reading Club.

171. Codrington, R. H., 1891, The Melanesians: Studies in their Anthropology and Folklore. Oxford: Oxford University Press.

172. Cohen, Ronald, 1967, The Kanuri of Bornu. New York: Holt, Rinehart & Winston.

173. Cole, Donald Powell, 1975, Nomads of the Nomads: The Al Murrah Bedouin of the Empty Quarter. Arlington Heights, IL: AMH.

174. Colle, R. P., 1913, Les Baluba (Congo Belge), Collection de Monographies Ethnographiques no. 11. Bruxelles: A. Dewit.

175. Colson, Elizabeth & Max Gluckman, 1951, Seven Tribes of British Central Africa. Manchester: Manchester University Press.

176.   Comas, Juan, 1960, Pigmeos en America. Mexico: Universidad Nacional Autonoma de Mexico.

177.   Condominas, George, 1977, We Have Eaten the Forest. New York: Hill & Wang.

178.   Conklin, Harold C., 1949, "Preliminary Report on Fieldwork on the Island of Mindoro and Palawan, Philippines." American Anthropologist 51:268-273.

179.   Conklin, Harold C., 1980, Ethnographic Atlas of Ifugao: A Study of Environment, Culture, and Society in Northern Luzon. New Haven, CT: Yale University Press.

180.   Coon, Carleton S., 1931, "Tribes of the Rif." Harvard African Studies 9.

181.   Cooper, J. M., 1946, "The Araucanians." HSAI 2:687-760.

182.   Cooper, John M., 1917, "Analytical and Critical Bibliography of the Tribes of Tierra del Fuego and Adjacent Territories." DBAE Bull. 63.

183.   Cooper, John M., 1917, "Fuegian and Chonoan Tribal Relations." International Congress of Americanists Proceedings 19.

184.   Cooper, John M., 1946, "Indian Hunters of South America." HSAI 1:13-17.

185.   Cooper, John M., 1946, "The Ona." HSAI 1:107-126.

186.   Cooper, John M., 1946, "The Yahgan." HSAI 1:81-106.

187.   Cooper, John M., 1946, "The Southern Hunters: An Introduction." HSAI 1:13-16.

188.   Cooper, Robert G., 1983, "Sexual Inequality Among the Hmong," in J. McKinnon & W. Bhruksasri, eds., pp. 173-186.

189.   Correa, A.A. Mendes, 1944, Timor Portugues. Lisbon: Impresa Nacional de Lisbon.

190.   Couper, Alastair, 1983, The Times Atlas of the Oceans. New York: Van Nostrand Reinhold.

191.   Crazzolara, J. R., 1950, The Lwoo, Pt. 1, Lwoo Migrations. Verona: Istituto Missioni Africane.

192.   Creanga, Ion, 1952, Folktales from Roumania. London: Routledge & Kegan Paul.

193.   Crocker, William H., 1974, "Extramarital Sexual Practices of the Ramkokamekra-Canela Indians," in P. Lyon, ed., pp. 184-194.

194.   Crow, John R. & Philip R. Obley, 1981, "Han," in J. Helm, ed., pp. 506-513.

195.   Crumrine, N. Ross, 1983, "Mayo," in A. Ortiz, ed., Vol. 10, pp. 264-275.

196.   Crystal, David, 1987, The Cambridge Encyclopedia of Language. New York: Cambridge University Press.

197.   Culwick, A. T. & G. M. Culwick, 1935, Ubena of the Rivers. London: Allen & Unwin.

198.   Cunha, Ayres Camara, 1960, Entre os Indios do Xingu. Sao Paulo: Livraria Exposicao do Livro.

199.   Cunnison, Ian, 1959, The Luapula Peoples of Northern Rhodesia. Manchester: Manchester University Press.

200.   Cunnison, Ian, 1966, Baggara Arabs: Power and the Lineage in a Sudanese Nomad Tribe. Oxford: Clarendon.

201.   Cureau, D. Ad, 1912, Les societes primitives de L'Afrique Equatoriale. Paris: Librairie Armand Colin.

202.   Czaplicka, M. A., 1914, Aboriginal Siberia: A Study in Social Anthropology. Oxford: Clarendon.

203.   D'Anglure, B. Saladin, 1984, "Inuit of Quebec," in D. Damas, ed., pp. 476-507.

204.   D'Azevedo, Warren L., 1984, "Washoe," in W. D'Azevedo, ed., pp. 467-498.

205.   D'Azevedo, Warren L., ed., 1986, Handbook of North American Indians. Vol. 11: Great Basin. Washington, DC: Smithsonian Institution Press.

206.   D'Hertefelt, M. et al., 1962, Les anciens royaumes de la zone interlacustre meridionale. ESOA, East Central Africa, Pt. 14.

207.   D'anglure, B. Saladin, 1984, "Inuit of Quebec," in D. Damas, ed., pp. 476-507.

208.   Damas, David, ed., 1984, Handbook of North American Indians. Vol. 5: Arctic. Washington, DC: Smithsonian Institution Press.

209.   Damas, David, 1984, "Copper Eskimo," in D. Damas, ed., pp. 397-414.

210.   Davenport, William, 1975, "The Population of the Outer Reef Islands, British Solomon Islands Protectorate," in V. Carroll, ed., pp. 64-116.

211.   Davies, D. Hywel, ed., 1971, Zambia in Maps. New York: Africana.

212.   Davis, Shelton H., 1977, Victims of the Miracle: Development and the Indians of Brazil. Cambridge: Cambridge University Press.

213.   De Almeida, Antonio, 1965, Bushmen and Other Non-Bantu Peoples of Angola. Pietermaritzburg: Witwatersrand University Press.

214.   De Arauz, Reina Torres, 1962, "Culturas Indigenas del Este de Panama." BICUA&ER no. 5, pp. 70-97.

215.   De Beauclair, Inez, 1974, Tribal Cultures of Southwest China. Taipei: Chinese Association of Folklore.

216.   De Fabrega, H. P., 1907, Ethnographic and Linguistic Notes on the Paez Indians of Tierra Adentro Cauca Colombia, AAAM no. 5, pp. 301-356.

217.   De Laguna, Frederica, 1972, Smithsonian Contributions to Anthropology. Vol. 7: Under Mount Saint Elias: The History and Culture of the Yakutat Tlingit. Washington, DC: Smithsonian Institution.

218.   De Laguna, Frederica & Catharine McClellan, 1981, "Ahtna," in J. Helm, ed., pp. 641-663.

219.   De Lima, Pedro, 1950, "Os Indios Waura." Boletim do Museu Nacional (Rio de Janerio), no. 9.

220.   De Williams, Anita Alvarez, 1983, "Cocopa," in A. Ortiz, ed., Vol. 10, pp. 99-112.

221.   Deacon, A. Bernard, 1934, Malekula: A Vanishing People in the New Hebrides. London: Routledge.

222.   Deagan, Kathleen A., 1985, "Spanish-Indian Interaction in Sixteenth-Century Florida and Hispaniola," in W. W. Fitzhugh, ed., pp. 281-318.

223.   Decicco, Gabriel, 1969, "The Chatino," in E. Vogt, ed., HMAI. Vol. 7: Ethnology, pp. 360-366.

224.   Delhaise, 1909, Les Warega, Collection de Monographies Ethnographiques no. 5. Bruxelles: A. Dewit.

225. Denevan, William M., 1971, "Campa Subsistence in the Gran Pajonal, Eastern Peru." Geographical Review 61(4):496-519.

226. Deng, Francis Mading, 1972, The Dinka of the Sudan. New York: Holt, Rinehart & Winston.

227. Denniston, 1981, "Sekani," in J. Helm, ed., pp. 433-450.

228. Dentan, Robert Knox, 1968, The Semai: A Nonviolent People of Malay. New York: Holt, Rinehart & Winston.

229. Diamong, R., 1969, K'un Shen: A Taiwan Village. New York: Holt, Rinehart & Winston.

230. Diebold, A. Richard, 1969, "The Huave," in Vogt, ed., HMAI. Vol. 7: Ethnology, pp. 478-488.

231. Dittmer, K., 1979, "Die Obervolta-Provinz." VA 2:495-542.

232. Dixon, R. B., 1907, "The Shasta." BAMNH 17:381-498.

233. Dixon, Roland B. & Alfred L. Kroeber, 1919, "Linguistic Families of California." UCP 16(3).

234. Doke, C. M., 1931, The Lambas of Northern Rhodesia. London: Harrap.

235. Dole, Gertrude, 1968, "Tribe as the Autonomous Unit," in J. Helm, ed., pp. 83-100.

236. Dolgikh, B. O., 1962, "Contributions to the History of the Buryat-People." AINA no. 2.

237. Dolgikh, B. O., 1962, "On the Origin of the Nganasans-Preliminary Remarks." AINA no. 2.

238. Domotor, Tekla, 1981, Hungarian Folk Beliefs. Bloomington: Indiana University Press.

239. Donner, Kai, 1954, Among the Samoyed in Siberia. New Haven, CT: HRAF.

240. Dostal, Walter, 1983, Ethnographic Atlas of 'Asir. Wien: Der Osterreichischen Akademie der Wissenschaften.

241. Doumenge, Jean-Pierre, 1975, Paysans Melanesiens, en pays canala-nlle Caledone. Talence: Centre d'etudes de geographie Tropicale.

242. Downs, James F., 1966, The Two Worlds of the Washo. New York: Holt, Rinehart & Winston.

243. Dozier, Edward P., 1954, "The Hopi-Tewa of Arizona." UCP 44(3).

244. Dozier, Edward P., 1966, Hano: The Tewa Indian Community in Arizona. New York: Holt, Rinehart & Winston.

245. Dozier, Edward P., 1967, The Kalinga of Northern Luzon. New York: Holt, Rinehart & Winston.

246. Dresch, Paul, 1982, "The Northern Tribes of Yemen, Their Organization and Place in Yemen." Unpublished Ph.D. Dissertation, Oxford, St. Catherines College.

247. Dreyfus, Simone, 1963, Les Kayapo du Nord, Etat de Para Brazil. Paris: Mouton.

248. Driberg, J. H., 1923, The Lango: A Nilotic Tribe of Uganda. London: Unwin.

249. Drucker, Philip, 1937, "The Tolowa and Their Southwest Oregon Kin." UCP 36(4).

250. Drucker, Philip, 1951, The Northern and Central Nootkan Tribes, BBAE no. 144.

251. Drucker, S., R. Escalante, & R. Weitlaner, 1969, "The Cuitlatec," in E. Vogt, ed., HMAI. Vol 7: Ethnology, pp. 565-576.

252. du Toit, Brian M., 1975, Akuna: A New Guinea Village Communtiy. Rotterdam: A. A. Balkema.

253. du Toit, Brian M., 1978, "Introduction," in B. du Toit, ed., Ethnicity in Modern Africa, pp. 1-16. Boulder, CO: Westview.

254. DuBois, Cora, 1944, The People of Alor. New York: Harper.

255. Dube, S. C., 1951, The Kamar. London: Universal.

256. Dubois, H. M., 1938, Monographie des Betsileo (Madagascar). Paris: Universite de Paris.

257. Duby, Gertrude & Franz Blom, 1969, "The Lacandon," in E. Vogt, ed., HMAI. Vol. 7: Ethnology, pp. 276-297.

258. Duff, Wilson, 1981, "Tsetsaut," in J. Helm, ed., pp. 455-457.

259. Dufour, Darna, 1983, "Nutrition in the Northwest Amazon," in R. Hames & W. Vickers, eds., pp. 329-355.

260. Dugast, Idelette, 1955, Monographie de la tribu des Ndiki, Travaux et Memoires de L'institut d E'thnologie 58. Paris: Universite de Paris.

261. Dumont, Jean Paul, 1972, Under the Rainbow. Austin: University of Texas Press.

262. Dundas, Charles, 1921, "Native Laws of Some Bantu Tribes of East Africa." JRAI 51:216-278.

263. Dunn, Stephen P., 1967, The Peasants of Central Russia. New York: Holt, Rinehart & Winston.

264. Dunnigan, Timothy, 1983, "Lower Pima," in A. Ortiz, ed., Vol. 10, pp. 217-229.

265. Dupuy, Andre, 1976, Historique de l'occitanie. Montpellier: Dupuy.

266. Durham, Margaret E., 1910, "High Albania and Its Customs in 1908." J. of RAI 40:453-472.

267. Durham, Margaret E., 1935, "Bride-Price in Albania." Man 35:102.

268. Durlach, T. M., 1928, "The Relationship Systems of the Tlingit, Haida and Tsimshan." Publications of the American Ethnological Society 11:1-177.

269. Durrenberger, E. Paul, 1983, "Lisu: Political Form, Ideology and Economic Action," in J. McKinnon & W. Bhruksasri, eds., pp. 215-226.

270. Durrenberger, E. Paul, 1983, "Changes in a Shan Village," in J. McKinnon & W. Bhruksasri, eds., pp. 112-122.

271. Dutt, Ashok K. & M. Margaret Geib, 1987, Atlas of South Asia: Fully Annotated. Boulder, CO: Westview.

272. Durham, M. E., 1928, Some Tribal Origins, Laws and Customs of the Balkins. London: Allen & Unwin.

273. Eells, Myron, 1887, "The Indians of Puget Sound." American Antiquarian 9(Jan.).

274. Eggan, Fred, 1937, "Historical Change in the Choctaw Kinship System." American Anthropologist 39:34-52.

275. Eggan, Fred, 1950, Social Organization of the Western Pueblos. Chicago: University of Chicago Press.

276. Eguilaz, Isabel, 1965, Publicaciones del Seminario de Antropologia Americana. Vol. 7: Los Indios del Norodeste de Mejico en el Siglo. Sevilla: Universidad de Sevilla.

277. Eickelman, Dale F., 1976, Moroccan Islam, Tradition and Society in a Pilgrimage Center. Austin: University of Texas Press.

278. Ekvall, Robert, 1968, Fields on the Hoof: Nexus of Tibetan Nomadic Pastoralism. New York: Holt, Rinehart & Winston.

279. Elkin, A. P., 1977, Aboriginal Men of High Degree, 2nd ed. New York: St. Martin's.

280. Elkin, A. P., 1978, Studies in Australian Totemism. New South Wales: Australian National Research Council.

281. Ellis, A. B., 1964, The Yoruba-Speaking Peoples of the Slave Coast of West Africa. Chicago: Benin.

282. Ellis, A. B., 1965, The Ewe-Speaking Peoples of the Slave Coast of West Africa. Chicago: Benin.

283. Elsasser, Albert B., 1978, "Mattole, Nongatl, Sinkyone, Lassik and Wailaki," in R. Heizer, ed., pp. 190-204.

284. Elwin, Verrier, 1947, The Muria and Their Ghotul. India: Oxford University Press.

285. Elwin, Verrier, 1968, The Kingdom of the Young. London: Oxford University Press.

286. Richards, Audrey, 1939, Land, Labour and Diet in Northern Rhodesia. London: Oxford University Press.

287. Embree, John F. & William L. Thomas, Jr., 1950, Ethnic Groups of Northern Southeast Asia. New Haven, CT: Yale University, Southeast Asian Studies.

288. Emley, E. D., 1927, "The Turkana of Kolosia District." JRAI 57:157-201.

289. Encyclopedia of Indians of the Americas, 1974, St. Clair Shores, MI: Scholarly Press.

290. Encyclopedie de la Pleiade, 1972, Paris: Ethnologie regionale.

291. Esterman, Carlos, 1976, The Ethnography of Southwestern Angola. New York: Africana.

292. Esterman, Carlos, 1957, Etnografia Do Sudoeste de Angola, Vol. 2. Memorias Serie Anthropologica e etnologica.

293. Evans, Ivor H. N., 1937, The Negritos of Malay. Cambridge: Cambridge University Press.

294. Evans-Pritchard, E. E., 1937, Witchcraft, Oracles and Magic Among the Azande. London: Oxford University Press.

295. Evans-Pritchard, E. E., 1940, The Nuer. Oxford: Oxford University Press.

296. Evans-Pritchard, E. E., 1949, The Sanusi of Cyrenaica. Oxford: Clarendon.

297. Ewers, John C., 1955, The Horse in Blackfoot Indian Culture, BBAE no. 159.

298. Ezell, Paul H., 1961, The Hispanic Acculturation of the Gila River Pimas, AAAM no. 90.

299. Ezell, Paul H., 1983, "History of the Pima," in A. Ortiz, ed., Vol. 10, pp. 149-160.

300. Faber, Richard, 1985, High Road to England. London: Faber and Faber.

301. Fage, J. D., 1978, An Atlas of African History. London: Edward Arnold.

302. Fallers, Margaret Chave, 1960, The Eastern Lacustrine Bantu. ESOA, East Central Africa, Pt. 11.

303. Farabee, William C., 1918, "The Central Arawaks." UPUM 9:13-131.

304. Farabee, William C., 1924, "The Central Caribs." UPUM 10:13-152.

305. Farabee, William C., 1922, PMP. Vol. 10: Indian Tribes of Eastern Peru.

306. Faron, Louis C., 1961, Mapuche Social Structure, ISA no. 1.

307. Faron, Louis C., 1964, Hawks of the Sun. Pittsburgh: University of Pittsburgh Press.

308. Fausz, J. Frederick, 1984, "Patterns of Anglo-Indian Aggression and Accommodation Along the Mid-Atlantic Coast, 1584-1636," in W. W. Fitzhugh, ed., pp. 225-268.

309. Feil, Daryl K., 1987, The Evolution of Highland Papua New Guinea Societies. Cambridge: Cambridge University Press.

310. Fejos, Paul, 1943, "Ethnography of the Yagua," Viking Fund Publications in Anthropology no. 1. New York: Wenner Gren.

311. Fenton, William N. & Elisabeth Tooker, 1978, "Mohawk," in B. Trigger, ed., pp. 466-480.

312. Ferdon, Edwin, 1981, Early Tahiti as the Explorers Saw it, 1767-1797. Tucson: University of Arizona Press.

313. Ferguson, T. J. & E. J. Hart, 1982, A Zuni Atlas. Norman: University of Oklahoma Press.

314. Fernandes, Jose L., 1962, "Os Indios da Serra dos Dourados." BICU no. 5, pp. 151-158.

315. Fernandez, James W., 1982, Bwiti: An Ethnography of the Religious Imagination in Africa. Princeton, NJ: Princeton University Press.

316. Field, Henry, 1939, Field Museum Anthropology Series. Vol. 29, no. 1: Contributions to the Anthropology of Iran. Chicago: Field Museum of Natural History.

317. Field, Henry, 1953, PMP. Vol. 48, no. 1: Contributions to the Anthropology of the Caucasus.

318. Field, Henry, 1956, PMP. Vol. 48, no. 2: An Anthropological Reconnaissance in the Near East, 1950.

319. Field, Henry, 1959, PMP. Vol. 52: An Anthropological Reconnaissance in West Pakistan, 1955.

320. Firth, Raymond, 1936, We the Tikopia. Boston: Beacon.

321. Firth, Raymond, 1959, Economics of the New Zealand Maori. Wellington: R. E. Owen.

322. Fischer, John L., 1966, The Eastern Carolines. New Haven, CT: HRAF.

323. Fischer, John L., 1956, "The Position of Men and Women in Truk and Ponape." Journal of American Folklore 69:55-62.

324. Fitz-Patrick, David G. & John Kimbuna, 1983, Bundi: The Culture of a Papua New Guinea People. Seattle: University of Washington Press.

325. Fitzhugh, William W., ed., 1985, Cultures in Contact. Washington, DC: Smithsonian Institution Press.

326. Fivaz, Derek & Patricia E. Scott, 1977, African Languages: A Genetic and Decimalised Classification for Bibliographic and General References. Boston: G. K. Hall.

327. Fletcher, A. C. & F. La Flesche, 1911, "The Omaha Tribe." ARBAE 27:17-654.

328. Flores, Anselmo M., 1967, "Indian Population and Its Identification," in M. Nash, ed., HMAI. Vol 6: Social Anthropology. Austin: University of Texas Press.

329. Fock, Niels, 1963, Waiwai: Religion and Society of an Amazonian Tribe. Copenhagen: National Museum.

330. Fock, Niels, 1960, "Urgent Ethnographical Tasks in the Argentine Chaco." International Congress of Americanists Proceedings 34:132-137.

331. Fock, Niels, 1967, Mataco Indians in Their Argentine Setting. Folk. Kobenhavn 9:89-104.

332. Fogel, Joshua A. & W. T. Rowe, ed., 198-, Perspectives on a Changing China. Boulder, CO: Westview.

333. Fogelson, Raymond D., 1961, "Cherokee Economic Cooperatives." UBBAE Bull. 180:82-123.

334. Fogelson, Raymond D., 1971, "The Cherokee Ballgame Cycle." Ethnomusicology 15(3):327-338.

335. Fogelson, Raymond D., 1978, The Cherokees: A Critical Bibliography. Bloomington: Indiana University Press.

336. Fogelson, Raymond D. & R. N. Adams, eds., 1977, The Anthropology of Power. New York: Academic Press.

337. Fogg, C. Davis, 1971, Small Holder Agriculture in Eastern Nigeria. Garden City, NJ: Natural History Press.

338. Folan, William J., 1985, Contributions to the Archaeology and Ethnohistory of Greater Mesoamerica. Carbondale: Southern Illinois University Press.

339. Foley, Douglas E., 1976, Philippine Rural Education: An Anthropological Perspective. Detroit: Center for Southwest Asian Studies.

340. Foley, William A., 1986, The Papuan Languages of New Guinea. New York: Cambridge University Press.

341. Fontana, Bernard, 1983, "Pima and Papago: Introduction," in A. Ortiz, ed., Vol. 10, pp. 125-136.

342. Ford, Clellan S., 1938, "The Role of the Fijian Chief." American Sociological Review 3:542-550.

343. Forde, C. Daryll, Paula Brown, & Robert Armstrong, 1955, Peoples of the Niger-Benue Confluence. ESOA, Western Africa, Pt. 10.

344. Forde, C. Daryll, 1931, "Ethnography of the Yuma Indians." UCP 28(2).

345. Forde, C. Daryll, 1951, The Yoruba-Speaking Peoples of Southwestern Nigeria. ESOA, Pt. 4.

346. Forde, C. Daryll, 1951, Marriage and the Family Among the Yako in Southwestern Nigeria. London: International African Institute.

347. Forde, C. Daryll, 1964, Yako Studies. London: Oxford University Press, for the International African Institute.

348. Fortes, Meyer & E. E. Evans-Pritchard, eds., 1940, African Political Systems. London: Oxford University Press.

349. Fortes, Meyer, 1949, The Web of Kinship Among the Tallensi. London: Oxford University Press.

350. Fortes, Meyer, 1945, The Dynamics of Clanship Among the Tallensi. London: Oxford University Press.

351. Fortune, Reo F., 1963, Sorcerers of Dobu. New York: Dutton.

352. Foster, Charles R., 1980, Nations Without a State: Ethnic Minorities in Western Europe. New York: Praeger.

353. Foster, George M., 1969, "The Mixe, Zoque & Popoluca," in E. Vogt, ed., HMAI. Vol. 7: Ethnology, pp. 448-476.

354. Fowler, Catherine & Sven Liljeblad, 1986, "Northern Paiute," in W. D'Azevedo, ed., pp. 435-465.

355. Fowler, Don D. & Catherine S. Fowler, 1971, "Introduction," in Anthropology of the Numa. Washington, DC: Smithsonian Institution Press.

356. Fox, Cyril E., 1919, "Social Organization in San Cristoval, Soloman Islands." JRAI 49:94-120.

357. Fraenkel, Merran, 1964, Tribe and Class in Monrovia. London: Oxford University Press.

358. Frake, Charles O., 1960, "The Eastern Subanun of Mindanao," in G. P. Murdock, ed., Social Structure in Southeast Asia, Viking Fund Publications in Anthropology no. 29. New York: Wenner Gren.

359. Frazer, James George, 1938, The Native Races of Africa and Madagascar. London: Percylund Humphries.

360. Freeman, J. Derek, 1983, Margaret Mead and Samoa. Cambridge, MA: Harvard University Press.

361. Freeman, J. Derek, 1955, Iban Agriculture: A Report on the Shifting Cultivation of Hill Rice by the Iban of Sarawak. London: Her Majesty's Stationery Office.

362. Fried, Jacob, 1969, "The Tarahumara," in E. Vogt, ed., HMAI. Vol. 8: Ethnology, pp. 846-870.

363. Fried, Morton H., 1968, "On the Concepts of 'Tribe' and 'Tribal Society,'" in J. Helm, ed., pp. 3-20.

364. Fried, Morton H., 1975, The Notion of Tribe. Menlo Park: Cummings.

365. Friedl, Ernestin, 1962, Vasilika: A Village in Modern Greece. New York: Holt, Rinehart & Winston.

366. Friedl, John, 1974, Kippel: A Changing Village in the Alps. New York: Holt, Rinehart & Winston.

367. Friedrich, Paul, 1960, Tarascan Political Homicide and Ethnographic Method." Philadelphia Anthropological Society Bulletin 13(3):1-6.

368. Fuchs, P., 1979, "Nordost-sudan." VA 2:189-228.

369. Fuchs, P., 1979, "Sahara und Sahel." VA 2:543-572.

370. Fuerst, Rene, 1969, "Gegenwartige Beilagen und dringoude volkerkundliche Forschungsaufgahen bei brasilianischen Wildbeutern." BICU no. 11

371. Fuller, Charles Edward, 1955, "An Ethnohistoric Study of Continuity and Change in Gwambe Culture." Ph.D. Dissertation, Northwestern University.

372. Furer-Haimendorf, Christoph von, 1969, The Konyak Nagas. New York: Holt, Rinehart & Winston.

373. Furer-Haimendorf, Christoph von, 1985, Tribal Populations and Cultures of the Indian Subcontinent. Leiden: Brill.

374. Furlong, C. W., 1917, "Tribal Distribution and Settlement of the Fuegians." Geographical Review 3:3-14.

375. Gailey, Harry A., 1967, The History of Africa in Maps. Chicago: Denoyer-Geppert.

376. Galvao, Eduardo, 1967, "Indigenous Culture Areas of Brazil 1900-1959," in J. Hopper, ed., pp. 167-206.

377. Gamble, David P., 1957, The Wolof of Senegambia. ESOA, Western Africa, Pt. 14.

378. Gamst, Frederick C., 1969, The Qemant. New York: Holt, Rinehart & Winston.

379. Garbarino, Merwyn S., 1972, Big Cypress: A Changing Seminole Community. New York: Holt, Rinehart & Winston.

380. Garfield, Viola E., 1939, Tsimshian Clan and Society. Seattle: University of Washington.

381. Garth, Thomas R., 1944, "Kinship Terminology, Marriage Practices and Behavior Towards Kin Among the Atsugewi." American Anthropologist 46:348-361.

382. Garth, Thomas R., 1978, "Atsugewi," in R. Heizer, ed., pp. 236-243.

383. Gatschet, Albert S., 1891, PMP. Vol. 1, no. 2: The Karankawa Indians.

384. Gauthier, J. G., 1979, Archeologie du pays Fali, nord Cameroun. Paris: Editions du Centre national de la recherche scientifique.

385. Geddes, William R., 1976, Migrants of the Mountains: The Cultural Ecology of the Blue Miao Chmong Njua of Thailand. Oxford: Clarendon.

386. Geertz, Clifford, 1960, The Religion of Java. London: Free Press.

387. Geertz, Clifford, 1973, The Interpretation of Culture. New York: Basic Books.

388. Gessain, Monique, 1967, Les migrations des Coniagui et Bassari. Paris: Societe des africanistes Musee de l'homme.

389. Geusau, Leo Alting von, 1983, "Dialects of Akhazan," in J. McKinnon & W. Bhruksasri, eds., pp. 242-277.

390. Gewertz, Deborah B., 1981, "A Historical Reconstruction Among the Chambri of Papua New Guinea." American Ethnologist 8(1):94-106.

391. Gewertz, Deborah B., 1983, Sepik River Societies: A Historical Ethnography of the Chambri and Their Neighbors. New Haven, CT: Yale University Press.

392. Giddings, Howard A., 1891, "The Nactchez Indians." Popular Science Monthly 1:201-206.

393. Gifford, Edward Winslow, 1932, "The Northfork Mono." UCP 31(2).

394. Gifford, Edward Winslow, 1931, The Kamia of Imperial Valley, BBAE no. 97.

395. Gifford, Edward Winslow, 1936, "Northwestern & Western Yavapai." UCP 34(4).

396. Gifford, Edward Winslow & Alfred L. Kroeber, 1937, "Culture Element Distributions: IV Pomo." UCP 37(4).

397. Gifford, Edward Winslow, 1918, "Clans and Moieties in Southern California." UCP 14(2).

398. Gilberg, Rolf, 1984, "Polar Eskimo," in D. Damas, ed., pp. 577-594.

399. Gilbert, William H., 1944, "Peoples of India," War Background Studies no. 18. Washington, DC: Smithsonian Institution.

400. Gillen, John & Curt Nimuendaju, 1948, "Tribes of the Guianas and the Left Amazon Tributaries." HSAI 3:799-860.

401. Gillespie, Beryl, 1981, "Bear Lake Indians," in J. Helm, ed., pp. 310-313.

402. Gitlow, Abraham Leo, 1947, Economics of the Mt. Hagen Tribes, New Guinea. New York: J. J. Augustin.

403. Glacken, Clarence J., 1955, The Great Loochoo. Berkeley: University of California Press.

404. Gladwin, Thomas & Seymour B. Sarason, 1954, Truk: Man in Paradise. New York: Wenner Gren Foundation for Anthropological Research.

405. Glasse, Robert M., 1959, "The Huli Descent System." Oceania 29(3)171-184.

406. Glasse, Robert M., 1968, Huli of Papua: A Cognatic Descent System. The Hague: Mouton.

407. Glazer, Nathan & Daniel P. Moynihan, 1975, Ethnicity: Theory and Experience. Cambridge, MA: Harvard University Press.

408. Gluckman, Max, 1955, The Judicial Process Among the Barotse of Northern Rhodesia. Manchester: Manchester University Press.

409. Gnielinski, Stefan von, ed., 1972, Liberia in Maps. New York: Africana.

410. Goddard, Pliny E., 1903, "Life and Culture of the Hupa." UCP 1:1-88.

411. Goddard, Pliny E., 1914, "Notes on the Chilua Indians of Northwestern California." UCPIAA&E 10(6).

412. Godelier, Maurice, 1985, The Making of Great Men: Male Domination and Power Among the New Guinea Baruya. New York: Cambridge University Press.

413. Goldman, Irving, 1963, The Cubeo: Indians of the Northwestern Amazon, ISA no. 2.

414. Goldschmidt, Walter, 1951, "Nomlaki Ethnography." UCP 42(4).

415. Goldschmidt, Walter, 1976, Culture and Behavior of the Sebei: A Study in Continuity and Adaptation. Berkeley: University of California Press.

416. Goldthorpe, J. E. & F. B. Wilson, 1960, Tribal Maps of East Africa and Zanzibar, East African Studies no. 3. Uganda: East African Institute of Social Research.

417. Goodale, Jane, 1971, Tiwi Wives: A Study of the Women of Melville Island, North Australia. Seattle: University of Washington Press.

418. Goodenough, Ward H., 1951, Property, Kin and Community on Truk, YUPA no. 46.

419. Goodman, James M., 1982, The Navajo Atlas: Environments Resources, People and History of the Dine Bikeyah. Norman: University of Oklahoma Press.

420. Goody, J. R., 1956, The Social Organization of the Lowilli. London: Her Majesty's Stationery Office.

421. Goody, Jack, 1957, "Fields of Social Control Among the Lodagaba." JRAI 87(1):75-104.

422.   Gorer, Geoffrey, 1938, Himalayan Village. London: M. Joseph.

423.   Gorer, Geoffrey & Margaret Mead, 1942, Balinese Character: A Photographic Analysis. New York: New York Academy of Sciences.

424.   Gough, E. Kathleen, 1968, "The Nayars and the Definition of Marriage," in Marriage, Family and Residence, pp. 49-71. Garden City, NY: Natural History Press.

425.   Gower, Chapman C., 1973, Milocca: A Sicilian Village. London: Allen & Unwin.

426.   Grant, Elihu, 1976, The People of Palestine. Westport, CT: Hyperion. (1921)

427.   Greenberg, Joseph H., 1955, Studies in African Linguistic Classification. New Haven, CT: Compass.

428.   Greenberg, Joseph H., 1962, The Languages of Africa. Bloomington: Indiana University Press.

429.   Greenberg, Joseph H., 1987, Language in the Americas. Stanford, CA: Stanford University Press.

430.   Gregor, Thomas, 1977, Mehinaku: The Drama of Daily Life in a Brazilian Indian Village. Chicago: University of Chicago Press.

431.   Griaule, Marcel, 1963, Masques Dogons, 2nd ed. Paris: Institut d'ethnologie.

432.   Griffen, William B., 1969, Culture Change and Shifting Populations in Central Northern Mexico, Anthropological Papers no. 13. Tucson: University of Arizona.

433.   Griffen, William B., 1983, "Southern Periphery: East," in A. Ortiz, ed., Vol. 10, pp. 329-342.

434.   Griffiths, Walter G., 1946, Monograph Series, Vol. 49: The Kol Tribe of Central India. Royal Asiatic Society of Bengal.

435.   Grigson, J. H., 1949, The Maria Gonds of Bastar. London: Oxford University Press.

436.   Grimble, Arthur, 1957, Return to the Islands: Life and Legend in the Gilberts. New York: Morrow.

437.   Grimes, Barbara, 1984, Ethnologue: Languages of the World, 10th ed. Dallas: Wycliffe Bible Trans.

438.   Grimes, Joseph E. & Thomas B. Hinton, 1969, "The Huichol and Cora," in E. Vogt, ed., HMAI. Vol. 8: Ethnology, pp. 792-813.

439.   Groves, Murray et al., 1957, "Blood Groups of the Motu and Koita Peoples." Oceania 28:222-238.

440.   Grunberg, Georg, 1966, "Urgent Research in Northwestern Mato Grosso." BICU no. 8:143-152.

441.   Gu-Konu, Yema, 1981, Atlas du Togo. Paris: Editions Jeune Afrique.

442.   Gulliver, Pamela & Philip H. Gulliver, 1968, The Central Nilo-Hamites. ESOA, East Central Africa, Pt. 7.

443.   Gunn, Harold D., 1953, Peoples of the Plateau Area of Northern Nigeria. ESOA, West Africa, Pt. 7.

444.   Gunn, Harold D., 1956, Pagan Peoples of the Central Area of Northern Nigeria. ESOA, West Africa, Pt. 12.

445.   Gunther, Erna, 1927, Publications in Anthropology. Vol. 1, no. 5: Klallam Ethnography. Seattle: University of Washington.

446.   Gurvich, I. S., 1962, The Ethnic Affiliation of the Population in the Northwest of the Yakut A.S.S.R., Anthro. of the North Sources no. 2. Arctic Inst. of N. America.

447.   Haberland, E. & H. Strande, 1979, "Nordost-Afrika." VA 2:69-156.

448.   Haddon, A. C., ed., 1908, Reports of the Cambridge Anthropological Expedition to Torres Straits, Vol. 6. Cambridge: Cambridge University Press.

449.   Hall, H. U., 1938, The Sherbro of Sierra Leone. Philadelphia: University of Pennsylvania Press.

450.   Hallpike, C. R., 1972, The Konso of Ethiopia: A Study of the Values of a Cushitic People. Oxford: Clarendon.

451.   Hallpike, C. R., 1977, Bloodshed and Vengance in the Papuan Mountains: The Generation of Conflict in Tauade Society. Oxford: Clarendon.

452.   Halpern, Joel, 1958, A Serbian Village. New York: Columbia University Press.

453.   Hamalainen, Pekka K., 1979, In Time of Storm: Revolution, Civil War and the Ethnolinguistic Issue in Finland. Albany: SUNY Press.

454.   Hambly, Wilfrid D., 1931, Field Museum Anthropological Series. Vol. 21, no. 1: Serpent Worship in Africa. Chicago: Field Museum of Natural History.

455.   Hambly, Wilfrid D., 1934, Field Museum Anthropological Series. Vol. 21: The Ovimbundu of Angola, pp. 89-362. Chicago: Field Museum of Natural History.

456.   Hambly, Wilfrid D., 1935, Field Museum Anthropological Series. Vol. 21, no. 3: Culture Areas of Nigeria. Chicago: Field Museum of Natural History.

457.   Hames, R. & W. Vickers, eds., 1983, Adaptive Responses of Native Amazonians. New York: Academic Press.

458.   Hamilton, James W., 1976, Pwo Karen, at the Edge of Mountain Plain. St. Paul: West.

459.   Hammel, Eugene, 1968, Alternative Social Structures and Ritual Relations in the Balkans. Englewood Cliffs, NJ: Prentice-Hall.

460.   Hammond-Tooke, W. D., 1955, The Tribes of Mount Frere District, Ethnological publication no. 33. Union of South Africa, Department of Native Affairs.

461.   Hammond-Tooke, W. D., 1956, The Tribes of Umtata District, Ethnological publication no. 35. Union of South Africa, Department of Native Affairs.

462.   Hammond-Tooke, W. D., 1958, The Tribes of King William's Town District, Ethnological publication no. 41. Union of South Africa, Department of Native Affairs.

463.   Hammond-Tooke, W. D., 1975, The Bantu Speaking Peoples of South Africa, 2nd ed. London: Routledge & Kegan Paul.

464.   Handelman, Don, 1975, The Social Anthropology of Israel. Tel Aviv: Institute for Social Research.

465.   Hanks, Lucien M., 1983, "The Yuan or Northern Thai," in J. McKinnon & W. Bhruksasri, eds., pp. 100-111.

466.   Harner, Michael, 1972, The Jivaro. Garden City, NJ: Natural History Press.

467.   Harris, Marvin, 1968, The Rise of Anthropological Theory. New York: T. Crowell.

468. Hart, C.W.M. & A. R. Pilling, 1960, The Tiwi of North Australia. New York: Holt, Rinehart & Winston.

469. Hart, David M., 1981, Dadda 'Atta and His Forty Grandsons: The Socio-Political Organization of the Ait 'Atta of Southern Morocco. Boulder: MENAS.

470. Hart, David M., 1984, The Ait 'Atta of Southern Morocco: Daily Life and Recent History. Boulder: Lynne Rienner.

471. Harvey, H. R. & Isabel Kelley, 1969, "The Totonac," in E. Vogt, ed., HMAI. Vol. 8: Ethnology, pp. 638-681.

472. Harwell, Henry O. & Marsha Kelly, 1983, "Maricopa," in A. Ortiz ed., Vol. 10, pp. 71-85.

473. Harwood, Alan, 1970, Witchcraft, Sorcery and Social Categories Among the Safwa. London: Oxford University Press.

474. Hasluck, F. W., 1921, "Heterodox Tribes of Asia Minor." JRAI 51:310-342.

475. Hegedus, Andras, 1977, The Structure of Socialist Society. New York: St. Martin's.

476. Heizer, Robert F., ed., 1978, Handbook of North American Indian. Vol. 8: California. Washington, DC: Smithsonian Institution Press.

477. Helm, June, 1981, "Dogrib," in J. Helm, ed., pp. 291-309.

478. Helm, June, ed., 1968, Essays on the Problem of Tribe. Seattle: University of Washington Press.

479. Helm, June, ed., 1981, Handbook of North American Indians. Vol. 6: Subarctic. Washington, DC: Smithsonian Institution Press.

480. Henley, P., 1982, The Panane: Tradition and Change on the Amazon Frontier. New Haven, CT: Yale University Press.

481. Henry, Jules, 1941, Jungle People: A Kaingang Tribe of the Highlands of Brazil. New York: J. J. Augustin.

482. Hernandez de Alba, Gregorio, 1948, "The Achagua and Their Neighbors." HSAI 4:399-412.

483. Herskovits, Melville J., 1938, Dahomey: An Ancient West African Kingdom, 2 vols. New York: J. J. Augustin.

484. Hewison, R. Neil, 1985, The Fayoum: A Practical Guide. Cairo: American University Press.

485. Hezel, Francis, 1983, The First Taint of Civilization: A History of the Caroline and Marshall Islands in Pre-Colonial Days 1521-1885. Honolulu: University of Hawaii Press.

486. Hicks, David, 1976, Tetum Ghosts and Kin. Palo Alto, CA: Mayfield.

487. Hiernaux, Jean, 1975, The People of Africa. New York: Scribner.

488. Hill, Ann Maxwell, 1983, "The Yunnanese," in J. McKinnon & W. Bhruksasri, eds., pp. 123-134.

489. Hill, Jonathan & Emilio Moran, 1983, "Adaptive Strategies of Wakuenai People to the Oligotrophic Rain Forest of the Rio Forest of the Rio Negro Basin," in R. Hames & W. Vickers, eds., pp. 113-135.

490. Hill, Jonathan D., 1984, "Social Equality and Ritual Hierarchy: The Arawakan Wakuenai of Venezuela." American Ethnologist 11(3):528-544.

491. Hill, Kim & Kristen Hawkes, 1983, "Neotropical Hunting Among the Ache of Eastern Paraguay," in R. Hames & W. Vickers, eds.

492. Hinton, Peter, 1983, "Do the Karen Really Exist?" in J. McKinnon & W. Bhruksasri, eds., pp. 155-172.

493. Hinton, Thomas B., 1969, "Remnant Tribes of Sonora: Opata, Pima, Papago and Seri," in E. Vogt, ed., HMAI. Vol. 8: Ethnology, pp. 879-890.

494. Hinton, Thomas B., 1983, "Southern Periphery: West," in A. Ortiz, ed., Vol. 10, pp. 315-328.

495. Hirschberg, Walter, 1979, "Das Crossflussgebiet und das kameruner Grasland." VA 2:355-372.

496. Hitchcock, John T., 1966, The Magars of Banyan Hill. New York: Holt, Rinehart & Winston.

497. Hobley, C. W., 1902, Eastern Uganda: An Ethnographic Survey, Occasional Paper no. 1. London: African Institute.

498. Hodgson, A.G.O., 1933, "Notes on the Achewa and Angoni of the Dowa District of Nyasaland Protectorate." JRAI 63:123-164.

499. Hoebel, E. Adamson, 1978, The Cheyennes. New York: Holt, Rinehart & Winston.

500 Hoernle, A. Winifred, 1925, "The Social Organization of the Nama Hottentots of Southwest Africa." American Anthropologist 27(1):1-24.

501. Hogbin, H. Ian, 1935, "Native Culture of the Wogeo." Oceania 5:308-337.

502. Hogbin, H. Ian, 1963, Kinship and Marriage in a New Guinea Village, MSA no. 26.

503. Hogbin, H. Ian, 1965, A Guadalcanal Society: The Kaoka Speakers. New York: Holt, Rinehart & Winston.

504. Holas, Bohumil, 1957, Les Senoufo (y Compris les minianka). Paris: Presses Universitairtes de France.

505. Hollis, Alfred C., 1969, The Nandi: Their Language and Folk-Lore. Westport, CT: Negro Universities Press.

506. Hollis, Alfred C., 1905, The Masai: Their Language and Folklore. New York: Freeport.

507. Holm, G., 1914, "Ethnological Sketch of the Angmagsalik Eskimo." Meddelelser om Gronland 39:1-47.

508. Holmberg, A., 1950, Nomads of the Long Bow: The Siriono of Eastern Bolivia. Washington, DC: Smithsonian Institution Press.

509. Honigmann, John J., 1946, Culture and Ethos of Kaska Society, YUPA No. 40.

510. Honigmann, John J., 1947, "Witch-Fear in Post Contact Kaska Society." American Anthropologist 49:222-243.

511. Honigmann, John J., 1963, "Sociology of an Austrian Village." American Philosophical Society Yearbook, pp. 418-421.

512. Hoppe, W., A. Medina, & R. Weitlaner, 1969, "The Popoloca," in E. Vogt, ed., HMAI. Vol. 7: Ethnology, pp. 489-498.

513. Hoppe, Walter & Roberto J. Weitlaner, 1969, "The Chocho," in E. Vogt, ed., HMAI. Vol. 7: Ethnology, pp. 505-515.

514. Hopper, Janice H., ed., 1967, Indians of Brazil in the Twentieth Century. Washington, DC: Institute for Cross-Cultural Research.

515.   Horrabin, Frank J., 1960, An Atlas of Africa. London: Victor Gollancz.

516.   Horton, Donald, 1948, "The Mundurucu." HSAI 3:271-282.

517.   Hose, Charles & William McDougall, 1912, The Pagan Tribes of Borneo. London: Macmillan.

518.   Hosley, Edward H., 1981, "Kolchan," in J. Helm, ed., pp. 618-622.

519.   Hostetler, J. A. & G. E. Huntington, 1980, The Hutterities in North America. New York: Holt, Rinehart & Winston.

520.   Hottot, Robert, 1956, "Teke Fetishes." JRAI 86(1):25-36.

521.   Howes, H. W., 1930, "Some Flemish Customes and Beliefs." Folklore 41:99-103.

522.   Howitt, A. W., 1904, The Native Tribes of South-East Australia. London: Macmillan.

523.   Hrbek, Ivan, 1984, "A List of African Ethnonyms," in African Ethnonyms and Toponyms, pp. 141-186. Paris: Imprimerie des Presses Universitaires de France.

524.   Hrdlicka, Ales, 1945, The Aleutian and Commander Islands and Their Inhabitants. Philadelphia: Wistar Institute.

525.   Hughes, Charles C., 1984, "Siberian Eskimo," in D. Damas, ed., pp. 247-261.

526.   Humphreys, Clarence Blake, 1926, The Southern New Hebrides. Cambridge: Cambridge University Press.

527.   Hunter, Monica, 1936, Reaction to Conquest: Effects of Contact with Europeans on the Pondo of South Africa. Oxford: Oxford University Press.

528.   Huntingford, G.W.B., 1929, "Modern Hunters: Some Account of the Kamelilo-Kapchendi Dorobo (Okiek) of Kenya Colony." JRAI 59:333-378.

529.   Huntingford, G.W.B., 1953, The Northern Nilo-Hamites. ESOA, East Central Africa, Pt. VI.

530.   Huntingford, G.W.B., 1953, The Nandi of Kenya. London: Routledge & Kegan Paul.

531.   Huntingford, G.W.B., 1953, The Southern Nilo-Hamites. ESOA, East Central Africa, Pt. 8.

532.   Huntingford, G.W.B., 1955, The Galla of Ethiopia, the Kingdom of Kafa and Janjero. ESOA, North Central Africa, Pt. 11.

533.   Hutton, John Henry, 1921, The Sema Nagas. London: Macmillan.

534.   Hutton, John Henry, 1969, The Angami Nagas, 2nd ed. London: Oxford University Press. (original work published 1921)

535.   Hymes, Dell, 1968, "Linguistic Problems in Defining the Concept of Tribe," in J. Helm, ed., pp. 23-48.

536.   Im, Tong-gwon, 1977, The Mores and Practices. Seoul: Korean Overseas Information Service.

537.   Imperial Gazetteer of India, 1908, Provincial Series, Burma, 2 vols. Calcutta: Spt. Government Printing.

538.   Im Thurn, Everard, 1883, Among the Indians of Guiana. New York: Dover. (republished 1967)

539.   Ingold, Tim, 1976, The Skolt Lapps Today. New York: Cambridge University Press.

540.   Institut Etnografii Imeni, N.N. Miklukho-Makaia, 1964, Atlas Narodov Mira. Moskva: Akademii Nauk CCCP (see also citation 1102).

541.   Irons, William, 1974, "Nomadism as a Political Adaptation: The Case of the Yomut Turkmen." American Ethnologist 1(4):635-658.

542.   Irons, William, 1975, The Yomut Turkmen: A Study of Social Organization Among a Central Asian Turkic-Speaking Population, APMAUM no. 58.

543.   Irving, Ronald E., 1980, The Flemings and Walloons of Belgium. London: Minority Rights Group.

544.   Ishii, Shinji, 1916, "The Island of Formosa and Its Primitive Inhabitants." London: Extract from the Transactions of the Japan Society.

545.   Ivinskis, V. et al., 1957, "A Medical and Anthropological Study of the Chimu Natives in the Central Highlands of New Guinea." Oceania 27:143-157.

546.   Jaenen, Cornelius J., 1956, "The Galla or Oromo of East Africa." Southwestern Journal of Anthropology 12:171-190.

547.   Jaspan, M. A., 1953, The Ila-Tonga Peoples of North-Western Rhodesia. ESOA, West Central Africa, Pt. 4.

548.   Jenks, Albert E., 1905, Ethnological Survey Publications, Vol. 1: The Bontoc Igorot. Manila: Department of Interior.

549.   Jenness, Diamond, 1922, "The Life of the Copper Eskimo." Report of the Canadian Arctic Expedition 1913-1918 12:A1-277.

550.   Jenness, Diamond, 1937, "The Sekani Indians of British Columbia." Bulletin of the Canadian Department of Mines and Resources 84:1-82.

551.   Jochelson, Waldemar, 1928, Peoples of Asiatic Russia. New York: American Museum of Natural History.

552.   Jochelson, Waldemar, 1933, APAMNH. Vol. 33, Pt. 2: The Yakut.

553.   Johnson, Allen, 1983, "Machiguenga Gardens," in R. Hames & W. Vickers, ed., pp. 29-64.

554.   Johnson, Allen & Timothy Earl, 1987, The Evolution of Human Societies. Stanford, CA: Stanford University Press.

555.   Johnson, Frederick, 1948, "The Post-Conquest Ethnology of Central America: An Introduction." HSAI 4:195-199.

556.   Johnson, Frederick, 1948, "Central American Cultures: An Introduction." HSAI 4:43-68.

557.   Jones, R., 1974, "Tasmanian Tribes," in N. Tindale, ed., pp. 210-247.

558.   Jones, Rex L. & Shirley K. Jones, 1976, The Himalayan Woman: A Study of Limbu Women in Marriage and Divorce. Palo Alto: Mayfield.

559.   Jones, William, 1913, "Kickapoo Ethnological Notes." American Anthropologist 15:332-335.

560.   Jones, William K., 1969, Smithsonian Contributions to Anthropology. Vol. 2, no. 5: Notes on the History and Material Culture of the Tonkawa Indians. Washington, DC: Smithsonian Institution.

561.   Josephides, Lisette, 1985, The Production of Inequality: Gender and Exchange Among the Kewa. London: Tavistock.

562. Johnson, Patti J., 1978, "Patwin," in R. Heizer, ed., pp. 350-360.

563. Junod, Henri, 1927, The Life of a South African Tribe, 2nd ed. New York: University Books. (republished 1962)

564. Kaberry, P. M., 1941, "The Abelam Tribe, Sepik District, New Guinea." Oceania 11:233-257, 245-367.

565. Kahn, Ed, 1972, Nauthars of Nepal. New Haven, CT: HRAF.

566. Kaplan, Joanna O., 1975, The Piaroa: A People of the Orinoco Basin. Oxford: Clarendon Press.

567. Karp, Ivan, 1978, Fields of Change Among the Iteso of Kenya. London: Routledge & Kegan Paul.

568. Karsten, Rafael, 1932, "Indian Tribes of the Argentine and Bolivian Chaco." Societas Scientiarum Fennica, Commentationes Humanorum Litterarum 4:1-236.

569. Kearney, Michael, 1972, The Winds of Ixtepeji: World View and Society in a Zapotec Town. New York: Holt, Rinehart & Winston.

570. Keesing, Felix M., 1939, "The Menomini Indians of Wisconsin." Memoirs of the American Philosophical Society 10.

571. Keesing, Felix M., 1962, The Ethnohistory of Northern Luzon. Stanford, CA: Stanford University Press.

572. Kelly, Isabel T., 1932, "Ethnography of the Surprise Valley Paiute." UCP 31(3):67-210.

573. Kelly, Isabel T. & Catherine Fowler, 1986, "Southern Paiute," in W. D'Azevedo, ed., pp. 368-397.

574. Kelly, Raymond, 1977, Etoro Social Structure: A Study in Structural Contradiction. Ann Arbor: University of Michigan Press.

575. Kelly, Raymond, 1985, The Nuer Conquest: The Structure and Development of an Expansionist System. Ann Arbor: University of Michigan Press.

576. Kemp, William B., 1984, "Baffinland Eskimo," in D. Damas, ed., pp. 462-475.

577. Kennedy, John G., 1977, Struggle for Change in a Nubian Community. Palo Alto, CA: Mayfield.

578. Kennedy, Raymond, 1943, "Islands and Peoples of the Indies," War Background Studies no. 14. Washington, DC: Smithsonian Institution.

579. Kennedy, John G., 1978, Nubian Ceremonial Life. Berkeley: University of California Press.

580. Kennedy, T. F., 1966, A Descriptive Atlas of the Pacific Islands. New York: Praeger.

581. Kenyatta, Jomo, 1961, Facing Mount Kenya: The Tribal Life of the Gikuyu. London: Secker & Warburg.

582. Key, Mary R., 1979, The Grouping of South American Indian Languages. Tubingen: Narr.

583. Kahn, Morton, 1971, Djuka: The Bush Negros of Dutch Guiana. New York: Viking.

584. Khera, Sigrid & Patricia S. Mariella, 1983, "Yavapai," in A. Ortiz, ed., Vol. 10, pp. 38-54.

585. Khleif, Bud B., 1980, Language, Ethnicity and Education in Wales. The Hague: Mouton.

586. Kiefer, Thomas Michael, 1972, The Tausug of the Philippines. New Haven, CT: HRAF Press.

587. Kietzman, Dale W., 1967, "Indians and Culture Areas of Twentieth Century Brazil," in J. Hopper, ed., pp. 1-68.

588. King, Chester & Thomas C. Blackburn, 1978, "Tataviam," in R. Heizer, ed., pp. 535-537.

589. Kirchhoff, Paul, 1948, "The Tribes North of the Orinoco River." HSAI 4:481-493.

590. Kirchhoff, Paul, 1948, "The Warrau." HSAI 3:869-881.

591. Kiste, Robert C., 1977, "The Relocation of the Bikini Marshallese," in M. Lieber, ed., pp. 80-120.

592. Klein, H., 1979, "Der Zentralsudan." VA 2:307-354.

593. Klima, George J., 1970, The Barabaig: East African Cattle-Herders. New York: Holt, Rinehart & Winston.

594. Kluckhohn, Clyde, 1944, Navaho Witchcraft. Boston: Beacon.

595. Knauft, Bruce M., 1985, Good Company and Violence: Sorcery and Social Action in a Lowland New Guinea Society. Berkeley: University of California Press.

596. Kniffen, Fred, Gordon Macgregor et al., 1935, Walapai Ethnography, AAAM no. 2.

597. Kottak, Conrad, 1977, "The Process of State Formation in Madagascar." American Ethnologist 4(1):136-155.

598. Kottak, Conrad, 1980, The Past in the Present: History, Ecology and Cultural Variation in Highland Madagascar. Ann Arbor: University of Michigan Press.

599. Kovalesky, M., 1888, "The Customs of the Ossetes." Journal of the Royal Asiatic Society n.s. 20:344-412.

600. Kozak, Vladimir et al., 1979, The Heta Indians: Fish in a Dry Pond. New York: American Museum of Natural History.

601. Kracke, Ward, 1978, Force and Persuasion: Leadership in an Amazonian Society. Chicago: University of Chicago Press.

602. Krader, Lawrence, 1966, Peoples of Central Asia. The Hague: Mouton.

603. Krader, Lawrence, 1963, Social Organization of Mongol-Turkic Pastoral Nomads. The Hague: Mouton.

604. Kramer, Augustin, 1927, West-Indonesien. Stuttgart: Franckhesche Verlagshandlung.

605. Krieger, Herbert W., 1942, "Peoples of the Philippines," War Background Studies no. 4. Washington, DC: Smithsonian Institution.

606. Krige, Eileen J. & J. D. Krige, 1943, The Realm of a Rain-Queen: A Study of the Pattern of Lovedu Society. London: Oxford University Press.

607. Krige, Eileen Jensen, 1936, The Social System of the Zulus. London: Longman, Green.

608. Kroeber, Alfred L., 1904, "The Languages of the Coast of California South of San Francisco." UCP 2(2).

609. Kroeber, Alfred L., 1907, "Shoshonean Dialects of California." UCP 4, Op. 164.

610. Kroeber, Alfred L., 1911, "The Languages of the Coast of California North of San Francisco." UCP 9(3).

611. Kroeber, Alfred L., 1917, "California Kinship Systems." UCP 12(9).

612.   Kroeber, Alfred L., 1917, "Zuni Kin and Clan." APAMNH 18:39-204.

613.   Kroeber, Alfred L., 1917, "California Kinship Systems." UCP 18:27-29.

614.   Kroeber, Alfred L., 1922, "Elements of Culture in Native California." UCP 13(8).

615.   Kroeber, Alfred L., 1925, Handbook of the Indians of California, BBAE No. 78.

616.   Kroeber, Alfred L., 1932, "The Patwin and Their Neighbors." UCP 29(4).

617.   Kroeber, Alfred L., 1935, "Walapai Ethnography." MAAA 42:1-193.

618.   Kroeber, Alfred L., 1939, Cultural and Natural Areas of Native North America. Berkeley: University of California Press.

619.   Kroeber, Alfred L., 1942, "The Chibcha." HSAI 2:887-909.

620.   Kroeber, Theodora, 1962, Ishi: In Two Worlds. Berkeley: University of California Press.

621.   Kronenberg, Andreas, 1979, "Die Niloten." VA 2:157-188.

622.   Kunstadter, Peter, ed., 1967, Southeast Asian Tribes, Minorities and Nations. Princeton, NJ: Princeton University Press.

623.   Kunstadter, Peter, 1983, "Animism, Buddhism and Christianity: Religion in the Life of Lua People of Pa Pae, North-Western Thailand," in J. McKinnon & W. Bhruksasri, eds., pp. 135-154.

624.   Kuper, Hilda, 1947, An African Aristocracy: Rank Among the Swazi. London: Oxford University Press.

625.   Kwamena-Poh, M., J. Tosh et al., 1982, African History in Maps. Essex: Longman.

626.   La Fontaine, Jean S., 1959, The Gisu of Uganda. ESOA, East Central Africa, Pt. 10.

627.   Laclavere, Georges, 1979, Atlas de la Republique Unie du Cameroun. Paris: Editions Jeune Afrique.

628.   Laclavere, Georges, 1980, Atlas du Niger. Paris: Editions Jeune Afrique.

629.   Lambert, Bernd, 1975, "Makin and the Outside World," in V. Carroll, ed., pp. 212-285.

630.   Lambert, H. H., 1956, Kikuyu Social and Political Institutions. International African Institute, London: Oxford University Press.

631.   Lane, Robert B., 1981, "Chilcotin," in J. Helm, ed., pp. 402-412.

632.   Lange, Werner, 1976, Dialectecs of Divine Kingship in the Kafa Highlands, Occasional Paper no. 15. University of California, African Studies Center.

633.   Langley, Myrtle, 1979, The Nandi of Kenya: Life Crisis Rituals in a Period of Change. New York: St. Martin's.

634.   Larson, Eric H., 1977, "Tikopia in the Russell Islands," in M. Lieber, ed., pp. 242-268.

635.   Laughlin, Charles D. & Ivan A. Brady, eds., 1978, Extinction and Survival in Human Populations. New York: Columbia University Press.

636.   Lawless, Robert, 1977, Papers in Anthropology. Vol. 18, no. 1: Societal Ecology in Northern Luzon: Kalinga Agriculture, Organization, Population, and Change. Norman: University of Oklahoma.

637.   Lawrence, David H., 1921, Sea and Sardinia. New York: T. Selzer.

638.   Lawrence, Peter, 1984, The Garia: An Ethnology of a Traditional Cosmic System in Papua New Guinea. Manchester: Manchester University Press.

639.   Lebar, Frank, 1964, The Material Culture of Truk, YUPA no. 68.

640.   Lebar, Frank, ed., 1975, Ethnic Groups of Insular Southeast Asia, Vols. 1, 2. New Haven, CT: HRAF Press.

641.   Lebar, Frank, ed., 1977, Insular Southeast Asia: Ethnographic Studies. Section 4: Philippines. New Haven, CT: HRAF Press.

642.   Le Roux, C.C.F.M., 1950, De Bergpapuea's van Nieuw-Guinea en Hun Woongebied. Leiden: E. J. Brill.

643.   Leach, Edmund R., 1954, Political Systems of Highland Burma. Boston: Beacon.

644.   Leach, Edmund R., 1961, Pul Eliya: A Village in Ceylon. London: Cambridge University Press.

645.   Leach, Jerry W. & Edmund Leach, 1983, The Kula: New Perspectives on Massim Exchange. New York: Cambridge University Press.

646.   Leakey, L.S.B., 1930, "Some Notes on the Masai of Kenya Colony." JRAI 60:185-209.

647.   Lebar, Frank, Gerald Hickey & John Musgrave, 1964, Ethnic Groups of Mainland Southeast Asia. New Haven, CT: HRAF Press.

648.   Lebeuf, Annie M.D., 1959, Les Populations du Tchad (nord du 10e parallele). Paris: Presses universitaires de France.

649.   Lederman, Rena, 1986, What Gifts Engender: Social Relationships in Mendi, Highland Papua New Guinea. New York: Cambridge University Press.

650.   Lee, Richard, 1979, The !Kung San: Men, Women and Work in a Foraging Society. New York: Cambridge University Press.

651.   Leeds, Anthony, 1961, "Yaruro Incipient Tropical Forest Horticulture," in J. Wilbert, ed., The Evolution of Horticulture Systems in Native South America, Antropologica Supplement Publication no. 2. Caracas.

652.   Lehman, Frederick K., 1963, The Structure of Chin Society, ISA no. 3.

653.   Lehmann, Walter, 1920, "Die Sprachen Zentral-Amerikas." Zentral-Amerikas, Pt. 1, Berlin.

654.   Leitch, Barbara A., 1979, A Concise Dictionary of Indian Tribes on North America. Algonac, MI: Reference Publications.

655.   Loeb, E. M., 1933, "Patrilineal & Matrilineal Organization in Sumatra: The Batak and the Minangkabau." American Anthropologist 35:16-50.

656.   Leonard, Arthur Glyn, 1968, The Lower Niger and Its Tribes. London: Frank Cass.

657.   Lessa, William A., 1966, Ulithi: A Micronesian Design for Living. New York: Holt, Rinehart & Winston.

658. Lestrade, G. P., 1937, "The Spelling of Names of Bantu Languages and Tribes in English." Bantu Studies 11:373-375.

659. Levi-Strauss, Claude, 1948, "The Nambicuara." HSAI 3:361-370.

660. Levin, M. G. & L. P. Potapov, 1964, The Peoples of Siberia. Chicago: University of Chicago Press.

661. Levine, Robert A. & Barbara B. Levine, 196-, Nyansongo: A Gusii Community in Kenya. New York: John Wiley.

662. Levy, Robert, 1973, Tahitians: Mind and Experience in the Society Islands. Chicago: University of Chicago.

663. Lewis, Paul & Elaine Lewis, 1984, Peoples of the Golden Triangle Six Tribes in Thailand. London: Thames & Hudson.

664. Lewis, Phillip H., 1969, The Social Context of Art in Northern New Ireland, Vol. 58. Fieldiana: Anthropology.

665. Lieber, Michael, ed., 1977, Exiles and Migrants in Oceania. Honolulu: University Press of Hawaii.

666. Liljeblad, Sven & Catherine S. Fowler, 1986, "Owens Valley Paiute," in W. D'Azevedo, ed., pp. 412-434.

667. Lindenbaum, Shirley, 1979, Kuru Sorcery. Palo Alto, CA: Mayfield.

668. Lingenfelter, Sherwood G., 1975, Yap, Political Leadership and Culture Change in an Island Society. Honolulu: University Press of Hawaii.

669. Linton, Ralph, 1933, "The Tanala." Field Museum of Natural History, Anthropological Series 22:1-334.

670. Little, Kenneth L., 1951, The Mende of Sierra Leone. London: Routledge & Kegan Paul.

671. Littlewood, R. A., 1972, Physical Anthropology of the Eastern Highlands of New Guinea. Seattle: University of Washington Press.

672. Lizondo Borda, Manuel, 1938, Tucuman Indigena. Talleres Grafico Miguel Violetto.

673. Lizot, Jacques, 1985, Tales of the Yanomami: Daily Life in the Venezuielan Forest. New York: Cambridge University Press.

674. Loeb, Edwin M., 1935, Sumatra: Its History and People. Wien: Verlag des Instituts fur Volkerkunde Universitat Wien.

675. Loeb, Edwin M. & Jan O.M. Brown, 1947, "Social Organization and the Long House in Southeast Asia." American Anthropologist 49:414-425.

676. Lothrop, Samuel K., 1928, The Indians of Tierra del Fuego. New York: Museum of the American Indian.

677. Loud, Llewellyn L., 1918, "Ethnogeography & Archaeology of the Wiyot Territory." UCP 14(3).

678. Loumala, Katharine, 1978, "Tipai & Ipai," in R. Heizer, ed., pp. 592-610.

679. Lowie, Robert H., 1935, The Crow Indians. New York: Farrar & Rinehart.

680. Lowie, Robert H., 1939, "Ethnographic Notes on the Washo." UCP 36:301-352.

681. Lowie, Robert H., 1946, "Eastern Brazil: An Introduction." HSAI 1:381-397.

682. Lowie, Robert H., 1948, "The Southern Cayapo." HSAI 1:519-520.

683. Lowie, Robert H., 1948, "The Cariri." HSAI 1:557-559.

684. Lowie, Robert H., 1948, "The Bororo." HSAI 1:419-434.

685. Lowis, Cecil Champain, 1919, The Tribes of Burma. Rangoon: Burma Government Printing Office.

686. Luzbetak, Louis J., 1966, Marriage and the Family in Caucasia. Vienna: St. Gabriel's Mission.

687. Lynch, Hannah, 1901, French Life in Town and Country. London: G. P. Putnam.

688. Lyon, Patricia J., ed., 1974, Native South Americans: Ethnology of the Least Known Continent. Boston: Little, Brown.

689. Lyons, A. P., 1926, "Notes on the Gogodara Tribe of Western Papua." JRAI 56:329-359.

690. Lystad, Robert, 1958, The Ashanti: A Proud People. New Brunswick, NJ: Rutgers University Press.

691. MacGregor, Gordon, 1934, "Anthropological Work of the Templeton Crocker Expedition, 1933." Bishop Museum Bull. no. 124, pp. 38-43.

692. MacLachlan, Bruce B., 1981, "Tahltan," in J. Helm, ed., pp. 458-468.

693. MacMichael, Harold Alfred, 1967, The Tribes of Northern and Central Kordofan. London: Frank Cass.

694. Mafeje, Archie, 1971, "The Ideology of 'Tribalism.'" Journal of Modern African Studies 9(2):253-261.

695. Magnarella, Paul J., 1979, The Peasant Venture. Cambridge, MA: Schenkman.

696. Majumdar, D. N., 1961, Races & Cultures of India. Bombay: Asia.

697. Malinowski, Branislaw, 1915, "The Natives of Mailu." Transactions and Proceedings of the Royal Society of South Australia 39:494-706.

698. Malinowski, Branislaw, 1922, Argonauts of the Western Pacific. New York: Dutton.

699. Malinowski, Branislaw, 1935, Coral Gardens and Their Magic. New York: Allen & Unwin.

700. Malinowski, Branislaw, 1929, The Sexual Life of Savages. London: Liss.

701. Mandelbaum, David G., 1940, The Plains Cree, APAMNH 37, Pt. 2.

702. Mann, M. & D. Dalby, 1986, Thesaurus of African Languages. London: Zed.

703. Manners, Robert A., 1957, "Tribe and Tribal Boundaries: The Walapai." Ethnohistory 4:1-26.

704. Manoukian, Madeline, 1950, The Akan and Ga-Adangme Peoples. ESOA, Western Africa, Pt. 1.

705. Manoukian, Madeline, 1951, Tribes of the Northern Territories of the Gold Coast. ESOA, Western Africa, Pt. 5.

706. Manoukian, Madeline, 1952, The Ewe-Speaking People of Togoland and the Gold Coast. ESOA, Western Africa, Pt. 6.

707. Manrique, Leonardo, 1969, "The Otomi," in E. Vogt, ed., HMAI. Vol. 8: Ethnology, pp. 638-681.

708. Maretzki, Thomas W. & Hatsumi Maretzki, 1974, Taira: An Okinawan Village. New York: John Wiley.

709. Markham, Clements, 1910, "A List of the Tribes of the Valley of the Amazons." JRAI 40:73-140.

710. Marks, S., 1976, Large Mammals and Brave People: Subsistence Hunters in Zambia. Seattle: University of Washington Press.

711. Marquardt, William T., 1987, The Calusa Social Formation in Protohistoric South Florida. Gainesville: University of Florida Press.

712. Marshall, Mac, 1972, "Changing Patterns of Marriage and Migration on Namoluk Atoll," in V. Carroll, ed., pp. 160-211.

713. Marshall, Mac, 1979, Weekend Warriors: Alcohol in a Micronesian Culture. Palo Alto, CA: Mayfield.

714. Marwick, Brian Allan, 1940, The Swazi: An Ethnographic Account of the Natives of the Swaziland Protectorate. London: Frank Cass.

715. Marx, Emanuel, 1977, "The Tribe as a Unit of Subsistence: Nomadic Pastoralism in the Middle East." American Anthropologist 79:343-363.

716. Mary-Rousseliere, Guy, 1984, "Iglulik," in D. Damas, ed., pp. 431-447.

717. Maurice, A. & G. Proux, 1954, Bulletin de la Societe des Etudes Indochinoises 29:149-177.

718. Maybury-Lewis, David, 1967, Akwe-Shavante Society. Oxford: Clarendon.

719. Mayer, Kurt, 1980, "Ethnic Tensions in Switzerland: The Jura Conflict," in C. R. Foster, ed., pp. 189-210.

720. McClellan, Catharine, 1981, "Inland Tlingit," in J. Helm, ed., pp. 469-480.

721. McClellan, Catharine, 1981, "Taghish," in J. Helm, ed., pp. 481-442.

722. McClellan, Catharine, 1981, "Tutchone," in J. Helm, ed., pp. 493-502.

723. McCulloch, Merran, 1952, The Ovimbundu of Angola. London: International African Institute.

724. McCulloch, Merran, M. Littlewood, & I. Dugast, 1954, Peoples of the Central Cameroons. ESOA, Western Africa, Pt. 9.

725. McCulloch, Merran, 1950, Peoples of Sierra Leone. ESOA, Western Africa, Pt. 2.

726. McCulloch, Merran, 1951, The Southern Lunda and Related Peoples. ESOA, Pt. 1.

727. McDonogh, Gary W., ed., 1986, Conflict in Catalonia. Gainesville: University Presses of Florida.

728. McDougal, Charles, 1963, "The Social Structure of the Hill Juang." Man in India 43:211-224.

729. McFarland, Curtis D., 1980, A Linguistic Atlas of the Philipines, Study of Languages and Cultures of Asia & Africa, Monograph Series no. 15.

730. McGee, W. J., 1898, "The Seri Indians." 17th ARBAE 1895-1896:9-298.

731. McGuire, Thomas R., 1983, "Walapai," in A. Ortiz, ed., Vol. 10, pp. 25-37.

732. McKaughan, Howard, ed., 1973, The Languages of the Eastern Family of the New Guinea Highland Stock. Seattle: University of Washington Press.

733. McKennan, Robert A., 1959, The Upper Tanana Indians, YUPA No. 55.

734. McKennan, Robert A., 1981, "Tanana," in J. Helm, ed., pp. 562-576.

735. McKinnon, John & Wanat Bhruksasri, 1983, Highlanders of Thailand. Kuala Lumpur: Oxford University Press.

736. McKnight, Robert K., 1977, "Commas in Microcosm," in M. Lieber, ed., pp. 10-23.

737. McNulty, Gerard E. & Louis Gilbert, 1981, "Attikamek (Tete de Boule)," in J. Helm, ed., pp. 208-216.

738. McQuown, Norman A., 1955, "The Indigenous Languages of Latin America." American Anthropologist 57:501-570.

739. McQuown, Norman A., ed., 1967, Handbook of Middle American Indians. Vol. 5: Linguistics. Austin: University of Texas Press.

740. Mead, Margaret, 1928, Coming of Age in Samoa. New York: Morrow.

741. Mead, Margaret, 1933, "Kinship in the Admiralty Islands." APAMNH 34:181-337.

742. Mednick, Melvin, 1977, "Ilanon," in F. Lebar, ed., pp. 209-228.

743. Mednick, Melvin, 1977, "The Maranao," in F. Lebar, ed., pp. 185-208.

744. Meek, Charles Kingsley, 1931, A Sudanese Kingdom: An Ethnological Study of the Jukan-Speaking Peoples of Nigeria. London: K. Paul Trench, Trubner & Co.

745. Meek, Charles Kingsley, 1931, Tribal Studies in Northern Nigeria. London: K. Paul Trench, Trubner & Co.

746. Meek, Charles Kingsley, 1937, Law and Authority in a Nigerian Tribe. London: Oxford University Press.

747. Meggitt, Mervyn J., 1956, "The Valleys of the Upper Wage and Lai Rivers." Oceania 27:90-135.

748. Meggitt, Mervyn J., 1962, Desert People: A Study of the Walbiri Aboriginies of Central Australia. Sydney: Angus & Robertson.

749. Meggitt, Mervyn J., 1965, The Lineage System of the Mae-Enga of New Guinea. New York: Barnes & Noble.

750. Meggitt, Mervyn J., 1977, Blood Is Their Argument: Warfare Among the Mae Enga Tribesmen of the New Guinea Highlands. Palo Alto, CA: Mayfield.

751. Melland, Frank H., 1923, In Witch-Bound Africa: An Account of the Primitive Kaonde Tribe and Their Beliefs. New York: Barnes & Noble.

752. Mercier, Paul, 1951, "The Social Role of Circumcision Among the Besorube." American Anthropologist 53:326-337.

753. Merlan, Francesca, 1982, "A Mangarrayi Representational System: Environment and Cultural Symbolism in Northern Australia." American Ethnologist 9(1):145-166.

754. Merrill, R. T., 1964, "Notes on Icelandic Kinship Terminology." American Anthropologist 66:867-872.

755. Merritt, Ruhlen, 1987, A Guide to the World's Languages. Vol. 1: Classification. Stanford, CA: Stanford University Press.

756. Messenger, John, 1969, Inis Beag: Isle of Ireland. New York: Holt, Rinehart & Winston.

757. Messerschmidt, Donald A., 1976, The Gurungs of Nepal. Warminster, England: Aris & Philips.

758. Metraux, Alfred, 1940, Ethnology of Easter Island. Bishop Museum Bull. no. 160.

759. Metraux, Alfred, 1942, The Native Tribes of Eastern Bolivia and Western Matto Grosso. BBAE Bull. no. 134.

760. Metraux, Alfred, 1946, "Ethnography of the Chaco." HSAI 1:197-370.

761. Metraux, Alfred, 1948, "Tribes of Eastern Bolivia and Madeira Headwaters." HSAI 3:381-424.

762. Metraux, Alfred, 1948, "The Guarani." HSAI 3:69-94.

763. Metraux, Alfred, 1948, "The Tupinamba." HSAI 3:95-133.

764. Metraux, Alfred, 1948, "Tribes of the Middle and Upper Amazon River." HSAI 3:687-712.

765. Metraux, Alfred, 1948, "Paressi." HSAI 3:349-360.

766. Metraux, Alfred, 1946, "The Guato." HSAI 1:409-418.

767. Metraux, Alfred, 1946, "Ethnography of Chaco." HSAI 1:197-370.

768. Metraux, Alfred & Herbert Baldus, 1946, "The Guayaki." HSAI 1:435-496.

769. Metraux, Alfred & Paul Kirchhoff, 1948, "The Northeastern Extension of Andean Culture." HSAI 4:349-368.

770. Meyerowitz, E.L.R., 1950, Akan Traditions of Origin. London: Faber & Faber.

771. Meyerowitz, E.L.R., 1951, The Sacred State of the Akan. London: Faber & Faber.

772. Michael, Henry N., ed., 1967, Lieutenant Zagoskin's Travels in Russian America, 1842-1844: The First Ethnographic Investigations in the Yukon and Kuskokwim Valleys in Alaska, AINA no. 8.

773. Middleton, John, 1960, Lugbara Religion. London: Oxford University Press.

774. Middleton, John, 1963, "The Yakan or Allah Water Cult Among the Lugbara." JRAI 93(1):80-108.

775. Middleton, John, 1965, The Lugbara of Uganda. New York: Holt, Rinehart & Winston.

776. Middleton, John & Greet Kershaw, 1965, The Kikuyu and Kamba of Kenya. ESOA, East Central Africa, Pt. 5.

777. Middleton, John, ed., 1978, Peoples of Africa. New York: Arco.

778. Milheiros, Mario, 1967, Notas de Etnografia Angolana. Luanda: Instituto de Investigasao Cientifica de Angola.

779. Mills, J. P., 1926, The Ao Nagas. Bombay: Oxford University Press.

780. Marquez, Miranda Fernando, 1942, "The Diaguita of Argentina." HSAI 2:637-659.

781. Mitchell, J. C., 1956, The Kalela Dance (Publication of the Rhodes-Livingstone Institute). Manchester: Manchester University Press.

782. Mole, Robert L., 1970, The Montagnards of South Vietnam. Rutland, VT: Charles E. Tuttle.

783. Montagu, M.F. Ashley, 1938, Coming into Being Among the Australian Aborigines. New York: Dutton.

784. Monteil, Vincent, 1966, Les Tribus du Fars et la sedentarisation des nomads. Paris: Mouton.

785. Moore, Arthur W., 1891, The Folklore of the Isle of Man. London: D. Nutt.

786. Moore, Sally Falk, 1985, Social Facts and Fabrications: Customary Law on Kilimanjaro, 1880-1980. New York: Cambridge University Press.

787. Morgan, Lewis Henry, 1877, Ancient Society. New York: Holt.

788. Morgan, Lewis Henry, 1951, League of the Iroquois. Secaucus, NJ: Citadel Press. (1962)

789. Moser, Leo J., 1985, The Chinese Mosaic. London: Westview.

790. Munn, Nancy D., 1986 Walbiri Iconography: Graphic Representation and Cultural Symbolism in a Central Australian Society. Chicago: University of Chicago Press.

791. Munn, Nancy D., 1986, The Fame of Gawa: A Symbolic Study of Value Transformation in a Massim (Papua New Guinea) Society. New York: Cambridge University Press.

792. Murdoch, John, 1892, "Ethnological Results of the Point Barrow Expedition." ARBAE 1887-1888:3-441.

793. Murdock, George P., 1934, "Kinship and Social Behavior Among the Haida." American Anthropologist 36:355-385.

794. Murdock, George P., 1934, Our Primitive Contemporaries. New York: Macmillan.

795. Murdock, George P., 1936, "The Witoto Kinship System." American Anthropologist 38:525-527.

796. Murdock, George P., 1959, Africa: Its Peoples and Their Culture History. New York: McGraw-Hill.

797. Murdock, George P., 1967, Ethnographic Atlas. Pittsburgh: University of Pittsburgh Press.

798. Murdock, George P., 1981, Atlas of World Cultures. Pittsburgh: University of Pittsburgh Press.

799. Murdock, George P. et al., 1983, Outline of World Cultures, 6th rev. ed. New Haven, CT: HRAF.

800. Murdock, George P. & Ward H. Goodenough, 1947, "Social Organization of Truk." Southwestern Journal of Anthropology 3:331-343.

801. Murphy, Robert & B. Quain, 1955, The Trumai Indians of Central Brazil, Monograph no. 24. Seattle: AES.

802. Murphy, Robert F., 1958, "Mundurucu Religion." UCP 49(1).

803. Murphy, Robert F. & Yolanda Murphy, 1986, "Northern Shoshone & Bannock," in W. D'Azevedo, ed., pp. 284-307.

804. Murphy, Yolanda & Robert F. Murphy, 1974, Women of the Forest. New York: Columbia University Press.

805. Murra, John V. et al., eds., 1986, The Anthropological History of Andean Polities. New York: Cambridge University Press.

806. Murra, John V., 1942, "The Historic Tribes of Ecuador." HSAI 2:785-821.

807. Murray, G. W., 1950, Sons of Ishmael: A Study of Egyptian Bedouin. New York: Humanities Press.

808. Musil, Alois, 1928, Manners and Customs of the Rwala Bedouins. New York: Charles R. Crane.

809. Myburgh, A. C., 1949, The Tribes of Barberton District. Pretoria: Union of South Africa, Department of Native Affairs.

810. Myerhoff, B., 1978, Number Our Days. New York: Dutton.

811. Myers, Fred R., 1986, Pintupi Country, Pintupi Self: Sentiment, Place and Politics Among Western Desert Aborigines. Washington, DC: Smithsonian Institution Press.

812. Nadel, Siegfried F., 1942, A Black Byzantium: The Kingdom of Nupe in Nigeria. London: Oxford University Press.

813. Nadel, Siegfried F., 1947, The Nuba: An Anthropological Study of the Hill Tribes in Kordofan. London: Oxford University Press.

814. Nai'ibi, Malam S. & Alhaji Hassan, 1969, Gwari Gade and Koro Tribes. Ibadan, Nigeria: Ibadan University Press.

815. Nance, John, 1975, The Gentle Tasaday. New York: Harcourt Brace Jovanovich.

816. Naroll, Raoul, 1964, "On Ethnic Unit Classification." Current Anthropology 5:283-291, 306-312.

817. Naroll, Raoul, 1968, "Who the Lue Are," in J. Helm, ed., pp. 72-79.

818. Needham, Rodney, 1962, Structure and Sentiment: A Test Case in Social Anthropology. Chicago: University of Chicago Press.

819. Nelson, Edward William, 1899, "The Eskimo About Bering Strait." 18th ARBAE 1896-1897:3-518, 965-997.

820. Neumann, Peter, 1967, Wirtschaft und materielle kultur der buschneger surinames, Band 26. Berlin: ABVMD.

821. Newcombe, W. W., 1983, "Karankawa," in A. Ortiz ed., Vol. 10, pp. 359-367.

822. Newman, James L., 1970, The Ecological Basis for Subsistence Change Among the Sandawe of Tanzania. Washington, DC: National Academy of Sciences.

823. Newman, M. T., A. Woodward et al., 1957, River Basin Surveys Papers, BBAE Bul. 166.

824. Newman, Philip L., 1965, Knowing the Gururumba. New York: Holt, Rinehart & Winston.

825. Nilles, J., 1943-1944, "Natives of the Bismarck Mountains, New Guinea." Oceania 14-15:104-123, 1-18.

826. Nimuendaju, Curt, 1939, "The Apinaye." Catholic University of America Anthropological Series, 8:1-189.

827. Nimuendaju, Curt, 1942, "The Serente." Publications of the Fredrick Webb Hodge Anniversary Publication Fund 4:1-106.

828. Nimuendaju, Curt, 1946, "The Eastern Timbira." UCP 41.

829. Nimuendaju, Curt, 1948, "The Cawahib, Parintintin, and Their Neighbors." HSAI 3:283-297.

830. Nimuendaju, Curt, 1948, "The Maue and Arapium." HSAI 3:245-254.

831. Nimuendaju, Curt, 1948, "The Cawahib, Parintintin, and Their Neighbors." HSAI 3:283-297.

832. Nimuendaju, Curt, 1948, "The Cayabi, Tapanyuna and the Apiaca." HSAI 3:307-320.

833. Nimuendaju, Curt, 1952, The Tukuna (Ed. by R. Lowie; Trans. by W. D. Hohenthal). UCP 45.

834. Nimuendaju, Curt, 1981, Mapa Etno-Historico de Curt Nimuendaju. Rio de Janeiro: IBGE.

835. Nimuendaju, Curt & Robert Lowie, 1937, "The Dual Organization of the Ramkokamekra (Canella) of Northern Brazil." American Anthropologist 39(4):565-582.

836. Norbeck, Edward, 1965, Changing Japan. New York: Holt, Rinehart & Winston.

837. Nordenskiold, Erland, 1938, "An Historical and Ethnological Survey of the Cuna Indians," in H. Wassen, ed., Comparative Ethnological Studies, Vol. 10, pp. 1-686. Goteborg: Hamentolg.

838. Norton, Robert, 1977, Race and Politics in Fiji. New York: St. Martin's.

839. Ntara, Samuel Josia, 1973, The History of the Chewa (Mbiri ya Achewa). Wiesbaden: Franz Steiner Verlag.

840. O'Brien, Denise & A. Ploeg, 1964, "Acculturation Movements Among the Western Dani." American Anthropologist Special Publication, pp. 281-292.

841. Obbo, Christine, 1980, African Women. London: Zed.

842. Oberg, Kalervo, 1953, Indian Tribes of Northern Mato Grosso Brazil, Social Anthropology Publication no. 15. Washington, DC: Smithsonian Institution.

843. Ohnuki-Tierney, Emiko, 1974, The Ainu of the Northwest Coast of Southern Sakhalin. New York: Holt, Rinehart & Winston.

844. Ojany, Francis F. & Reuben B. Ogendo, 1973, Kenya: A Study in Physical and Human Geography. Nairobi: Longman.

845. Oliver, Douglas L., 1949, PMP. Vol. 39, nos. 1-4: Studies in the Anthropology of Bougainville, Solomon Islands.

846. Oliver, Douglas L., 1955, A Solomon Island Society. Cambridge, MA: Harvard University Press.

847. Oliver, Douglas L., 1981, The Tahitian Villages. Hawaii: Institute for Polynesian Studies.

848. Olson, Ronald L., 1933, "Clan and Moiety in Native America." UCP 33(4):351-422.

849. Olson, Ronald L., 1936, Publications in Anthropology. Vol. 6, no. 1: The Quinault Indians, pp. 1-190. Seattle: University of Washington.

850. Olson, Ronald L., 1936, Publications in Anthropology. Vol. 6, no. 1: The Quinault Indians, pp. 1-190. Seattle: University of Washington

851. Oosterwal, G., 1961, People of the Tor. Assen, the Netherlands: Royal Van Gorcum.

852. Opler, Morris E., 1941, An Apache Life-Way. Chicago: University of Chicago Press.

853.   Opler, Morris E., 1969, Apache Odyssey: A Journey Between Two Worlds. New York: Holt, Rinehart & Winston.

854.   Opler, Morris E., 1983, "Chiricahua Apache," in A. Ortiz, ed., Vol. 10, pp. 401-418.

855.   Opler, Morris E., 1983, "Mescalero Apache," in A. Ortiz, ed., Vol. 10, pp. 419-440.

856.   Ortiz, Alfonso, ed., 1983, Handbook of North American Indians, Vols. 9, 10: Southwest. Washington, DC: Smithsonian Institution.

857.   Ortiz, Sergio Elias, 1947, "The Native Tribes and Languages of Southwestern Columbia." HSAI 2:911-914.

858.   Ortiz, William B., 1983, "Southern Periphery: East," in A. Ortiz, ed., Vol. 10, pp. 329-342.

859.   Osgood, Cornelius, 1936, The Distribution of the Northern Athapaskan Indians, YUPA No. 7.

860.   Osgood, Cornelius, 1936, Contributions to the Ethnography of the Kutchin, YUPA no. 14, pp. 1-189.

861.   Osgood, Cornelius, 1937, The Ethnography of the Tanaina, YUPA no. 16.

862.   Osgood, Cornelius, 1940, Ingalik Material Culture, YUPA no. 22.

863.   Osgood, Cornelius, 1958, Ingalik Social Culture, YUPA no. 53.

864.   Osgood, Cornelius, 1959, Ingalik Mental Culture, YUPA no. 56.

865.   Overbergh, Cyr Van, 1909, Les Mangbetu, Collection de Monographies Ethnographiques no. 4. Bruxelles: A. Dewit.

866.   Panikkar, K. M., 1918, "Some Aspects of Nayar Life." JRAI 47:254-293.

867.   Paques, Viviana, 1954, Les Bambara. Paris: Presses Universitaires de France.

868.   Parry, Nevill Edward, 1932, The Lakhers. London: Macmillan.

869.   Parsons, Elsie C., 1928, "Notes on the Pima 1926." American Anthropologist 30:455-464.

870.   Parsons, Elsie C., 1929, "The Social Organization of the Tewa of New Mexico." AAAM 36:1-309.

871.   Parsons, Elsie C., 1936, "Taos Pueblo." General Series in Anthropology, 11:1-121.

872.   Pataki-Schweizer, K. J., 1980, A New Guinea Landscape: Community, Space and Time in the Eastern Highlands. Seattle: University of Washington Press.

873.   Paul, A., 1954, A History of Beja Tribes of the Sudan. London: Cambridge University Press.

874.   Peake, Frederick G., 1961, Change at St. Boswell's. Galashiels: John MacQueen.

875.   Pearsall, Marion, 1947, "Distributional Variations of Bride-Wealth in the East African Cattle Area." Southwestern Journal of Anthropology 3(1):15-31.

876.   Pelissier, Paul, 1980, Atlas du Senegal. Paris: Editions Jeune Afrique.

877.   Pelto, Pertti J., 1973, The Snowmobile Revolution: Technology and Social Change in the Arctic. Menlo Park, CA: Cummings.

878.   Pennington, Campbell W., 1983, "Tarahumara," in A. Ortiz, ed., Vol. 10, pp. 276-289.

879.   Pennington, Campbell W., 1983, "Northern Tepehuan," in A. Ortiz, ed., Vol. 10, pp. 306-314.

880.   Peristiany, J. G., 1939, The Social Institutions of the Kipsigis. New York: Humanities.

881.   Peron, Yves, 1975, Atlas de la Haute-Volta. Paris: Editions Jeune Afrique.

882.   Petersen, Glenn T., 1982, One Man Cannot Rule a Thousand: Fission in a Ponapean Chiefdom. Ann Arbor: University of Michigan Press.

883.   Peterson, Nicolas, ed., 1976, Tribes and Boundaries in Australia. Atlantic Highlands, NJ: Humanities.

884.   Petrullo, Vincenzo, 1969, Los Yaruros del Rio Capanaparo. Caracas: Instituto de Antropologia e Historia.

885.   Philipps, T., 1948, "Etymology of Some African Names." Geographical Journal 110(1-3):142-144.

886.   Pi-Sunyer, Oriol, 1973, Zamora: Change and Continuity in a Mexican Town. New York: Holt, Rinehart & Winston.

887.   Pierce, Earl B., 1973, The Cherokee People, Indian Tribal Series. Phoenix: Arizona State University Press.

888.   Pierce, Joe E., 1964, Life in a Turkish Village. New York: Holt, Rinehart & Winston.

889.   Pike, Eunice, 1964, "The Phonology of New Guinea Highlands Languages." American Anthropologist 66 (Special Publication):121-132.

890.   Pinto, Estevao, 1956, Etnologia Brasileira. Sao Paulo: Companhia Editora Nacional.

891.   Pitt-Rivers, Julian, 1961, The People of the Sierra. Chicago: University of Chicago Press.

892.   Polunin, Ivan & P.H.A. Sneath, 1953, "Studies of Blood Groups in South-Eastern Asia." JRAI 83(1):214-251.

893.   Pospisil, Leopold, 1958, Kapauku Papuans and Their Law, YUPA no. 54.

894.   Pospisil, Leopold, 1963, The Kapauku Papuans of West New Guinea. New York: Holt, Rinehart & Winston.

895.   Powdermaker, Hortense, 1933, Life in Lesu. London: Williams & Norgue.

896.   Preuss, K. T., 1922, Religion und mythologie der Uitoto. Leipzig: J. L. Hinrichs.

897.   Price, David, 1981, "Nambiquara Leadership." American Ethnologist 8(4):686-708.

898.   Price, P. David & Cecil Cook, 1969, "The Present Situation of the Nambiquara." American Anthropologist 71:688-693.

899.   Prins, A.H.J., 1961, The Swahili Speaking Peoples of Zanzibar and the East African Coast. ESOA, East Central Africa, Pt. 12.

900.   Pristinger, Flavia, 1980, "Ethnic Conflict and Modernization in the South Tyrol," in C. R. Foster, ed., pp. 153-188.

901.   Quimby, George, 1948, "Culture Contact on the Northwest Coast 1785-1795." American Anthropologist 50:247-255.

902.   Quinlivan, Paul J., 1954, "Afek of Telefolmin." Oceania 25:17-22.

903.   Radcliffe-Brown, A. R., 1913, "Three Tribes of Western Australia." JRAI 43:143-170.

904.   Radcliffe-Brown, A. R., 1933, The Andaman Islanders. Cambridge: Cambridge University Press.

905.   Radcliffe-Brown, A. R., 1938, The Social Organization of Australian Tribes, Oceania Monographs no. 1. Sydney: Australian National Research Council.

906.   Radin, Paul, 1923, "The Winnebago Tribe." ARBAE 37:35-560.

907.   Rambo, Terry, 1985, Primitive Polluters: Semang Impact on the Malaysian Tropical Rain Forest Ecosystem, APMAUM no. 76.

908.   Rappaport, Roy A., 1968, Pigs for the Ancestors: Ritual in the Ecology of a New Guinea People. New Haven, CT: Yale University Press.

909.   Rattray, Robert Sutherland, 1932, The Tribes of the Ashanti Hinterland. Oxford: Clarendon.

910.   Ravicz, Robert & A. K. Romney, 1969, "The Mixtec," in E. Vogt, ed., HMAI. Vol. 7: Ethnology, pp. 367-399.

911.   Ray, Dorthy J., 1984, "Bering Strait Eskimo," in D. Damas, ed., pp 285-302.

912.   Ray, Verne F., 1932, Publications in Anthropology. Vol. 5: The Sanpoil and Nespelem. Seattle: University of Washington.

913.   Ray, Verne F., 1938, Publications in Anthropology. Vol. 7, no. 2: Lower Chinook Ethnographic Notes. Seattle: University of Washington.

914.   Read, Kenneth E., 1954, "Cultures of the Central Highlands New Guinea." Southwestern Journal of Anthropology 10:1-43.

915.   Read, Kenneth E., 1965, The High Valley. New York: Scribner.

916.   Reay, Marie, 1959, The Kuma: Freedom and Conformity in the New Guinea Highlands. Melbourne: University Press for the Australian National University.

917.   Reefe, Thomas Q., 1981, The Rainbow and the Kings: A History of the Luba Empire to 1891. Berkeley: University of California Press.

918.   Reeves, Carolyn K., 1985, The Choctaw Before Removal. Jackson: University Press of Mississippi.

919.   Rehfisch, F., 1961, "Marriage and the Elementary Family Among Scottish Tinkers." Scottish Studies 5:121-147.

920.   Reichard, Gladys A., 1933, Melanesian Design. New York: Columbia University Press.

921.   Reina, Ruben E., 1969, "Eastern Guatemalan Highlands: The Pokomames & Chorti," in E. Vogt, ed., HMAI. Vol. 7: Ethnology, pp. 101-132.

922.   Reynolds, Barrie, 1978 "Beothuk," in B. Trigger, ed., pp. 101-108.

923.   Ribeiro, Darcy, 1967, "Indigenous Cultures and Languages of Brazil," in J. Hopper, ed., pp. 77-166.

924.   Reichard, Gladys A., 1928, "Social Life of the Navajo Indians." Columbia University Contributions to Anthropology 7:1-239.

925.   Richards, Audrey I., 1939, Land, Labour and Diet in Northern Rhodesia. London: Oxford University Press.

926.   Richards, Audrey I., 1956, Chisungu: A Girls' Initiation Ceremony Among the Bemba of Northern Rhodesia. New York: Grove.

927.   Riddell, Francis A., 1978, "Maidu & Kowkow," in R. Heizer, ed., pp. 370-386.

928.   Ridington, Robin, 1981, "Beaver," in J. Helm, ed., pp. 350-360.

929.   Rieckmann, K. et al., 1961, "Blood Groups and Hemoglobin Values in the Telefolmin Area New Guinea." Oceania 31:296-304.

930.   Riesenberg, Saul H., 1968, Smithsonian Contributions to Anthropology. Vol. 10: The Native Polity of Ponape. Washington, DC: Smithsonian Institution.

931.   Rigby, Peter, 1969, Cattle and Kinship Among the Gogo, A Semi-Pastoral Society of Central Tanzania. Ithaca: Cornell University Press.

932.   Riley, Carroll L., 1969, "The Southern Tepehuan and Tepecano," in E. Vogt, ed., HMAI. Vol. 8: Ethnology, pp. 814-821.

933.   Rivers, W.H.R., 1906, The Todas. Oosterhout, the Netherlands: Anthropological Publications.

934.   Rivers, W.H.R., 1914, The History of Melanesian Society. Oosterhout, the Netherlands: Anthropological Publications.

935.   Riviere, Peter, 1969, Marriage Among the Trio: A Principle of Social Organization. Oxford: Clarendon.

936.   Robbins, Sterling, 1982, Auyana: Those Who Held onto Home. Seattle: University of Washington Press.

937.   Rodd, Francis R., 1926, People of the Veil. London: Macmillan.

938.   Rogers, Edward S. & Eleanor Leacock, 1981, "Montagnais—Naskapi," in J. Helm, ed., pp. 169-189.

939.   Rogers, Edward S. & J. Garth Taylor, 1981, "Northern Ojibwa," in J. Helm, ed., pp. 231-243.

940.   Rohner, Ronald P. & Evelyn C. Rohner, 1970, The Kwakiutl. New York: Holt, Rinehart & Winston.

941.   Rojas, Alfonso Villa, 1969, "Maya Lowlands: The Chontal, Chol and Kekchi," in E. Vogt, ed., HMAI. Vol. 7: Ethnology, pp. 230-243.

942.   Rojas, Alfonso Villa, 1969, "The Tzeltal," in E. Vogt, ed., HMAI. Vol. 7: Ethnology, pp. 195-225.

943.   Romney, A. Kimball, 1966, The Mixtecans of Juxtlahauaca, Mexico. New York: John Wiley.

944.   Rosenblat, Angel, 1936, "Los Otomacas y taparitos de los llanos de Venezuela." Tierra Firme Ano 2(1):131-153.

945.   Roth, H. Ling, 1899, The Aborigines of Tasmania. London: Halifax.

946.   Roth, Walter E., 1924, An Introductory Study of the Arts, Crafts and Customs of the Guiana Indians. 38th ARBAE 1916-1916:25-745.

947.   Rouch, Jean, 1954, Les Songhay. Paris: Presses universitaires de France.

948.   Rouse, Irving, 1948, "The Arawak." HSAI 4:507-546.

949.   Rouse, Irving, 1948, "The Ciboney." HSAI 4:497-503.

950.   Rowe, John H., 1974, "Map: Indian Tribes of South America," in P. J. Lyon, ed.

951.   Rozo Gauta, Jose, 1978, Los Muiscas. Bogot : Fondo Editorial Suramerica.

952.   Rubel, Paula & Abraham Rosman, 1978, Your Own Pigs You May Not Eat. Chicago: University of Chicago Press.

953.   Rubin, Morton, 1974, The Walls of Acre. New York: Holt, Rinehart & Winston.

954.   Ruby, Robert H. & John A. Brown, 1986, A Guide to the Indian Tribes of the Pacific Northwest, Civilization of the American Indian Series no. 173. Norman: University of Oklahoma Press.

955.   Ruhen, Olaf, 1966, Harpoon in My Hand. Sydney: Angus & Robertson.

956.   Rutter, Owen, 1929, The Pagans of North Borneo. London: Hutchinson.

957.   Ryan, D. J., 1955, "Clan Organization in the Mendi Valley." Oceania 26:79-90.

958.   Sahlins, Marshall, 1958, Social Stratification in Polynesia. Seattle: University of Washington Press.

959.   Sahlins, Marshall, 1968, Tribesmen. Englewood Cliffs, NJ: Prentice-Hall.

960.   Sahlins, Marshall, 1981, Historical Metaphors and Mythical Realities. Ann Arbor: University of Michigan Press.

961.   Salisbury, Richard F., 1956, "Asymmetrical Marriage Systems." American Anthropologist 58:639-655.

962.   Salzmann, Z. & V. Scheufler, 1974, Komarov: A Czech Farming Village. New York: Holt, Rinehart & Winston.

963.   Swanson, John R., 1908, Social Condition, Beliefs and Linguistic Relationship of the Tlingit Indians. ARBAE 26:391-485.

964.   Santandrea, P. Stefano, 1964, A Tribal History of the Western Bahr el Ghazal. Bologna: Nigrizia.

965.   Sapir, Edward, 1907, "Notes on the Takelma Indians of Southwestern Oregon." American Anthropologist 9:250-275.

966.   Sapir, Edward & Morris Swadesh, 1939, Nootka Texts: Tales and Ethnological Narratives with Grammatical Notes and Lexical Materials. Philadelphia: Linguistic Society of America.

967.   Sarat, Roy Chandra, 1935, The Hill Bhuiyas of Orissa. Ranchi: Man in India Office.

968.   Sato, Shun, 1980, Pastoral Movements and the Subsistence of the Rendille of Northern Kenya: With Special Reference to Camel Ecology, African 2, Ethnological Series no. 6. Osaka: Senri.

969.   Sausse, Andre, 1951, Populations primitives du Maroni (Guyane Francaise). Paris: Institut Geographiqque National.

970.   Savigear, Peter, 1980, "Corsica and the French State," in C. R. Foster, ed., pp. 116-135.

971.   Savishinsky, Joel & Hiroki Hara, 1981, "Hare," in J. Helm, ed., pp. 314-325.

972.   Schapera, Issaac, 1929, "A Working Classification of the Bantu Peoples of Africa." Man 29:82-87.

973.   Schapera, Issaac, 1930, The Khoisan Peoples of South Africa. London: Routledge & Kegan Paul.

974.   Schapera, Issaac, 1937, The Bantu-Speaking Tribes of South Africa. London: Routledge & Kegan Paul.

975.   Schapera, Issaac, 1940, Married Life in an African Tribe. New York: Sheridan.

976.   Schapera, Issaac, 1952 The Ethnic Composition of Tswana Tribes. London: London School of Economics and Political Science.

977.   Schapera, Issaac, 1956, A Handbook of Tswana Law and Custom, 2nd ed. London: Oxford University Press.

978.   Schapera, Issaac, ed., 1937, The Bantu-Speaking Tribes of South Africa: An Ethnographical Survey. London: Routledge.

979.   Schebesta, Paul, 1952, Die Negrito Asiens. Studia Instituti Anthropos, Vol. 6, Band 1. Wien-Modling: St. Gabriel Verlag.

980.   Schefold, Reimer, 1966, Versuch einer Stilanalyse der Aufhangehaken vom Mittleren Sepik in Neu Guinea, Band 4. Basler Beitrage zur Ethnologie.

981.   Schildkrout, Enid, 1974, Islam and Politics in Kumas, APAMNH 52, Pt. 2.

982.   Schneider, David M., 1984, A Critique of the Study of Kinship. Ann Arbor: University of Michigan.

983.   Schumacher, P., 1939, Exploration du Parc National Albert. Bruxelles: Institut des Parcs Nationaux du Congo Belge.

984.   Schwab, George, 1947, PMP. Vol. 31: Tribes of the Liberian Hinterland.

985.   Schwab, George, 1947, Tribes of the Liberian Hinterland. Cambridge: Peabody Museum.

986.   Schwartz, Douglas W., 1983, "Havasupai," in A. Ortiz, ed., Vol. 10, pp. 13-24.

987.   Schwimmer, Erik, 1973, Exchange in the Social Structure of the Orokaiva. New York: St. Martin's.

988.   Scott, W. H., 1966, On the Cordillera. Manila: MCS Inderprises.

989.   Seabrook, William B., 1931, Jungle Ways. New York: Harcourt, Brace.

990.   Seeger, Anthony, 1981, Nature and Society in Central Brazil: The Suya Indians of Mato Grosso. Cambridge, MA: Harvard University Press.

991.   Seligmann, C. G., 1909, "A Classification of the Natives of British New Guinea." JRAI 39:314-333.

992.   Seligmann, C. G., 1911, The Veddas. Cambridge: Cambridge University Press.

993.   Seligmann, C. G. & Brenda Seligmann, 1932, Pagan Tribes of the Nilotic Sudan. London: Routledge.

994.   Seligmann, C. G., 1976, The Melanesians of British New Guinea. New York: AMS.

995.   Service, Elman R., 1969, "The Northern Tepehuan," in E. Vogt, ed., HMAI. Vol. 8: Ethnology, pp. 822-829.

996.   Shack, William A., 1963. "Some Aspects of Ecology and Social Structure in the Ensete Complex in South-West Ethiopia." JRAI 93(1):72-79.

997. Shack, William A., 1974, The Central Ethiopians Amhara, Tigerina, and Related People. ESOA, North-Eastern Africa, Pt. 4.

998. Shapiro, Harry L., 1933, The Physical Characteristics of the Ontong Javanese, APAMNH 33, Pt. 3.

999. Sheddick, V.G.J., 1953, The Southern Sotho. ESOA, Southern Africa, Pt. 3.

1000. Shimkin, Demitri B., 1986, "Eastern Shoshone," in W. D'Azevedo, ed., pp. 308-335.

1001. Shirokogoroff, Sergei M., 1977, Social Organization of the Northern Tungus. Shanghai: Commercial Press.

1002. Shostak, Marjorie, 1981, Nisa. New York: Vintage.

1003. Silberbauer, George B., 1965, Report to the Government of Bechuanaland on the Bushman Survey. Gaberones: Bechuanaland Government.

1004. Silberbauer, G., 1981, Hunter and Habitat in the Central Kalahari Desert. New York: Cambridge University Press.

1005. Sillitoe, Paul, 1983, Roots of the Earth: Crops in the Highlands of Papua New Guinea. Manchester: University of Manchester Press.

1006. Singe, Bhupinder & J. Bhandari, eds., 1978, The Tibal World and Its Transformations. New Delhi: Concept.

1007. Siskind, Janet, 1973, To Hunt in the Morning. New York: Oxford University Press.

1008. Skeat, W. W. & C. O. Blagden, 1906, Pagan Races of the Malay Peninsula. London: Macmillan.

1009. Skinner, Alanson, 1911, Notes on the Eastern Cree and Northern Saulteaux, APAMNH 9, Pt. 1.

1010. Skinner, Elliot, 1964, The Mossi of Upper Volta. Stanford, CA: Stanford University Press.

1011. Slobodin, Richard, 1981, "Kutchin," in J. Helm, ed., pp. 514-532.

1012. Smith, Anne M., 1974, Ethnography of the Northern Utes. Santa Fe: Museum of New Mexico Press.

1013. Smith, Edwin W., 1920, The Ila-Speaking Peoples of Northern Rhodesia. London: Macmillan.

1014. Smith, James G.E. 1981, "Chipewyan," in J. Helm, ed., pp. 271-290.

1015. Smith, James G.E., 1981, "Western Woods Cree," in J. Helm, ed., pp. 256-270.

1016. Smith, James G.E., 1987. "The Western Woods Cree: Anthropological Myth and Historical Reality." American Ethnologist 14(3):434-448.

1017. Smith, Mary F., 1954, Baba of Karo: A Woman of the Muslim Hausa. London: Faber & Faber.

1018. Smith, Marian W., 1940, The Puyallup-Nisqually, Contributions to Anthropology no. 32. New York: Columbia University.

1019. Smith, Richard C., 1982, The Dialects of Domination in Peru, Occasional Papers in Cultural Survival no. 8. Cambridge, MA: Harvard University.

1020. Snow, Jeanne H., 1981, "Ingalik," in J. Helm, ed., pp. 602-617.

1021. Sorenson, Richard E., 1976, The Edge of the Forest. Washington, DC: Smithsonian Institution Press.

1022. Soret, Marcel, 1959, Les Kongo, Nord-occidentaux Paris: Presses Universitaires de France.

1023. Southall, Aidan, 1970, "The Illusion of Tribe." Journal of Asian and African Studies 5(1-2):28.

1024. Gearing, Frederick, 1970, The Face of the Fox. Chicago: Aldine.

1025. Speck, Frank G., 1909, "Ethnology of the Yuchi Indians." Philadelphia: University of Pennsylvania Museum.

1026. Speck, Frank G., 1918, "Kinship Terms and the Family Band Among the Northeastern Algonquian." Proceedings of the International Congress of Americanists 19:143-161.

1027. Speck, Frank G., 1924, "The Ethnic Position of the Southeastern Algonkian." American Anthropologist 26:184-200.

1028. Speck, Frank G., 1931, "Montagnais-Naskapi Bands and Early Eskimo Distributions in the Labrador Peninsula." American Anthropologist 33:557-600.

1029. Spencer, Baldwin & Francis J. Gillen, 1927, The Arunta, 2 vols. London: Macmillan.

1030. Spencer, Baldwin & Francis J. Gillen, 1938, The Native Tribes of Central Australia. London: Macmillan.

1031. Spencer, J. E. & W. L. Thomas, 1969, Cultural Geography. New York: John Wiley.

1032. Spencer, J. E. & W. L. Thomas, 1971, Asia, East by South: A Cultural Geography. New York: John Wiley.

1033. Spencer, Robert F., 1957, An Ethno-atlas: A Student's Manual of Tribal, Linguistic and Racial Groupings. Dubuque, IA: William C Brown.

1034. Spencer, Robert F., 1959, The North Alaskan Eskimo, BBAE Bul. 171.

1035. Spencer, Robert F. & Elden Johnson, 1960, Atlas For Anthropology, 2nd ed. Dubuque, IA: William C Brown.

1036. Sperry, John R., 1986, " 'Eskimo' not a Racist Slur." The Musk-Ox 34:105.

1037. Spicer, Edward H., 1969, "The Yaqui and Mayo," in E. Vogt, ed., HMAI. Vol. 8: Ethnology, pp. 830-845.

1038. Spicer, Edward H., 1983, "Yaqui," in A. Ortiz, ed., Vol. 10, pp. 250-263.

1039. Spier, Leslie & Edward Sapir, 1930, Publications in Anthropology. Vol. 3: Wishram Ethnography, pp. 151-300. Seattle: University of Washington.

1040. Spier, Leslie, 1925, Publications in Anthropology. Vol. 1, no. 2: The Distribution of Kinship Systems in North America. Seattle: University of Washington.

1041. Spier, Leslie, 1930, "Klamath Ethnography." UCP 30:171-314.

1042. Spier, Leslie, 1933, Yuman Tribes of the Gila River. Chicago: University of Chicago Press.

1043. Spier, Leslie, 1936, Tribal Distribution in Washington. Menasha: George Banta.

1044. Spier, Robert F.G., 1978, "Monache," in R. Heizer, ed., pp. 426-436.

1045.   Spindler, George D. & Louise E. Spindler, 197-, Dreamers Without Power: The Menomini Indians. New York: Holt, Rinehart & Winston.

1046.   Spindler, George D., 1973, Burgbach: Urbanization and Identity in a German Village. New York: Holt, Rinehart & Winston.

1047.   Staden, Hans, 1928, The True Story of his Captivity. London: Routledge & Kegan Paul.

1048.   Stanislawski, Dan, 1947, "Tarascan Political Geography." American Anthropologist 49:46-55.

1049.   Stayt, H. A., 1931, The Bavenda. London: Frank Cass.

1050.   Steadman, Lyle B., 1971, "Neighbors and Killers: Residence and Dominance Among the Hewa of New Guinea." Ph.D. Dissertation, Australian National University.

1051.   Stearmen, Allyn Maclean, 1984, "The Yuqui Connection: Another Look at Siriono Deculturation." American Anthropologist 86(3):630-650.

1052.   Stefansson, Vilhjalmur, 1914, The Stefansson-Anderson Expedition of the American Museum: Preliminary Ethnological Report, APAMNH 14, Pt. 1.

1053.   Stein, Aurel, 1923, Memoir on Maps of Chinese Turkistan and Kansu; from the Surveys Made During Sir Aurel Stein's Expeditions 1900-1, 1906-8, 1913-15. Dehra Dun: Trigonometrical Survey Office.

1054.   Steinbring, Jack H., 1981, "Saulteaux of Lake Winnipeg," in J. Helm, ed., pp. 244-255.

1055.   Stephfen, Alexander M., 1893, "The Navajo." American Anthropologist 4(4):345-362.

1056.   Stern, Bernhard J., 1934, The Lummi Indians of Northwest Washington. New York: Columbia University Press.

1057.   Sternberg, L., 1933, Semya, Rod u Narodov Severo-Vostochnoi Azii. Leningrad.

1058.   Stevenson, H.N.C., 1943, The Economics of the Central Chin Tribes. Bombay: Times of India Press.

1059.   Stevenson, R. C., 1984, The Nuba People of Kordofan Province. Khartoum: University of Khartoum.

1060.   Steward, Julian H., 1937, "Linguistic Distributions and Political Groups of the Great Basin Shoshoneans." American Anthropologist 39:625-634.

1061.   Steward, Julian H., 1938, Basin-Plateau Aboriginal Sociopolitical Groups, BBAE Bul. 120.

1062.   Steward, Julian H., 1946, HSAI. Vol. 1: The Marginal Tribes, BBAE Bul. 143.

1063.   Steward, Julian H., 1946, HSAI. Vol. 2: The Andean Civilization, BBAE Bul. 143.

1064.   Steward, Julian H., 1948, "Tribes of the Montana and Bolivian East Andes." HSAI 3:507-657.

1065.   Steward, Julian H., 1948, HSAI. Vol. 4: The Circum-Caribbean Tribes, BBAE Bul. 143.

1066.   Steward, Julian H., 1948, HSAI. Vol. 3: The Tropical Forest Tribes, BBAE Bul. 143.

1067.   Steward, Julian H., 1949, HSAI. Vol. 5: Comparative Ethnology of South American Indians, BBAE Bul. 143.

1068.   Steward, Julian H., 1950, HSAI. Vol. 6: Physical Anthropology, Linguistic and Cultural Geography of South American Indians, BBAE Bul. 143.

1069.   Steward, Julian H. & Alfred Metraux, 1948, "Tribes of the Peruvian and Ecuadorian Montana." HSAI 3:535-656.

1070.   Steward, Julian H. & Louis C. Faron, 1959, Native Peoples of South America. New York: McGraw-Hill.

1071.   Steward, T. Dale, 1939, Field Museum Anthropological Series. Vol. 31, no. 1: Anthropometric Observations of the Eskimo and Indians of Labrador. Chicago: Field Museum of Natural History.

1072.   Stewart, Kenneth W., 1983, "Mohave," in A. Ortiz, ed., Vol. 10, pp. 55-70.

1073.   Stewart, Omer C., 1943, "Notes on Pomo Ethnogeography." UCP 40(2).

1074.   Stimson, John F., 1971, Tuamotuan Religion, Bul. no. 103 Honolulu: Bishop Museum.

1075.   Stirling, Matthew W., 1938, Historical and Ethnographical Materials on the Jivaro Indians, BBAE Bul. 117.

1076.   Stites, Sara H., 1905, Bryn Mawr College Monographs. Vol. 1, no. 3: Economics of the Iroquois. Bryn Mawr, PA: Bryn Mawr College.

1077.   Stocks, Anthony, 1978, "The Invisible Indians." Ph.D. Dissertation, University of Florida, Department of Anthropology.

1078.   Stocks, Anthony, 1983, "Cocamilla Fishing: Patch Modifications and Environmental Buffering in the Amazon Varzea," in R. Hames & W. Vickers, eds.

1079.   Strauss, Herman & Herbert Tischner, 1962, Die Mikultur der Hagenberg-stamme im Ostlichen Zentralneuguinea. Hamburg: Kommissionsverlag Cram.

1080.   Stubel, Hans, 1958, The Mewu Fantzu: A Tibetan Tribe of Kansu. New Haven, CT: HRAF.

1081.   Sturtevant, William C. (general ed.), 1978, Handbook of North American Indians. Washington, DC: Smithsonian Institution Press.

1082.   Stewart, Omer C., 196-, Ethnohistorical Bibliography of the Ute Indians of Colorado, Series in Anthropology. Boulder: University of Colorado.

1083.   Sullivan, Louis R., 1918, "Racial Types in the Philippine Islands." APAMNH 23, Pt. 1.

1084.   Sutton, J.E.G., 1973, The Archaeology of the Western Highlands of Kenya, Memoir no. 3. Nairobi: British Institute in Eastern Africa.

1085.   Swan, James G., 1974, The Haidah Indians of Queen Charlottes Island. Seattle: Shorey Reprints.

1086.   Swanton, John R., 1904, "The Development of the Clan System and of Secret Societies Among the Northwestern Tribes." American Anthropologist 6:476-485.

1087.   Swanton, John R., 1911, Indian Tribes of the Lower Mississippi Valley and Adjacent Coast of the Gulf of Mexico, BBAE Bul. 43.

1088.   Swanton, John R., 1911, "Indian Tribes of the Lower Mississippi Valley." BBBAE 43:1-274.

1089. Swanton, John R., 1928, "Social Organization and Social Usages of the Indians of the Creek Confederacy." ARBAE 42:23-472.

1090. Swanton, John R., 1928, "Social and Religious Beliefs and Usages of the Chickasaw Indians." ARBAE 44:169-273.

1091. Swanton, John R., 1946, The Indians of Southeastern United States, BBAE Bul. 137.

1092. Swanton, John R., 1952, The Indian Tribes of North America, BBAE Bul. 145.

1093. Sweet, Louise E., 1965, "Camel Raiding of North Arabian Bedouin." American Anthropologist 67:1132-1150.

1094. Taggart, James M., 1983, Nahuat Myth and Social Structure. Austin: University of Texas Press.

1095. Tait, David, 1961, The Konkomba of Northern Ghana. London: Oxford University Press.

1096. Tam, L. et al., 1973, Vietnamese Studies: Ethnographic Data, Vol. 2.

1097. Tanner, Helen Hornbeck, ed., 1987, Atlas of Great Lakes Indian History. Norman: University of Oklahoma Press.

1098. Tanganyika Geographical Division, 1955, Tribal and Ethnographic Map of Tanganyika, 3rd ed.

1099. Tanner, Helen H., ed., 1987, Atlas of Great Lakes Indian History. Norman: University of Oklahoma Press.

1100. Taylor, Brian K., 1962, The Western Lacustrine Bantu. ESOA, East Central Africa, Pt. 13.

1101. Taylor, Garth J., 1974, Labrador Eskimo Settlements of the Early Contact Period, Publications in Ethnology no. 9 Ottawa: National Museum of Man.

1102. Telberg, V. G., 1965, Telberg Translation to: Atlas Narodov Mira. New York: Telberg.

1103. Teschauer, P. C., 1914, "Die Caingang oder Coroados-Indianer." Anthropos 9:16-35.

1104. Thesiger, Wilfred, 1959, Arabian Sands. New York: Viking.

1105. Thomas, A.E.Y. Arima, 1970, t'a:t'a:qsapa A Practical Orthography for Nootka, Publications in Anthropology no. 1. Ottawa: National Museum of Canada.

1106. Thomas, Bertran, 1932, "Anthropological Observations in Southern Arabia." JRAI 62:83-103.

1107. Thomas, Cyrus & John R. Swanton, 1911, Indian Languages of Mexico and Central America and Their Geographical Distribution, BBAE Bul. 44.

1108. Thomas, David Hurst et al., 1986, "Western Shoshone," in W. D'Azevedo, ed., pp. 262-283.

1109. Thomas, Northcote W., 1910, Anthropological Report on the Edo-Speaking Peoples of Nigeria, Pt. 1: Law and Custom. New York: Negro Universities Press.

1110. Thomson, Donald F., 1934, "The Dugong Hunters of Cape York." JRAI 64:237-264.

1111. Thomson, Donald F., 1934, "Notes on an Hero Cult from the Gulf of Carpentaria North Queensland." JRAI 64:217-235.

1112. Tibet Institut, 1980, "Ethnish-kulturhistorische Karte."

1113. Tiesler, Frank, 1969, Die Intertribalen Beziehungen an der Nordkuste Neuguineas im Gebiet der Kleinen Schouten-inseln, Band 30. ABVMB.

1114. Tiesler, Frank, 1975, Topfereie Erzeugnisse aus demTorricelli-gebirge, Sepik District (Nord-Neuguinea), Band 34, pp. 605-627. ABVMD.

1115. Tiller, Veronica E., 1984, "Jicarilla Apache," in A. Ortiz, ed., Vol. 10, pp. 440-461.

1116. Tindale, Norman B., 1940, "Results of the Harvard-Adelaide Universities' Anthropological Expedition." Transactions of the Royal Society of South Australia 64:140-231.

1117. Tindale, Norman B., ed., 1974, Aboriginal Tribes of Australia. Los Angeles: University of California Press.

1118. Tobey, Margaret L., 1981, "Carrier," in J. Helm, ed., pp. 413-932.

1119. Tonkinson, Robert, 1977, "Exploration of Ambiguity: A New Hebrides Case," in M. Lieber, ed., pp. 269-296.

1120. Tooker, Elisabeth, 1978, "The League of the Iroquois: Its History, Politics, and Ritual," in B. Trigger, ed., pp. 418-441.

1121. Torday, E. & T. A. Joyce, 1907, "On the Ethnology of the South-Western Congo Free State." JRAI 37:133-156.

1122. Toupet, Charles, 1977, Atlas de la Republique Islamique de Mauritanie. Paris: Editions Jeune Afrique.

1123. Townsend, Joan B., 1981, "Tanaina," in J. Helm, ed., pp. 623-640.

1124. Traore, Mamadou, 1980, Atlas du Mali. Paris: Editions Jeune Afrique.

1125. Trigger, Bruce, 1969, The Huron: Farmers of the North. New York: Holt, Rinehart & Winston.

1126. Trout, Frank E., 1969, Morocco's Saharan Frontiers. Geneva: Libraire Droz.

1127. Trowell, Margaret & K. P. Wachsmann, 1953, Tribal Crafts of Uganda. London: Oxford University Press.

1128. Tschopik, Harry F., Jr., 1946, "The Aymara." HSAI 147(ii):501-573.

1129. Tschopik, Harry F., Jr., 1951, The Aymara of Chucuito Peru, APAMNH 44, Pt. 2.

1130. Tucker, A. Winifred & Charles S. Myers, 1910, "A Contribution to the Anthropology of the Sudan." JRAI 40:141-163.

1131. Turnbull, Colin M., 1965, The Mbuti Pygmies: An Ethnographic Survey, APAMNH 50, Pt. 3.

1132. Turnbull, Colin M., 1965, Wayward Servants: The Two Worlds of the African Pygmies. Garden City, NJ: Natural History Press.

1133. Turnbull, Colin M., 1961, The Forest People. New York: Simon & Schuster.

1134. Turnbull, Colin M., 1972, The Mountain People. New York: Simon & Schuster.

1135. Turner, Paul R., 1971, The Highland Chontal. New York: Holt, Rinehart & Winston.

1136. Turner, Edwin Randolph, 1984, "Sociopolitical Organization Within the Powhatan Chiefdom and the Effects of European Contact," in W. W. Fitzhugh, ed., pp. 193-224.

1137.   Turner, Edwin Randolph, 1979, An Archaeological and Ethnohistorical Study on the Evolution of Rank Societies in the Virginia Coastal Plain. Ann Arbor: University of Michigan Microfilms.

1138.   Turner, Victor W., 1952, The Lozi Peoples of Northwest Rhodesia. ESOA, West Central Africa, Pt. 3.

1139.   Turner, Victor W., 1957, Schism and Continuity in an African Society: A Study of Ndembu Village Life. Manchester: Manchester University Press.

1140.   Turner, Victor W., 1967, The Forest of Symbols. Ithaca: Cornell University Press.

1141.   Turney-High, Harry H., 1937, "The Flathead Indians of Montnan." AAAM 47:1-161.

1142.   Turnwald, Richard, 1916, "Banaro Society." AAAM 3:251-391.

1143.   Tuzin, Donald F., 1976, The Ilahita Arapesh. Berkeley: University of California Press.

1144.   UNESCO, 1963, Nomades et Nomadisme au Sahara. Paris: Fountenoy.

1145.   UNESCO, 1984, African Ethnonyms and Toponyms. Paris: Imprimerie des Presses Universitaires de France.

1146.   USSR Geographical Society, 1985, Small and Dispersed Ethnic Groups in the European U.S.S.R. [in Russian]. Moscow: Academy of Sciences.

1147.   United Bible Societies, 1986, Scriptures of the World. London: United Bible Societies.

1148.   United Nations, 1974, Second United Nations Conference on the Standardization of Geographical Names. New York: United Nations.

1149.   Vader, Artur, 1974, Equal Among Equals. Tallinn: Perioodika.

1150.   Van Ball, J., 1966, Dema. The Hague: Martinus-Nijhoff.

1151.   Van Geluwe, H., 1957, Les Bira. ESOA, Central Belgian Congo, Pt. 2.

1152.   Van Geluwe, H., 1957, Mamvu-Mangutu et Balese-Mvuba. ESOA, Central Africa Belgian Congo, Pt. 3.

1153.   Van Geluwe, H., 1960, Les Bali. ESOA, Central Africa Belgian Congo, Pt. 5.

1154.   Van Stone, J., 1974, Athapaskan Adaptations: Hunters and Fishermen of the Subartic Forest. Chicago: Aldine.

1155.   Van Warmelo, N. J., 1932, Contributions Towards Venda History, Religion and Tribal Ritual, Ethnological Publications no. 3. Pretoria: Union of South Africa, Department of Native Affairs.

1156.   Van Warmelo, N. J., 1951, Notes on the Kaokoveld and Its People, Ethnological Publications no. 26. Pretoria: Republic of South Africa, Department of Bantu Administration.

1157.   Van Wouden, F.A.E., 1968, Types of Social Structure in Eastern Indonesia. The Hague: Martinus Nijhoff.

1158.   Vanden Bergh, Leonard John, 1921, On the Trial of the Pygmies. New York: J. A. McCann.

1159.   Vansina, J., 1954, Les Tribus Ba-Kuba. ESOA, Central Africa Belgian Congo, Pt. 1.

1160.   Vanstone, James W. & Ives Goddard, 1981, "Territorial Groups of West Central Alaska Before 1898," in J. Helm, ed., pp. 556-561.

1161.   Variot, Jean, 1936, Contes populaires et traditions orales de l'Alsace. Paris: Firmin-Didot.

1162.   Vayda, Andrew P., ed., 1968, Peoples and Cultures of the Pacific. Garden City, NJ: Natural History Press.

1163.   Uchendu, Victor C., 1965, The Igbo of Southeast Nigeria. New York: Holt, Rinehart & Winston.

1164.   Vennetier, Pierre, 1977, Atlas de la Republique Populaire du Congo. Paris: Editions Jeune Afrique.

1165.   Vergouwen, J. C., 1964, The Social Organization and Customary Law of the Toba-Batak of Northern Sumatara. The Hague: Martinus Nijhoff.

1166.   Vickers, William T., 1983, "Territorial Dimensions of Siona-Secoya and Encabellado Adaptation," in R. Hames & W. Vickers, eds., pp. 451-478.

1167.   Viveiros de Castro, Eduardo, 1986, Arawete os deuses Canibais. ANPOCS.

1168.   Voegelin, E. W., 1938, "Tubatulabal Ethnography." Anthropological Records 2(i):1-82.

1169.   Vogt, Evon Zartman, ed., 1969, Handbook of Middle American Indians. Vol. 8: Ethnology.

1170.   Vogt, Evon Zartman, ed., 1969, Handbook of Middle American Indians. Vol. 7: Ethnology.

1171.   Vogt, Evon Zartman, 1970, The Zinacantecos of Mexico: A Modern Maya Way of Life. New York: Holt, Rinehart & Winston.

1172.   Wauchope, Robert (series ed.), 1964-1976, Handbook of Middle American Indians. Austin: University of Texas Press.

1173.   Wagley, Charles, 1977, Welcome of Tears: The Tapirape Indians of Central Brazil. New York: Oxford University Press.

1174.   Wagley, Charles & Eduardo Galvao, 1948, "The Tenetehara." HSAI 3:137-148.

1175.   Wagley, Charles & Eduardo Galvao, 1949, The Tenetehara Indians of Brazil: A Culture in Transition. New York: Columbia University Press.

1176.   Wagner, Roy, 1986, Asiwinarong: Ethos, Image and Social Power Among the Usen Barok of New Ireland. Princeton, NJ: Princeton University Press.

1177.   Waldman, Carl, 1985, Atlas of the North American Indian. New York: Facts on File.

1178.   Walker, Anthony R., 1983, "The Lahu People: An Introduction," in J. McKinnon & W. Bhurksasri, eds., pp. 227-241.

1179.   Wallerstein, Emmanuel, 1960, "Ethnicity and National Integration in West Africa." Cahiers d'Etudes Africaines 1(3):129-139.

1180.   Walter, Bob J., 1970, Territorial Expansion of the Nandi of Kenya 1500-1950, African Series No. 90. Athens: Ohio University, Center for International Studies.

1181.   Walter, Lavina E., 1911, The Fascination of Brittany. London: A & C Black.

1182.   Warner, William Lloyd., 1937, A Black Civilization. New York: Harper.

1183. Warren, Charles, 1977, "Palawan," in F. Lebar, ed., pp. 229-290.

1184. Waterman, T. T., 1918, "The Yana Indians." UCP 13(2).

1185. Waterman, T. T., 1920, "Yorok Geography." UCP 16(5).

1186. Watson, James, 1983, Tairora Culture: Contingency and Pragmatism. Seattle: University of Washington Press.

1187. Watson, James B., 1973, "Tairora: The Politics of Despotism in an Small Society," in R. Brendt et al., eds., Politics in New Guinea, pp. 224-276, Seattle: University of Washington Press.

1188. Watson, James B., ed., 1973, The Languages of the Eastern Family of the East New Guinea Highland Stock. Seattle: University of Washington Press.

1189. Wedel, Waldo R., 1936, An Introduction to Pawnee Archaeology, BBAE Bull. 112.

1190. Wedgwood, Camilla, 1936, "Report on Research Work in Naru Island, Central Pacific." Oceania 6-7:359-391, 1-33.

1191. Wedgwood, Camilla H., 1942, "Notes on the Marshall Islands." Oceania 13:1-23.

1192. Weeks, John H., 1914, Among the Primitive Bakongo. London: Seeley, Service.

1193. Weinberg, Daniela, 1975, Peasant Wisdom: Cultural Adaptation in a Swiss Village. Berkeley: University of California Press.

1194. Weinrich, A.K.H., 1971, Chiefs and Councils in Rhodesia. Columbia: University of South Carolina Press.

1195. Wente-Luka, Renate, 1985, Handbook of Ethnic Units in Nigeria. Stuttgart: Franz Steiner.

1196. Werner, Dennis, 1983, "Why do the Mekranoti Trek?" in R. Hames & W. Vickers, eds., pp. 225-238.

1197. Weslager, Clinton A., 1977, The Delaware Indians: A History. New Brunswick, NJ: Rutgers University Press.

1198. White, Leslie A., 1930, "The Acoma Indians." ARBAE 47:17-192.

1199. White, Marian E., W. E. Engelbrecht, & Elisabeth Tooker, 1978, "Cayuga," in B. Trigger, ed., pp. 500-504.

1200. White, Marian E., 1979, "Erie," in B. Trigger, ed., pp. 412-417.

1201. White, Raymond C., 1963, "Luiseno Social Organization." UCP 48(2).

1202. Whiteley, Wilfred et al., 1950, Bemba and Related Peoples of Northern Rhodesia. ESOA, East Central Africa, Pt. 2.

1203. Whiting, J. W., 1941, Becoming a Kwoma. New Haven, CT: Yale University Press.

1204. Wiens, Herold J., 1954, China's March Toward the Tropics. Hamden, CT: Shoe String.

1205. Wilkenson, J. C., 1977, Water and Tribal Settlement in South East Arabia: A Study of the Aflaj of Oman. Oxford: Clarendon.

1206. Wilks, Ivor, 1975, Asante in the Nineteenth Century: The Structure and Evolution of a Political Order. London: Cambridge University Press.

1207. Will, G. F. & H. J. Spinden, 1906, PMP. Vol. 3, pp. 81-219: The Mandans.

1208. Willamson, Robert W., 1939, Essays in Polynesian Ethnology. London: Cambridge University Press.

1209. Willems, Emilio, 1962, "On Portuguese Family Structure." International Journal of Comparative Sociology 3:65-79.

1210. Williams, Thomas R., 1965, The Dusun. New York: Holt, Rinehart & Winston.

1211. Williams, Francis Edgar, 1936, Papuans of the Trans-Fly. Oxford: Clarendon.

1212. Williams, Francis Edgar, 1940, "Natives of Lake Kutubu, Papua." Oceania 11(2).

1213. Williams, Francis Edgar, 1930, Orokaiva Society. London: Oxford University Press.

1214. Williamson, Robert W., 1912, The Mafulu Mountain People of British New Guinea. London: Macmillan.

1215. Williamson, Robert W., 1924, The Social and Political Systems of Central Polynesia. Cambridge: Cambridge University Press.

1216. Williamson, Robert W., 1939, Essays in Polynesian Ethnology. London: Cambridge University Press.

1217. Willis, Roy G., 1966, The Fipa and Related Peoples of Southwest Tanzania and Northeast Zambia. ESOA, East Central Africa, Pt. 15.

1218. Wilson, Monica, 1951, Good Company: A Study of Nyakusa Age Villages. London: Oxford University Press.

1219. Wilson, Monica, 1959, Communal Rituals of the Nyakyusa. Oxford: Oxford University Press.

1220. Wilson, Monica, 1979, Reaction to Conquest, Effects of Conduct with Europeans on the Pondo of South Africa. London: Oxford University Press.

1221. Winter, Edward H., 1956, Bwamba: A Structural-Functional Analysis of a Patrilineal Society. Cambridge: W. Heffer.

1222. Wirz, Paul, 1922, Die Marind-anim von Hollandisch-Sud-Neu-Guinea, Band 1. Hamburg: L. Friederitchsen.

1223. Wissler, Clark, 1912, "The Social Life of the Blackfoot Indians." APAMNH 7:1-64.

1224. Wissler, Clark, ed., 1916, Societies of the Plains Indians. APAMNH 11.

1225. Wurm, S. A., 1962, "The Languages of the Eastern, Western and Southern Highlands Territory of Papua New Guinea," in A. Capell, ed., A Linguistic Survey of the SW Pacific, Technical Paper no. 136, pp. 105-128. Noumea: South Pacific Commission.

1226. Wurm, S. A., 1964, "Australian New Guinea Highlands Language and the Distribution of their Typological Features." American Anthropologist 66(4, Pt. 2):77-96.

1227. Wylie, Laurence, 1957, Village in the Vaucluse: An Account of Life in a French Village. Cambridge, MA: Harvard University Press.

1228. Yalman, Nur, 1967, Under the Bo Tree. Berkeley: University of California Press.

1229. Yen, D. E. & J. Nance, eds., 1976, Further Studies on the Tasaday. Makati, Philippines: Panamin Foundation.

1230. Yost, J., 1981, "People of the Forest: The Waorani," in G. Ligabue, ed., Ecuador in the Shadow of the Volcanoes, pp. 95-115. Venice: Ediciones Libri Mundi.

1231. Young, Michael W., 1983, "Ceremonial Visiting in Goodenough Island," in J. Leach & E. Leach, eds., pp. 395-410.

1232. Young, O. Gordon, 1961, The Hilltribes of Northern Thailand. Bangkok: United States Operations Mission to Thailand.

1233. Young, Philip D., 1971, Ngawbe. ISA.

1234. Zagoskin, L. A., 1967, Lieutenant Zagoskin's Travels in Russian America, 1842-1844. Toronto: University of Toronto Press.

1235. Zegwaard, Gerard A., 1968, "Headhunting Practices of the Asmat of Netherlands New Guinea," in A. Vayda, ed., pp. 421-450.

1236. Zerries, Otto, 1962, "Die volkerkundliche Forschungssituation in Sudost-Venezuela." BICU no. 5, pp. 97-111.

1237. Zigmond, Maurice L., 1986, "Kawaiiso," in W. D'Azevedo, ed., pp. 398-411.

CULTURE INDEX

Cite 1	Cite 2	Culture	Map	No.	HRAF	Murdock's Atlas
71	0	Alawa	30	142	OI5	
753	0	Alawa . . . see Alagwa	0	0		
267	266	Albanians	37	2	EG1	
807	0	Aleiqat	19	5	MR11	
540	0	Aleut	36	1	NA6	Na7
1092	0	Algonkin	2	22	NH4	
1092	0	Algonkin	3	14	NH4	
77	0	Ali Bin Morrah	19	79	MK1	
0	0	Aliab . . . see Dinka	0	0	FJ12	
187	0	Allentiac	13	9	SI6	
640	0	Aloene	28	83	OH9	
254	0	Alor	28	11	OF5	Ic2
1161	0	Alsatians	37	24	EW10	
74	0	Alsea	4	9	NR5	Nb28
0	523	Alulu . . . see Alur	0	0		
0	523	Alunda . . . see Lunda	0	0	FO27	
416	0	Alur	21	34	FK5	Aj17
0	523	AmaNgwane . . . see Swazi	0	0		
135	0	Amahuaca	11	48	SE6	Se8
1139	0	Amahumbu	22	31		
0	0	Amale . . . see Qashqai	0	0		
826	0	Amanaye	10	56	SQ2	
1116	0	Amangu	29	87	OI5	
0	523	Amara . . . see Amhara	0	0		
873	0	Amarar	19	143	MR9	Ca35
318	0	Amarat Bedu	38	11	MH8	
1113	0	Amarken	32	102	OJ1	
0	523	Amaswati . . . see Swazi	0	0		
0	523	Amaswazi . . . see Swazi	0	0		
0	523	Amazulu . . . see Zulu	0	0		
1221	416	Amba	21	86	FO6	Ae1
647	0	Amberbaken	32	162	OJ1	
502	0	Ambo	23	58	FX8	Ab19
926	0	Ambo	22	16	FX8	Ab19
1214	0	Ambo	32	203	OJ1	Ab19
0	523	Ambuela . . . see Mbwela	0	0		
455	0	Ambuella	22	37	FP12	
0	523	Ambundu . . . see Mbundu	0	0		
0	523	Ambuun . . . see Mbundu	0	0		
64	0	Amdo	39	43	AJ1	
1092	0	Ameralik	1	11	NB6	
1092	0	Ameyao	7	69	SX5	
997	532	Amhara	19	129	MP5	Ca7
152	640	Ami	27	55	AD16	Ia9
1092	0	Ammassalimiut	1	8	NB4	Na24
834	0	Amoipira	12	5	SN7	
1205	0	Amr	19	74	MK1	
973	0	Amraal Hottentots	22	80	FX13	
1019	0	Amuesha	11	20	SE9	
71	0	Amurag	29	5	OI5	
133	0	Amyu	32	137	OJ1	
0	523	Ana . . . see Bideyat	0	0		
99	0	Anadyr Eskimo	1	68	RY5	
154	0	Anakazza	18	98	MS5	
1092	0	Anarkat	1	5	NB4	
0	0	Anasazi . . . see Hopi	0	0		
904	0	Andamanese	26	25	AZ2	Eh1
466	0	Andoa	9	61	SE22	
0	523	Andreleba . . . see Lugbara	0	0		
0	523	Anfue . . . see Aja	0	0		
767	0	Angaite	11	121	SK10	
1063	0	Angara	11	21	SE13	
507	0	Angmagsqlik	37	39	NB4	Na24
498	1098	Angoni	23	30	FR5	Ac9
217	0	Angoon	4	117	NA12	
412	0	Angu	32	15	OJ1	
532	0	Ania	21	211	MP13	
77	0	Anizah	19	17	MJ4	
1093	77	Anizah	38	2	MJ4	
648	0	Ankaza	18	97	MS5	
416	302	Ankole	21	93	FK11	Ad45
4	0	Anlo	17	35	FE6	
441	0	Anoufo	17	54	FA13	
0	0	Antankarama . . . see Tankarana	0	0	FY9	
0	0	Antanosy . . . see Tanosy	0	0	FY14	
0	0	Antimanambondro . . . see Timanambondro	0			
0	523	Anzakara . . . see Nzakara	0	0		
373	0	Apa tani	25	56	AR11	
53	852	Apache, Chiricahua	6	56	NT8	Nh1
1115	0	Apache, Jicarilla	6	30	NT26	Nh16
1092	44	Apache, Kiowa	4	45	NQ16	
855	0	Apache, Mescalero	6	57	NT25	Nh15
855	0	Apache, Mescalero	8	66	NT25	Nh15
1092	0	Apache, Western	5	23	NT21	Nh17
222	0	Apalachee	7	47	NN14	
834	946	Apalai	10	25	SQ3	
0	523	Apambia . . . see Pambia	0	0		
39	988	Apayao	27	52	OA5	
832	0	Apiaca	11	97	SP2	
826	826	Apinaye	10	49	SP3	Sj7
718	0	Apinaye	12	17	SP3	
759	0	Apolista	11	82	SF14	
0	523	Appa . . . see Jukun	0	0		
318	0	Aqaidat Bedu	38	9	MD5	
187	0	Arachane	13	32	SM4	
60	296	Arafah ('Arafah)	16	22	MT9	
94	0	Arago	17	82	FF27	
519	0	Arago	18	55	FF27	
685	458	Arakanese	26	44	AP4	
828	0	Arake	10	44		
0	0	Aranda . . . see Arunta	0	0	OI8	
582	759	Araona	11	74	SF23	
1092	0	Arapaho	3	32	NQ6	Ne9
1092	0	Arapaho	6	27	NQ6	
1143	133	Arapesh	32	105	OJ6	Ie3
830	0	Arapium	10	36	SQ12	
57	0	Arara	11	58	SQ6	
1092	0	Araraibos	9	115		
829	946	Arauaki	9	96	SQ22	
181	176	Araucanians	14	13	SG4	Sg2
176	0	Araucanians	13	4	SG4	Sg2
303	948	Arawak	7	74	SR6	
125	0	Arawak	10	1	SR10	
1167	0	Arawete	10	46		
0	523	Are . . . see Baka	0	0	Fj18	
946	0	Arecuna	9	162	SS16	
997	997	Argobba	21	212	MP5	
647	0	Arguni	32	154	OJ1	
0	0	Ari . . . see Baka	0	0		
1063	0	Arica	11	138	SE13	
834	0	Aricobi	12	12	SO8	
1092	0	Arikara	3	28	NQ7	Ne10
57	0	Arikemes	11	59	SP5	
0	523	Arimi . . . see Nyaturu	0	0		
946	0	Arinagoto	9	161	SS16	
540	0	Armenians	38	30	RJ3	Ci10
648	154	Arna	18	90	MS22	
439	0	Aroma	32	231	OJ1	
0	523	Arringeu . . . see Pongo	0	0		
1092	0	Arsuk	1	10	NB6	
133	0	Aru Islands	32	170	OH5	
400	0	Arua	10	54	SQ5	
0	523	Arund . . . see Lunda	0	0		
1029	1030	Arunta	30	118	OI8	Id1
0	523	Arusa . . . see Arusha	0	0		
61	0	Arusha	21	154	FL7	
532	996	Arusi, Galla	21	208	MP13	Ca11
1092	0	Arviligyuarmiut	3	46	ND13	
22	1092	Arviquurmiut	1	35	ND13	
0	523	Asanti . . . see Ashanti	0	0		
0	523	Asenga . . . see Senga	0	0		
316	0	Ashan	19	110		
1206	690	Ashanti	17	42	FE12	Af3
767	0	Ashluslay	11	122	SK5	
1092	0	Asiagmiut	1	42	ND8	
1235	133	Asmat	32	138	OJ1	
643	0	Assam	26	50	AR1	
1092	0	Assiniboin	4	47	NF4	Ne11
1092	0	Assiniboin	3	17	NF4	Ne11
0	523	Asu . . . see Aka	0	0	FN4	
0	523	Asu . . . see Pare	0	0	FN4	
828	0	Asurini	10	45	SQ26	
950	0	Atacama	13	11	SG5	
950	0	Atacama	11	131	SG5	
1092	0	Atakapa	7	1	NO4	
1092	0	Atakapa	6	3	NO4	
640	0	Atayal	27	55	AD8	Ia1
873	0	Atbara	19	141	MR9	
0	523	Atemne . . . see Temne	0	0		
0	523	Ateo . . . see Teke	0	0		

Cite 1	Cite 2	Culture	Map	No.	HRAF	Murdock's Atlas
290	0	Atie	17	109	FE12	
647	0	Atjehnese	28	37	OD4	
217	0	Atlin	4	124	NA12	
317	0	Atmanika	38	29		
217	0	Atna	1	77	NA5	
189	647	Atoni	28	6	OF20	
125	0	Atorai	10	9	SR13	
0	523	Atsam . . . see Chawai	0	0		
1092	0	Atsina	3	34	NQ13	Ne1
381	0	Atsugewi	5	78	NS5	Nc4
737	0	Attikamek	2	30	NG4	
226	0	Atwot, Dinka	21	9	FJ12	
0	523	Atyap . . . see Katab	0	0		
522	0	Auanbura	30	88	OI5	
820	0	Aucaners	10	11	SR8	
487	0	Auen	22	72	FX10	
487	0	Auen	24	4	FX10	
198	0	Aueti	12	24	SP6	Si9
406	0	Augu	32	71	OJ1	
217	0	Auk	4	122	NA12	
296	0	Aulad Soliman	16	13	MT9	
947	1144	Aulliminden	17	80	MS25	
199	0	Aushi	22	4	FQ5	
511	0	Austrians	37	13	EKI	
889	872	Auyana	32	18	OJ1	
317	0	Avar	38	47	RH8	
946	0	Averiano	9	145		
316	0	Avil	19	104		
775	0	Avukaya	18	148	FJ19	
671	0	Awa	32	17	OJ1	
116	0	Awai	32	115	OJ4	
0	0	Awak . . . see Ponape	0	0		
1104	0	Awamir	19	82	MK1	
296	0	Awaqir ('Awaqir)	16	24	MT4	
0	523	Awasira . . . see Shila	0	0		
0	523	Awasira . . . see Shilluk	0	0		
77	0	Awazim	19	27	MJ4	
94	0	Awe	18	48	MS5	
718	0	Aweikoma	12	47	SM2	Sj3
807	0	Awlad 'Ali	16	2	MT9	
133	0	Awyu	32	135	OJ1	
807	0	Ayaida	19	2	MR11	
807	0	Ayaida	16	9	MR11	
133	0	Ayamaro	32	160	OJ1	
1139	0	Ayisenga	22	34		
1129	115	Aymara	11	26	SF5	Sf2
767	0	Ayoreo (Moro)	11	108	SF3	
294	47	Azande	21	27	FO7	Ai3
1135	0	Azande	18	144	FO7	Ai3
123	0	Azande	20	39	FO7	Ai3
540	0	Azerbaidzhan	38	26	RK1	
738	0	Aztec	8	39	NU7	Nj2
154	0	Azzas	18	80	MS22	
45	0	Baadu . . . see Badi	0	0		
77	10	Baalahmah	19	41	MJ4	
77	10	Baalasmar	19	35	MJ4	
1214	0	Baba	32	209	OJ1	
0	523	Babemba . . . see Bemba	0	0		
0	523	Babisa . . . see Bisa	0	0		
0	523	Babwili . . . see Bwile	0	0		
0	523	Bachoko . . . see Chokwe	0	0		
0	0	Bad . . . see Badi	0	0		
0	523	Badama . . . see Padhola	0	0		
45	0	Badi	29	36	OI5	
72	0	Badimaia	29	77	OI5	
522	0	Badjeri	30	50	OI5	
0	523	Badondo . . . see Dondo	0	0		
578	0	Badui	28	27	OE4	
996	0	Badutu	21	203		
0	523	Bafau . . . see Fo	0	0		
724	0	Bafia	18	16	FH10	Ae48
0	523	Bafilache . . . see Fulbe	0	0		
0	523	Bafo . . . see Fo	0	0		
0	523	Bafokeng . . . see Fokeng	0	0		
0	523	Bafu . . . see Bafia	0	0		
0	0	Bafut . . . see Bafia	0	0		
145	0	Baga	17	153	FA7	Ag14
0	523	Baganda . . . see Ganda	0	0		
200	0	Baggara Arabs	16	11	MQ5	
0	523	Bagishu . . . see Gishu	0	0		

Cite 1	Cite 2	Culture	Map	No.	HRAF	Murdock's Atlas
729	0	Bagobo	27	10	OA7	
71	0	Bagu	29	30	OI5	
0	523	Baha . . . see Ha	0	0		
725	0	Bahar-Lu	19	87		
0	523	Bahaya . . . see Haya	0	0		
0	523	Bahima . . . see Hima	0	0		
782	0	Bahnar	27	69	AM15	
0	523	Baholo . . . see Holo	0	0		
201	523	Baia	18	9	FI9	Ai7
285	285	Baiga	25	44	AW24	Eg9
0	523	Baila . . . see Ila	0	0		
1092	0	Bainoa	7	70	SX4	
1104	0	Bait Imani	19	67	MJ4	
1104	0	Bait Kathir	19	68	MJ4	
0	523	Bajinja . . . see Zinza	0	0		
993	0	Baka	21	24	FJ18	
990	0	Bakairi	12	31	SP7	Si3
973	0	Bakalahari	22	74	FV4	
201	0	Bakamba	20	72	FO21	
0	523	Bakare . . . see Kare	0	0		
0	0	Bakele	20	13	FI14	
141	0	Bakere	20	19	FI14	
316	0	Bakhtiari	38	15	MA12	Ea8
725	0	Bakhtiari	19	93	MA12	
0	523	Bakiga . . . see Kiga	0	0		
155	0	Bakil	19	50		
0	0	Bako . . . see Baka	0	0		
0	0	Bakongo . . . see Kongo	0	0	FO20	
0	523	Bakonjo . . . see Konjo	0	0		
0	523	Bakota . . . see Kota	0	0		
159	0	Bakovi	32	244	OM8	Ig15
0	523	Bakuria . . . see Kuria	0	0		
985	0	Bakwe	17	114	FD7	Af46
0	523	Bakwena . . . see Kwena	0	0		
0	523	Balala . . . see Lala	0	0		
201	0	Balali	20	75	FI33	
0	523	Balamba . . . see Lamba	0	0		
647	0	Balantak	28	70	OG5	
876	0	Balante	17	167	FB6	Ag15
71	1116	Balardong	29	89	OI5	
1152	0	Bale	21	85	FO13	
0	523	Bale . . . see also Lendu	0	0		
0	523	Balegu . . . see Lendu	0	0		
0	523	Balengola . . . see Lengola	0	0		
0	0	Balenje . . . see Lenje	0	0		
1152	0	Balese Ndake	21	83	FO31	
1152	0	Balese Ndake	18	142	FO31	
77	0	Balgarn	19	43	MR11	
495	0	Bali	18	27	FF51	Ae49
1153	0	Bali	20	34	FO9	
520	0	Bali	20	79	FO9	
387	423	Balinese	28	23	OF7	Ih3
876	0	Ballouk	17	168	FB6	
0	523	Balojash . . . see Luchazi	0	0		
201	0	Baloulou (Mongo)	20	44	FO32	
0	523	Balozi . . . see Lozi	0	0		
1121	0	Balua	20	98	FO28	
0	0	Baluba . . . see Luba	0	0	FO27	
0	523	Balubalo . . . see Luena	0	0		
27	0	Baluchi	19	119	AT2	
99	0	Baluchi	39	3	AT2	
99	0	Baluchi	25	39	AT2	
0	523	Balumba . . . see Lumbu	0	0		
0	523	Balunda . . . see Lunda	0	0		
0	523	Baluyia . . . see Luyia	0	0		
0	0	Bamana . . . see Bambara	0	0		
0	523	Bamananke . . . see Bambara	0	0		
0	523	Bamanga . . . see Mba	0	0		
0	523	Bamangwato . . . see Ngwato	0	0		
0	523	Bamba . . . see Amba	0	0		
0	523	Bambala . . . see Mbala	0	0		
867	947	Bambara	17	89	FA8	Ag1
444	0	Bambara	18	79	FA8	
0	523	Bambata . . . see Mbata	0	0		
0	523	Bambuti . . . see Mbuti	0	0		
0	523	Bamekom . . . see Kom	0	0		
724	0	Bamileke	18	38	FH19	Ae5
133	0	Bamu	32	188	OJ4	
0	0	Bamum . . . see Mum	0	0		

Cite 1	Cite 2	Culture	Map	No.	HRAF	Murdock's Atlas
0	523	Banande . . . see Konjo	0	0		
1142	133	Banaro	32	95	OJ8	Ie27
0	523	Bandi . . . see Gbande	0	0		
1164	0	Bandza	20	26		
724	0	Banen	18	12	FH10	Ae51
201	0	Bangala	20	32	FO12	
723	0	Bangala	20	85	FP10	
647	0	Banggai	28	76	OG5	
71	0	Banggala	30	33	OI5	
0	523	Bangwaketse . . . see Ngwaketse	0	0		
1092	0	Bani	7	67	SX5	
77	0	Bani Hajir	19	84	MK1	
77	0	Bani Hilal	19	45	MJ4	
77	0	Bani Khalid	19	28	MJ4	
1104	0	Bani Kitab	19	81	MK1	
77	0	Bani Shahr	19	44	MJ4	
77	1104	Bani Yam	19	54	MJ4	
946	0	Baniwa	9	112	SQ27	
604	0	Banka	28	30	OD8	
0	523	Bankoya . . . see Ankole	0	0		
133	0	Banks Islands	33	16	OO7	
74	0	Bannock	4	35	NR14	Nd63
204	0	Bannock	5	57	NR14	
0	523	Banu . . . see Baya	0	0		
0	253	Banu . . . see Berta	0	0		
647	0	Banyak	28	38	OD1	
0	523	Banyanga . . . see Nyanga	0	0		
348	523	Banyanhkole (Ankole)	21	100	FK11	
0	523	Banyoro . . . see Nyoro	0	0		
985	0	Banyua	17	128	FA29	
201	0	Banzirti	18	130	FI18	
0	523	Bapet . . . see Bafia	0	0		
201	0	Bapoto	18	135	FO40	
201	0	Bapoto	20	36	FO40	
77	0	Baqum	19	37	MJ4	
598	0	Bara	23	17	FY13	
946	0	Bara	9	70	SQ19	
71	0	Baraba-Baraba	30	6	OI5	
416	593	Barabaig	21	116	FN26	
316	0	Baranzai	19	109	AU4	
0	0	Barba . . . see Bariba	0	0		
1092	0	Barbacoa	7	66	SX5	
769	0	Barbacoan	9	37	SC12	
0	0	Bard . . . see Badi	0	0		
946	0	Bare	9	111	SQ27	
0	523	Bare . . . see Belanda	0	0		
0	523	Bargu . . . see Bariba	0	0		
58	59	Bari	9	19	SS13	
1220	0	Bari	21	17	FJ5	Aj8
345	0	Bariba	17	60	FA9	
77	0	Bariyah	19	26	MJ4	
522	0	Barkinji	30	42	OI9	
1182	0	Barlamomo	30	148	OI17	
1176	0	Barok	32	249	OM10	
0	523	Baroka . . . see Roka	0	0		
0	523	Barolong . . . see Rolong	0	0	FV6	
0	523	Barotse . . . see Lozi	0	0		
0	523	Barozi . . . see Lozi	0	0		
522	0	Barrumbinya	30	47	OI5	
540	0	Bartangs	39	26		
0	523	Barundi . . . see Rundi	0	0	FO42	
522	0	Barunga	30	45	OI5	
412	309	Baruya	32	1	OJ1	
412	0	Baruya	32	16	OJ1	
724	0	Basakomo	18	15	FF8	Ah12
0	523	Basamia . . . see Samia	0	0		
0	523	Bashila . . . see Shila	0	0		
0	0	Bashilange	20	66	FO10	Ae13
1159	0	Bashilele	20	103	FO24	
540	0	Bashkirs	38	62	RF3	
201	0	Basiri	18	132	FJ20	
996	0	Basketo	21	195	MP26	Ca28
0	523	Basoga . . . see Soga	0	0		
0	523	Basotho . . . see Sotho	0	0		
165	0	Basques	37	19	EX8	Ce4
985	0	Bassa	17	139	FF8	
876	0	Bassari	17	157	FA41	Ag21
35	0	Basseri	19	88	MA13	Ea6
0	523	Basuto . . . see Sotho	0	0		
368	0	Batahin	18	114	MQ15	

Cite 1	Cite 2	Culture	Map	No.	HRAF	Murdock's Atlas
655	1165	Batak	28	34	OD5	Ib4
178	0	Batak	27	27	OA9	
1165	647	Batak	28	34	OD5	Ib4
0	0	Batatela	20	55	FO47	
0	0	Batek	26	14	AN7	
0	523	Bateke . . . see Teke	0	0		
647	0	Batjan	28	86	OH7	
973	0	Batlaro	22	71	FV6	
0	523	Batoro . . . see Toro	0	0		
0	523	Batumbwe . . . see Tumbwe	0	0		
704	0	Baule	17	107	FA5	Af9
0	523	Baunga . . . see Unga	0	0		
759	0	Baure	11	66	SF15	
0	523	Baushanga . . . see Lushange	0	0		
0	0	Bavenda . . . see Venda	0	0		
0	523	Bavesma . . . see Venda	0	0		
0	523	Bavili . . . see Vili	0	0		
133	0	Bawaki	32	233	OJ4	
1164	0	Baya	20	24	FI9	Ai7
201	0	Baya	20	33	FI9	
201	0	Bayaka	20	17	FI4	
1121	201	Bayaka	20	87	FO49	
726	0	Bayaka	20	97	FO49	
1092	0	Bayamo	7	68	SX5	
1092	0	Bayaquitiri	7	68	SX5	
0	523	Bayeke . . . see Yeke	0	0		
0	0	Bazenda . . . see Azande	0	0		
0	523	Baziba . . . see Haya	0	0		
0	523	Bazinza . . . see Zinza	0	0		
0	523	Bazombo . . . see Zombo	0	0		
401	0	Bear Lake	1	92	ND14	
401	0	Bear Lake	4	131	ND14	
928	0	Beaver	4	108	NF5	Na29
0	523	Bechuana . . . see Tswana	0	0		
0	0	Bedamini . . . see Petamini	0	0		
0	0	Bedawir . . . see Beja	0	0		
0	523	Bedawiye . . . see Beja	0	0		
368	693	Bederiat	18	124	MQ5	
876	0	Bedik	17	160	FA36	
0	523	Bedja . . . see Beja	0	0		
0	523	Beer-Landa . . . see Belanda	0	0		
532	0	Begemder	19	131	MP5	
807	0	Beheria	16	1	MR13	
993	0	Beir	21	11	FJ6	
124	0	Belanda	21	7		
228	0	Belandas	26	10	AN4	
1092	0	Bellabella	4	106	NE5	Nb23
1092	0	Bellacoola	4	105	NE6	Nb9
985	0	Belle	17	137	FD7	
317	0	Bellikan	38	35		
1202	0	Bemba	23	51	FQ5	Ac3
1202	0	Bemba	20	111	FQ5	
199	0	Bemba	20	119	FQ5	
1126	1144	Ben Guil	15	30	MW3	
197	1098	Bena	21	146	FN9	Ac3
1098	197	Bena	23	31	FN9	
309	0	Benabena	32	20	OJ1	
796	0	Bende	21	129	FN18	Ad18
0	0	Benguet . . . see Igorot	0	0	OA20	
873	0	Beni Amer	19	135	MR9	Ca36
277	0	Beni Amer	15	31	Ca36	
77	0	Beni Atiyah	19	19	MJ4	
318	0	Beni Hajar	19	86	MJ4	
807	0	Beni Sakhr Bedu	19	13	MG2	
807	0	Beni Suef	16	7	MR11	
1092	922	Beothuk	2	69	NI4	
1144	0	Berabiche	17	5	MS29	Cc7
1144	0	Berabiche	17	95	MS29	Cc7
147	0	Berber	15	1	MT10	
6	0	Berberi Hazaras	39	14	A45	
973	0	Bergdama	22	85	FX9	Aa4
0	523	Beri . . . see Bideyat	0	0		
0	523	Beri . . . see Zaghawa	0	0		
522	0	Berriat	30	23	OI5	
973	0	Berseba Hottentots	22	77	FX13	
938	0	Bersimis	2	37	NH6	
993	0	Berta	19	124	FJ7	
873	0	Besharin	19	139	MR9	
752	0	Besorube	17	52	FA9	
290	0	Bete	17	112	FD7	Af7

Cite 1	Cite 2	Culture	Map	No.	HRAF	Murdock's Atlas
973	0	Bethanie Hottentots	22	78	FX13	
106	0	Betsileo	23	8	FY11	Eh10
598	0	Betsimisaraka	23	4	FY4	
598	0	Bezanozano	23	7	FY19	
463	0	Bhaca	24	26	FX20	
0	523	Bhaka ... see Bhaca	0	0		
696	0	Bhil	25	32	AW25	Ef5
373	0	Bhota	39	48		
412	0	Biagai	32	197	OJ1	
133	0	Biak	32	256	OJ9	
0	523	Biara ... see Konjo	0	0		
782	0	Biat	26	63	AM31	
782	0	Biat	27	62	AM31	
71	0	Bibelmen	29	98	OI26	
154	0	Bideyat	18	101	MS5	
72	0	Bidjandjadjara	29	61	OI5	
540	0	Bielorussians	38	72	RC1	
0	0	Biet ... see Biat	0	0		
72	0	Bigambul	30	62	OI5	
522	0	Bikalbura	30	97	OI5	
591	0	Bikini	34	22	OR11	If12
1083	729	Bikol	27	34	OA32	
0	523	Bikom ... see Kom	0	0		
0	0	Bilaan	27	7	OA10	Ia17
77	0	Billi	19	12	MJ4	
604	0	Billiton	28	32	OD8	
1121	0	Biloxi	7	3	NN14	
1121	0	Biloxi	6	2	NN14	
647	0	Bimanese	28	21	OF18	
133	0	Binandere	32	211	OJ1	
71	1116	Bindjareb	29	91	OI5	
71	0	Bindubi	29	59	OI5	
1131	0	Binga	20	30	FI15	
522	0	Bingabura	30	113	OI5	
656	0	Bini	17	7	FF21	
309	0	Binumarien	32	2	OJ1	
1151	1151	Bira	21	89	FO11	Ae30
316	0	Birdi	19	117		
201	0	Biri	18	137	FJ20	
290	0	Birifor	17	104	FE4	Ag5
443	0	Birom	18	60	FF9	Ah17
926	0	Bisa	23	54	FA12	Ag53
199	0	Bisa	20	118	FQ5	
0	523	Bisano ... see Busansi	0	0		
1083	0	Bisayan	27	28	OA11	Ia18
517	0	Bisayas	28	58	OC7	
0	523	Bisi Kota ... see Kota	0	0		
391	0	Bisis	32	100	OJ1	
1223	297	Blackfoot	4	51	NF6	Ne12
522	0	Boanbura	30	111	OI5	
133	0	Boardji	32	178	OJ1	
867	0	Bobo	17	91	FA11	Ag30
57	0	Bocas Negras	11	68	SP10	
0	523	Bogung ... see Bariba	0	0		
187	0	Bohane	13	29	SJ5	
0	523	Bolea ... see Bolewa	0	0		
456	0	Bolewa	18	61	FF10	Cb7
133	0	Boli	32	228	OJ1	
522	0	Bombarabua	30	108	OI5	
123	0	Bombesa	20	42	FO13	Ae36
463	0	Bomvana	24	23	FX17	Ab21
771	0	Bona	17	62	FE7	
416	61	Bondei	21	165	FN28	
373	0	Bondo	25	25	AW30	
199	0	Bongo	18	134	FJ8	Ai35
201	0	Bongo	20	35	FJ8	
844	0	Boni	21	183	FL6	
0	523	Bonkese ... see Ndenges	0	0		
796	0	Bono	17	43	FE12	
547	548	Bontoc Igorot	27	48	OA12	Ia8
416	529	Boran	21	178	FL7	
0	523	Borana ... see Boran	0	0		
0	0	Borgawa ... see Bariba	0	0		
0	523	Borgu ... see Bariba	0	0		
1064	0	Boro	9	67	SC19	
828	684	Bororo	12	32	SP8	Si1
684	828	Bororo	11	105	SP8	
556	0	Boruca	8	1	SA19	
556	0	Boruca	9	4	SA19	
133	0	Boskien	32	58	OJ1	
201	0	Bosyeba	20	10		
834	0	Botocudo	13	34	SN2	Sj5
834	0	Botocudo	12	10	SN2	
0	523	Bouaka ... see Bwaka	0	0		
845	846	Bougainville Islands	33	9	ON4	
1182	0	Boun	30	147	OI5	
653	0	Boyaca	7	67	SX5	
947	0	Bozo	17	88	MS6	Ag7
154	0	Braoya	18	84	MS22	
0	523	Brawiya ... see Teda	0	0		
1181	0	Bretons	37	25	EW8	
300	8	British	37	40	ES1	
517	0	Brunei	28	61	OC11	
72	0	Budidjara	29	64	OI5	
1152	0	Budu	21	82	FO14	Ae31
456	0	Buduma	18	75	MS7	Cb5
0	523	Bufu ... see Bafia	0	0		
302	0	Bugusu (Luyia)	21	73	FL4	Ad41
206	0	Buha	21	104		
178	0	Buhid	27	31	OA18	
640	0	Bukidnon	27	16	OA13	
517	0	Bukitans	28	63	OC10	
302	0	Bukuli	21	71		
0	0	Bul ... see Nuer	0	0	FJ22	
522	0	Bulalli	30	38	OI5	
459	0	Bulgarians	37	11	EE1	Ch5
540	0	Bulgarians	38	69	EE1	
166	0	Bullom	17	148	FC8	
495	0	Bum	18	25	FF5	
771	0	Bumbu	17	106	FA31	
1121	0	Bunda	20	100	FO17	Ac21
1121	0	Bunda	20	104	FO17	Ac21
324	324	Bundi	32	57	OJ1	
0	473	Bungu	21	142	FN21	
522	0	Buntamurra	30	70	OI5	
522	0	Bunurong	30	8	OI5	
567	0	Bunyole	21	51	FL4	
0	0	Bunyoro ... see Nyoro	0	0		
652	647	Burman	26	43	AP1	Ei3
647	675	Buru	28	82	OH8	
302	0	Buruli	21	74		
0	523	Burum ... see Birom	0	0		
993	0	Burun	19	127	FJ9	
416	206	Burundi	21	101	FO52	
416	0	Burungi	21	118	FN5	
603	172	Buryats, Khorin	40	16	RW1	Eb6
981	0	Busansi	17	65	FA12	
583	0	Bush Negro	10	4	SR8	Sc18
0	0	Bushongo ... see Songo	0	0	FO23	
317	0	Butlikh	38	48	RH8	
647	0	Butung	28	78	OG7	
133	0	Bwaidoga	32	241	OM8	Ig16
199	0	Bwaka	18	131	FI11	Ai23
201	0	Bwaka	20	31	FI11	Ai23
1221	0	Bwamba ... see Amba	0	0		
199	0	Bwile	21	132	FQ5	
199	0	Bwile	20	116	FQ5	
556	0	Cabo	8	16		
769	0	Cabre	9	116	SC5	
834	0	Caete	12	1	SO9	
416	0	Caga	21	14		
176	0	Cagaba	9	14	SC7	Sb2
1092	0	Cahibo	7	71	SV5	
609	0	Cahuilla	5	19	NS20	Nc31
718	0	Caingua	12	42	SM4	
1092	0	Caizcimu	7	71	SV5	
981	0	Calabar	17	1	FF25	
74	0	Calapuya	4	26	NR9	
946	0	Calayua	10	21	SQ8	
711	0	Calusa	7	62	NN7	
834	0	Camacan	12	9	SO2	
1092	0	Camaguey	7	76	SX5	
1063	0	Camana	11	140	SE13	
225	0	Campa	11	34	SE9	Sf7
1063	0	Cana	11	27	SE13	
829	0	Canamari	9	85	SQ6	
1064	0	Canamari	11	45	SQ6	
769	0	Canari	9	51	SD4	
1063	0	Canchi	11	28	SF5	
114	0	Candoshi	9	56	SE22	
835	718	Canella	10	69	SO8	

Cite 1	Cite 2	Culture	Map	No.	HRAF	Murdock's Atlas
1092	0	Cape Fear Indians	7	36	NN13	
769	0	Caquetio	9	16	SS7	
769	0	Cara	9	42	SD11	
769	0	Caraca	9	153	SS8	
187	0	Caracara	13	24	SI11	
946	0	Carahyaby	9	108	SQ27	
1063	0	Caranga	11	137	SF5	
1063	0	Caravaya	11	29	SE3	
15	0	Caribou Eskimo	3	42	ND6	Na21
304	0	Caribs	7	73	ST11	
946	0	Caribs	9	158	SR9	
946	0	Cariguano	10	28	SR7	
834	0	Carijo	13	33	SM4	
834	0	Carijo	12	44	SM4	
946	0	Carijona	9	69	SC8	
946	0	Caripuna	9	97	SF19	
761	57	Caripuna	11	69	SF19	
683	0	Cariri	10	58	SO3	
683	0	Cariri	12	4	SO3	
322	0	Caroline Islands	34	19	OR4	
1118	0	Carrier	4	104	NE7	Na19
74	0	Cascade	4	22	NR6	
950	0	Casma	11	14	SE13	
727	540	Catalonians	37	18	EX9	
829	0	Catawishi	9	86	SQ7	
829	0	Catawisi	9	91	SQ7	
1064	0	Catukuina	11	53	SQ7	
829	0	Catukuina	9	90	SQ7	
0	0	Cauatambo	11	17	SE13	
582	0	Cavinena	11	77	SF23	
829	831	Cawahib	11	62	SP10	
832	0	Cayabi	11	98	SP2	
1092	0	Cayaguayo	7	67	SX5	
32	62	Cayapa	9	43	SD6	Sf3
247	31	Cayapo, Northern	12	18	SP13	
682	682	Cayapo, Southern	12	11	SP11	
1199	1092	Cayuga	2	18	NM9	
74	0	Cayuse	4	39	NR18	
1092	0	Cazcan	8	49	NU9	
647	0	Ceram	28	84	OH9	
1144	105	Chaamba	15	11	MV5	Cc16
1069	0	Chachapoya	11	4	SE17	
582	0	Chacobo	11	76	SF19	Se11
416	262	Chagga	21	168	FN4	Ad3
392	0	Chakchiuma	7	5	NN9	
1204	649	Cham	26	59	AM5	Ej11
782	649	Cham	27	60	AM5	Ej11
582	0	Chama	11	75	SE10	
767	0	Chamacoco	11	114	SK14	Sh6
94	0	Chamba	18	35	FF15	Ah28
390	0	Chambri	32	109	OJ1	
187	0	Chana	13	27	SJ5	
187	0	Chana-Timbu	13	26	SI11	
767	0	Chane	11	129	SF8	
761	0	Chapakura	11	78	SP12	
997	0	Chara	21	196	FF32	
761	0	Characa	11	134	SS17	
142	0	Chari River Groups	18	67		
973	0	Chariguriqua, Hottentot	24	13	FX13	
187	0	Charrua	13	31	SJ5	
223	0	Chatino	8	33	NU44	
1092	0	Chatot	7	46	NN14	
443	0	Chawai	18	59	FF16	Ah10
1064	0	Chayahuita	11	5	SE8	
1092	0	Chayane . . . see Cheyenne	0	0		
187	0	Chechehet	13	1	SI10	
317	0	Chechen	38	77	RI5	Ci7
913	0	Chehalis	4	65	NR15	
71	0	Chepara	30	51	OI5	
887	0	Cherokee	7	24	NN8	Ng5
74	0	Chetco	4	2	NR22	
175	0	Chewa	23	53	FR4	Ac10
499	0	Cheyenne	3	26	NQ8	Ne5
619	951	Chibcha	9	11	SC11	Sf6
769	0	Chibcha	9	21	SC11	
761	0	Chicha	11	111	SE13	
1090	0	Chickasaw	7	7	NN9	Ng14
1090	0	Chickasaw	6	14	NN9	Ng14
938	0	Chicoutimi	2	34	NH6	
925	0	Chikunda	23	55	FR4	
631	0	Chilcotin	4	103	NE8	Na18
1097	0	Chilkat	4	135	NA12	
0	0	Chiloe Araucanians	14	10	SG4	
411	0	Chilula	5	87	NS11	
1092	0	Chimakum	4	79	NR16	
761	0	Chimane	11	85	SF16	
1092	0	Chimariko	5	82	NS6	Nb33
115	545	Chimbu	32	42	OJ1	
938	0	Chimo	2	57	NH6	
1059	652	Chin	26	45	AP5	Ei19
1059	647	Chin	40	1	AP5	Ei19
0	0	Chincha	11	23	SE13	
0	0	Chinchacha	11	18	SE13	
1030	0	Chingali	30	139	OI5	
913	0	Chinook	4	66	NR6	Nb19
582	0	Chipaya	11	136	SF24	
1014	0	Chipewyan	4	128	ND7	Na30
1014	0	Chippewa	3	15	NG6	Na36
761	0	Chiquito	11	109	SF9	
187	0	Chiquiyami	13	6	SI10	
767	761	Chiriguano	11	115	SF10	Sh7
133	0	Chirma	32	222	OJ1	
796	0	Chishinga	22	1	FQ5	
1065	0	Chisos	6	63	NU14	
1092	0	Chitimacha	7	2	NO4	Ng15
1092	0	Chitimacha	6	1	NO4	Ng15
769	0	Choco	9	10	SC12	Sa4
274	0	Choctaw	6	11	NN10	Ng12
918	0	Choctaw	7	8	NN10	Ng12
6	0	Choiah	39	10		
455	926	Chokwe	22	33	FP4	Ac12
926	0	Chokwe	20	91	FP4	Ac12
1092	0	Chol	8	25	NV6	
0	523	Cholo . . . see Shilluk	0	0		
1064	0	Cholon	11	12	SE14	
647	0	Chong	26	60	AM7	
183	0	Chono	14	7	SH3	
1135	941	Chontal	8	29	NV7	
796	0	Chonyi	21	173	FL14	
463	0	Chopi	23	78	FT4	Ab22
769	0	Choque	9	34	SC20	
921	767	Choroti	11	127	SK6	Sa3
542	0	Choudor Turkomen	38	60	RM2	
782	0	Chrau Jro	27	59	AM17	
1215	0	Christmas Islands	31	8	OV6	
782	0	Chru	27	64	AM18	
146	0	Chuabo	23	25	FT5	
0	0	Chuan . . . see Miao	0	0		
1092	0	Chuckbukmiut	2	63	NI5	
772	0	Chugach	1	78	NA13	Na10
540	99	Chukchi	1	67	RY2	Ec3
540	660	Chukchi	36	5	RY2	Ec3
608	0	Chumash	5	36	NS7	Nc28
0	0	Chupayachu	11	15	SE19	
202	0	Chuvanzy	1	96	RV3	
539	0	Chuvanzy	36	4	RV3	
0	0	Ciara . . . see Chara	0	0		
949	222	Ciboney	7	70	SX4	
514	0	Cint Larga	11	55		
723	0	Cipungu	22	117	FP17	
723	0	Cisama	20	82	FP6	
723	0	Cisanji	22	113	FP6	
74	0	Clackamas	4	23	NR6	
74	0	Clatskanie	4	15	NR11	
74	0	Clatsop	4	13	NR6	
131	383	Coahuiltecan	8	80	NU12	Ne21
131	383	Coahuiltecan	6	61	NU12	Ne21
131	0	Coahuiltecans	6	61	NU12	
1066	0	Coani	10	43	SQ26	
1064	0	Cocama	9	76	SE11	
1077	1078	Cocamilla	9	75	SE11	
1078	0	Cocamilla	11	9	SE11	
761	0	Cochapampa	11	86	SE13	
1092	0	Cochimi	5	11	NU13	
1092	0	Cochimi	8	73	NU13	
220	344	Cocopa	5	6	NT30	Nh19
556	0	Coiba	9	6	SB5	
1063	0	Collagua	11	143	SF5	
769	0	Colorado	9	47	SD7	
1092	0	Colville	4	58	NR19	
0	0	Comanche . . . see Shoshoni	0	0	NO6	Ne3
187	0	Comechingon	13	12	SI5	

Cite 1	Cite 2	Culture	Map	No.	HRAF	Murdock's Atlas
1092	0	Comox	4	98	NE13	Nb14
858	0	Concho	8	65	NU14	
432	432	Concho	6	62	NU14	
0	0	Concho	8	56	NU14	
0	0	Conchuco	11	11	SE13	
0	0	Congo . . . see Kongo	0	0		
1064	0	Conibo	11	36	SE10	Se9
1137	0	Conoy	7	28	NM11	
113	0	Cook Islands	31	9	OZ9	
74	0	Coos	4	5	NR7	Nb21
849	0	Copalis	4	69	NR15	
209	549	Copper Eskimo	1	93	ND8	Na3
74	0	Coquille	4	4	NR22	
438	0	Cora	8	50	NU15	Sj9
834	0	Coroado	12	39	SN6	
158	0	Corsicans	37	7	EZ4	
970	0	Corsicans	37	17	EZ4	
608	0	Costano	5	43	NS8	
1064	0	Coto	9	72	SE12	
946	0	Coussari	10	24	SR12	
1092	0	Cowichan	4	95	NE13	Nb26
913	0	Cowlitz	4	63	NR15	
1092	0	Cree	3	36	NG4	
938	1092	Cree, Barren Ground	2	56	NG4	
1092	1009	Cree, Barren Ground	3	39	NG4	
1015	0	Cree, Rocky	3	35	NG4	
1092	0	Cree, Springwoods	3	45	NG4	
1092	0	Cree, Swampy	3	16	NG4	
1089	0	Creek	7	23	NN11	Ng3
540	0	Croats	37	12	EF4	
679	1224	Crow	4	46	NQ10	Ne4
730	1224	Crow	6	26	NQ10	Ne4
730	679	Crow	3	31	NQ10	Ne4
782	0	Cua	27	72	AM19	
0	523	Cuale . . . see Kuvale	0	0		
738	0	Cuauhcomeca	8	47		
653	0	Cubanacan	7	67	SX5	
413	0	Cubeo	9	57	SQ19	Se5
1092	0	Cuciba	7	68	SX5	
829	0	Culino	9	89	SQ23	
829	0	Culino	11	41	SQ23	
0	0	Cumana	9	159	SS9	
769	0	Cumanagoto	9	154	SS9	
769	841	Cuna	9	9	SB5	Sa1
954	0	Cuniba	11	44	SQ9	
0	0	Cupaca	11	141	SE13	
1201	0	Cupeno	5	18	NS20	Nc32
1062	0	Curuminaca	11	103	SF18	
1092	0	Cusabo	7	39	NN12	
0	523	Cwana . . . see Tswana	0	0		
962	0	Czechs	37	28	EB1	Ch3
0	523	Dabosa . . . see Dodos	0	0		
705	0	Dagaba	17	61	FE4	
189	647	Dagada	28	3	OF20	
865	0	Dagati	17	58	FE4	
0	523	Dagbamba . . . see Dagomba	0	0		
1095	0	Dagomba	17	50	FE5	Ag44
1104	0	Dahm	19	55	MJ4	
4	1099	Dahomey (Fon)	17	31	FA18	Af1
1182	0	Dai	30	146	OI17	
133	0	Daiomoni	32	237	OJ1	
1189	0	Dakota	3	18	NQ11	
1189	0	Dakota	6	25	NQ11	
1092	0	Dakota, Santee	3	21	NQ11	Ne20
1092	0	Dakota, Teton	3	27	NQ11	Ne8
201	0	Dakwa	18	129	FI6	
522	0	Dalebura	30	106	OI5	
67	0	Dalleburra	30	125	OI5	
487	0	Dama	22	84	FH6	
0	0	Dama . . . see Padhola	0	0	FH6	
316	0	Damani	19	105		
937	0	Damergu	18	82	MS25	
985	0	Dan	17	130	FA29	
796	0	Danakil (Afar)	19	121	MN4	Ca6
146	0	Danda	23	73		
0	0	Danes	37	33	EM1	
71	0	Dangani	30	26	OI5	
0	523	Dango . . . see Dongo	0	0		
840	107	Dani	32	134	OJ1	Ie38

Cite 1	Cite 2	Culture	Map	No.	HRAF	Murdock's Atlas
0	523	Dankali . . . see Afar	0	0		
0	523	Dankil . . . see Afar	0	0		
316	0	Darab Khani	19	103		
996	0	Darasa	21	204	MP23	Ca15
1064	0	Darawa	11	42		
316	0	Darazi	19	98		
296	0	Dars	16	23	MT4	
1092	812	Daru	19	80	MK1	
316	0	Darusar	19	114		
1126	0	Darwa	15	36		
0	0	Davan . . . see Atoni	0	0		
938	0	Davis Inlet	2	55	NH6	
647	0	Dayaks	28	41	OC8	
648	0	Daza	18	100	MS22	Cc14
985	0	De	17	136	FD7	
133	0	Dea	32	68	OJ1	
133	0	Dea	32	184	OJ1	
6	0	Dehi Hazaras	39	15	AU5	
316	0	Dehwar	19	111		
1197	1092	Delaware	2	6	NM7	Ng6
1197	0	Delaware	7	26	NM7	
0	0	Denaxdax . . . see Kwakiutl	0	0		
113	0	Denca	31	18		
107	0	Dern	32	144	OJ1	
317	0	Dersimili	38	34		
1066	0	Desana	9	119	SQ19	
0	523	Dewoi . . . see De	0	0		
285	284	Dhurwa	25	27		
780	187	Diaguita	13	10	SG6	
876	0	Diakhanke	17	159	FA27	
867	145	Dialonke	17	152	FA33	
317	0	Didi	38	46	RH8	
529	0	Didinga	21	13	FJ10	Aj19
0	523	Die . . . see Jie	0	0		
397	0	Diegueno	5	14	NS9	Nc6
0	523	Dieng . . . see Dinka	0	0		
45	0	Dieri	30	74	OI10	Id4
0	523	Dierma . . . see Djerma	0	0		
154	0	Dietko	18	77	MS22	
796	0	Digo	21	164	FL14	Ad30
575	226	Dinka	21	3	FJ12	Aj11
575	124	Dinka	18	151	FJ12	Aj11
876	0	Diola	17	166	FA14	Ag19
1092	0	Diria	8	10		
522	0	Dirityangura	30	72	OI5	
1092	0	Disko	1	21	NB6	
0	523	Diwala . . . see Duala	0	0		
154	0	Djagada	18	99	MS22	
72	0	Djalendi	29	69	OI5	
71	0	Djamadjong	29	19	OI5	
71	0	Djara	29	38	OI5	
71	0	Djargudi	29	58	OI5	
0	523	Djerawa . . . see Jerawa	0	0		
628	0	Djerma	17	68	MS20	
0	523	Djie . . . see Jie	0	0		
1182	0	Djinba	30	151	OI17	
72	0	Djiwali	29	72	OI5	
0	523	Djiwe . . . see Jie	0	0		
0	523	Djok . . . see Chokwe	0	0		
0	523	Djukun . . . see Jukun	0	0		
0	523	Djur . . . see Jur	0	0		
351	0	Dobu	32	239	OL4	Ig5
416	0	Dodos	21	39	FK8	
416	523	Dodoth . . . see Dodos	0	0		
431	369	Dogon	17	90	FA16	Ag3
154	0	Dogorda	18	93	MS22	
477	0	Dogrib	4	130	ND14	Na15
0	0	Dok . . . see Nuer	0	0		
123	0	Doko	20	41	FD34	Ae38
237	540	Dolgan	1	102	RV2	
914	0	Dom	32	40	OJ1	
133	0	Domu	32	234	OJ1	
1022	0	Dondo	20	74	FO21	
1152	0	Dongo	21	81	FO26	
316	0	Dorazai	19	112		
284	285	Dorla Gond	25	22	AW32	
416	528	Dorobo	21	70	FL6	Aa2
522	0	Dorobura	30	109	OI5	
1144	1126	Dou Menia	15	20		
0	523	Douala . . . see Duala	0	0		
696	0	Doubla	25	34	AW47	

Cite 1	Cite 2	Culture	Map	No.	HRAF	Murdock's Atlas
439	0	Doura	32	224	OJ1	
217	0	Dry Bay	1	85	NA12	
0	523	Dsebu ... see Ijebu	0	0		
0	523	Dsuku ... see Jukun	0	0		
13	0	Duala	18	29	FH7	Ae12
13	0	Duala	20	3	FH7	Ae12
782	0	Duan	27	73	AM23	
1216	0	Ducie	31	21	OW1	
0	523	Duela ... see Duala	0	0		
0	0	Duke of York Isl	0	0		
277	0	Dukkala	15	40	MW10	
175	0	Duma	23	70	FS5	
133	0	Dumu	32	38	OJ1	
406	0	Duna	32	91	OJ1	
0	0	Dunjol ... see Dinka	0	0		
6	0	Durrani	39	4	AU4	
1210	0	Dusun	28	57	OC7	Ib5
1092	0	Duwamish	4	82	NR15	
77	0	Duwasir	19	33	MJ4	
316	0	Duzdgah	19	97		
0	523	Dyabarma ... see Djerma	0	0		
0	0	Dzawadenox ... see Kwakiutl	0	0		
64	0	Dzayul	39	51		
38	758	Easter Island	31	22	OY12	Ij9
767	0	Ebidoso	11	116	SK14	
1109	0	Edo	17	17	FF21	Af24
1109	523	Edo ... see Bini	0	0	FF21	Af24
78	0	Egba	17	23	FF62	Af32
0	523	Egbura ... see Igbira	0	0		
1092	0	Egedesminde	1	19	NB6	
0	523	Egun ... see Gu	0	0		
340	0	Ekagi	32	150	OJ1	
487	0	Ekonda	20	49	FO32	Ae20
144	0	El Arbaa	15	16		
9	0	Elato	34	8	OR21	
929	0	Eliptamin	32	114	OJ1	
416	0	Elmolo	21	47	FL12	
416	581	Embu	21	182	FL5	
125	0	Emerillon	10	17	SQ8	
522	0	Emon	30	67	OI5	
1064	0	Encabellado	9	65	SE12	
647	0	Endenese	28	16	OF9	
750	1226	Enga	32	81	OJ1	Ie7
116	0	Enga, Kyaka	32	78	OJ1	Ie7
116	0	Enga, Raiapu	32	79	OJ1	Ie7
647	0	Engganese	28	31	OD6	
133	0	Erema	32	205	OJ4	
71	0	Eri	29	6	OI5	
1200	328	Erie	3	1	NM8	
328	0	Erie	2	7	NM8	
873	0	Eritrea	19	136	MN1	
696	0	Erukala	25	15	AW52	
938	0	Escoumains	2	36	NH6	
723	0	Esele	22	118	FP6	
68	0	Esmeralda	9	48	SD8	
608	0	Esselen	5	42	NS8	
1149	0	Estonians	38	75	RG4	
1149	0	Estonians	37	35	RG4	
1092	0	Etchaottine	4	132	ND14	
1092	0	Etchaottine	4	133	ND14	
627	0	Eton	18	10	FH9	
574	0	Etoro	32	70	OJ1	
856	0	Eudeve	8	76	NU25	
99	0	Even-Lamoot	1	98	RU5	
99	0	Even-Lamoot	36	3	RU5	
540	0	Evenki	1	107	RU5	
540	0	Evenki	36	9	RU5	
540	0	Evenki	40	18	RU5	
540	0	Evens	1	105	RU5	
706	282	Ewe	17	37	FA17	Af36
206	0	Eyak	1	83	NA7	Nb5
0	0	Fafoyo ... see Luyia	0	0		
993	0	Fajelu	21	29	FJ5	
0	523	Fajulu ... see Pojulu	0	0	FJ5	Aj13
0	0	Fakfak	32	155	OJ1	
384	0	Fali	18	46	FH8	Ai12
315	0	Fang	18	2	FH9	Ae3
21	315	Fang	20	6	FH9	Ae3
0	523	Fante ... see Fanti	0	0		
981	0	Fanti	17	41	FE12	Af42
1212	649	Fasu	32	61		
318	0	Fauara Bedu	38	5	MJ4	
133	0	Faur	32	153	OJ1	
296	0	Fawakhir	16	19	MT9	
807	0	Fawayid	16	6	MT9	
318	0	Fedaan Bedu	38	7	MH8	
0	523	Fellata ... see Fulbe	0	0		
929	0	Feramin	32	113	OJ4	
160	0	Fergusson Island	33	2	OL4	
147	0	Fezzan	16	26	MT5	
342	103	Fiji	31	1	OQ1	
103	838	Fiji	33	22	OQ1	
0	523	Fika ... see Bolewa	0	0		
0	523	Filani ... see Fulbe	0	0		
460	0	Fingo	24	19	FX20	
453	0	Finns	37	36	EO1	
0	523	Fioti ... see Vili	0	0		
1217	0	Fipa	21	135	FN6	Ad19
1141	1092	Flathead	4	52	NR8	Nd12
521	0	Flemish	37	26	EV2	
706	0	Fo	17	29	FF40	
463	0	Fokeng	24	44		
133	0	Foll	32	49	OJ4	
48	0	Fon	17	25	FA18	Af1
667	1021	Fore	32	27	OJ1	Ie31
0	523	Foula ... see Fulbe	0	0		
510	0	Fox	3	10	NP5	Nf7
1227	687	French	37	23	EW1	
1092	0	Fresh Water Indians	7	52	NN18	
495	0	Fugon	18	34		
0	523	Fula ... see Fulbe	0	0		
345	0	Fulani ... see also Fulbe	17	55	MS11	
345	0	Fulani ... see also Fulbe	18	62	MS11	
0	523	Fulanke ... see Fulbe	0	0		
881	345	Fulbe	17	55	MS11	
890	0	Fulnio	12	3	SO3	
1022	0	Fumbu	20	77	FF51	
368	0	Fur	18	107	MQ8	Cb17
0	523	Fuulbe ... see Fulbe	0	0		
451	0	Fuyughe	32	218	OJ1	
704	0	Ga	17	39	FE6	Af43
0	0	Gaawar ... see Nuer	0	0		
439	0	Gabadi	32	223	OJ19	
873	0	Gabail Ukhra	19	142	MR9	
416	0	Gabbra	21	190	FL7	
201	0	Gabou	18	138	FI6	
609	0	Gabrielino	5	32	NS10	Nc29
373	0	Gadaba	25	26	AW52	
40	0	Gaddang	27	45	OA20	
100	0	Gade	17	71	FF24	
71	0	Gadjerong	29	26	OI5	
648	0	Gadoa	18	91	MS22	
116	0	Gadsup	32	13	OJ1	
72	0	Gadudjara	29	57	OI5	
9	0	Gaferut	34	6	OR21	
71	0	Gagadju	29	7	OI5	
290	0	Gagu	17	111	FA21	Af51
914	0	Gahuku-Gama	32	23	OJ1	
502	0	Gaidemoe	32	4	OJ1	
502	0	Gaiwa	32	201	OJ1	
1116	0	Galago	29	85	OI5	
133	0	Galeva	32	232	OJ1	
125	0	Galibi	10	3	SR9	
532	0	Galla	21	200	FL7	
532	0	Galla	19	122	FL7	
540	0	Gallacians	37	22	EX6	
0	523	Gallina ... see Vai	0	0		
113	0	Gambier Islands	31	16	0X5	
1111	0	Gammatti	30	136	OI5	
696	0	Gamta	25	33	AW47	
0	523	Gan ... see Acholi	0	0		
416	0	Ganda	21	75	FK7	Ad7
71	0	Gandju	30	129	OI5	
1116	0	Ganeang	29	96	OI5	
0	523	Gang ... see Acholi	0	0		
72	0	Gangulu	30	92	OI5	
72	0	Garadjeri	29	47	OI5	
71	0	Gari	29	3	OI5	

Cite 1	Cite 2	Culture	Map	No.	HRAF	Murdock's Atlas
789	0	Han	27	77	AF1	
789	215	Han	35	2	AF1	
789	0	Han	40	6	AF1	
1092	0	Hanamana	7	65	SX4	
463	0	Hananwa	23	80		
1052	1092	Haneragmiut	1	45	ND8	
1092	0	Haningayogmiut	3	41	ND13	
178	640	Hanunodo	27	30	OA18	Ia5
291	0	Hanya	22	116	FP15	
807	0	Harabi	16	5	MT9	
574	0	Harado	32	66	OJ4	
997	0	Harari	21	214	MP12	
1104	0	Harasis	19	70	MK1	
77	0	Harb	19	21	MJ4	
971	0	Hare	1	91	ND9	
15	0	Harvaqtormiut	3	43	ND6	
1104	0	Hasa	19	29	MJ1	
246	155	Hashid	19	48	MJ4	
317	0	Hassananli	38	38		
1236	0	Haue	9	148	SQ18	
1017	0	Hausa	17	69	MS12	
1017	0	Hausa	18	52	MS12	
0	523	Hausawa . . . see Hausa	0	0		
676	0	Haush	14	1	SH4	
1092	0	Havana	7	65	SX4	
986	730	Havasupai	5	24	NT14	Nd3
82	960	Hawaiians	31	7	OV5	Ij6
368	0	Hawawir	18	113	MQ9	
807	0	Haweitat	19	4	MR11	
807	0	Haweitat	16	8	MR11	
844	0	Hawiyah	21	187	MO4	
206	0	Haya	21	97	FN8	Ad42
0	0	Hayo . . . see Luyia	0	0		
416	62	Hehe	21	148	FN9	Ad8
1157	647	Helong	28	8	OF20	
1218	1219	Henga	23	40	FR6	
1216	0	Henkison	31	19		
217	0	Henya	4	116	NA12	
292	487	Herero	22	83	FX12	Ab1
487	973	Herero	24	1	FX12	Ab1
973	0	Hessequa	24	14	FX13	
187	0	Het	14	15	SI10	
600	0	Heta	12	46	SP1	
1050	649	Hewa	32	98	OJ1	
1064	0	Hibito	11	7	SE14	
1092	0	Hidatsa	3	30	NQ14	Ne15
973	487	Hiechware	22	58	FX10	
729	603	Hiligaynon	27	19	OA14	
522	0	Hilleri	30	36	OI5	
1152	1221	Hima	21	87	FK1	
291	0	Himba	22	91	FX12	
1092	0	Hitchiti	7	40	NN11	
371	24	Hlengwe	23	72	FT6	
463	0	Hlubi	24	27	FX20	
188	663	Hmong	26	35	AE5	
640	0	Hoanya	27	54	AD13	
1144	0	Hodh	17	99		
849	0	Hoh	4	74	NR16	
206	0	Holoholo	21	127	FO18	
174	0	Holoholo	20	110	FO18	
1092	0	Holsteins Borg	1	16	NB6	
595	0	Honibo	32	86	OJ4	
74	0	Hood River	4	36	NR15	
217	0	Hoonah	4	120	NA12	
395	0	Hopi	6	40	NT9	Nh18
275	243	Hopi	5	27	NT9	Nh18
0	0	Horin . . . see Yoruba	0	0		
316	0	Hot Baluch	19	113	AT2	
500	0	Hottentot . . . see also				
		Nama & Bergdam	0	0	FX13	
77	0	Howitat	38	1	MG2	
77	0	Hozayl	19	40	MJ4	
782	0	Hroy	27	68	AM22	
667	0	Hua	32	31	OJ4	
114	0	Huambisa	9	58	SD9	
0	0	Huambo	11	3	SE21	
769	0	Huancavilca	9	50	SD10	
187	0	Huarpe	13	8	SI6	
230	0	Huave	8	31	NU18	Nj6
0	0	Huaylas	11	13	SE13	
1092	0	Hubabo	7	71	SV5	

Cite 1	Cite 2	Culture	Map	No.	HRAF	Murdock's Atlas
1205	0	Huddan	19	78	MK1	
1092	0	Huereo	7	69	SX5	
540	0	Hui	35	3	AF1	
540	0	Hui	40	8	AF1	
187	0	Huilliche (Araucanians)	14	11	SG4	
487	973	Hukwe Bushmen	22	81	FX10	
406	405	Hula	32	229	OJ1	
406	750	Huli	32	83	OJ1	
849	0	Humptulips	4	68	NR15	
368	0	Humr	18	123	MQ5	Cb15
155	1106	Humum	19	63	MJ1	
475	238	Hungarians	38	70	EC1	Ch8
238	475	Hungarians	37	29	EC1	Ch8
410	611	Hupa	5	83	NS11	Nb35
611	410	Hupa, East	5	80		
1092	0	Huron	3	3	NG5	Ng1
463	0	Huruthse	22	69	FV6	
463	0	Huruthse	24	45	FV6	
77	0	Hutaim	19	18	MJ4	
463	0	Hwaduba	24	43	FX18	
46	952	Iatmul	32	108	OJ11	Ie35
640	0	Ibaloi	27	44	OA20	
361	517	Iban	28	66	OC6	Ib1
605	40	Ibanag Ilokano	27	51	OA29	
0	0	Ibenama	9	100	SQ25	
346	0	Ibibio	18	28	FF25	Af10
155	0	Ibn Amir	19	49	MJ4	
0	523	Ibo . . . see Igbo	0	0	FF26	Af10
0	0	Icelanders	37	45	EQ1	
0	0	Idjebu . . . see Ijebu	0	0	EQ1	
343	0	Idoma	18	42	FF27	Af29
0	523	Idsebu . . . see Ijebu	0	0		
122	0	Ifaluk	34	5	OR21	If4
1109	0	Ife-Ilesha	17	20	FF62	Af34
1144	937	Iforas, Tuareg	17	92	MS25	Cc12
1144	0	Iforas, Tuareg	15	5	MS25	Cc12
39	179	Ifugao	27	47	OA19	Ia3
1109	0	Igara	17	10	FF28	Ap30
1109	0	Igbira	17	13	FF29	Af13
1163	42	Igbo	17	2	FF26	Af10
346	1163	Igbo	18	41	FF26	Af10
1092	0	Igidlorssuit	1	24	NB6	
0	0	Iglulik . . . see Iglulikmiut	0	0		
716	1092	Iglulikmiut	1	37	ND5	Na22
548	0	Igorot	27	51	OA20	
345	0	Ijebu	17	22	FF62	
656	0	Ijo	17	4	FF30	
1134	0	Ik	21	15		
1109	0	Ika	17	9	FF26	
1013	547	Ila	22	23	FQ6	Ac1
547	1013	Ila	22	23	FQ12	
742	0	Ilanon	27	12	0A22	
1030	0	Iliaura	30	119	OI5	
130	0	Illinois	3	7	NP6	
40	0	Ilongot	27	41	0A21	
1092	0	Imaklimuit	1	66	RY5	
0	523	Imoshagh . . . see Tuareg	0	0		
0	523	Imoshar . . . see Tuareg	0	0		
105	0	Imraguen	15	45	MY5	
801	0	Inahukwa	12	29	SP25	
725	0	Inan-lu	19	94		
71	0	Indjinandi	30	138	OI5	
863	864	Ingalik	1	74	NA8	Na8
993	0	Ingassana	19	125	FJ13	Ai4
72	0	Inggada	29	73	OI5	
1092	0	Inguklimiut	1	65	NA13	
317	0	Ingushi	38	57	RI5	
71	0	Iningai	30	114	FI23	
112	0	Injibandi	29	56	OI5	
973	0	Inqua, Hottentot	24	15	FX13	
0	0	Ioullemeden . . . see				
		Aulliminden	0	0		
1092	0	Iowa	6	21	NQ19	Nf10
1092	0	Iowa	3	19	NQ19	Nf10
946	0	Ipeka	9	114	SQ27	
406	0	Ipili	32	92	OJ1	
1064	0	Ipurina	11	46	SQ9	
1064	0	Iquito	9	73	SE22	
416	0	Iramba	21	115	FN19	
416	0	Irangi	21	117	FN16	Ad25

Cite 1	Cite 2	Culture	Map	No.	HRAF	Murdock's Atlas
751	926	Kaonde	22	28	FQ7	Ac32
412	0	Kapau	32	196	OJ4	
894	107	Kapauku	32	151	OJ29	Ie1
759	0	Kapechene	11	47		
159	0	Kapore	32	245	OM8	
627	0	Kapsiki	18	64	FF12	Ah38
1106	0	Karabi	19	65	MJ4	
317	0	Karachai	38	54	RH7	
867	0	Karago	17	97	FA27	
990	0	Karaja	12	20	SP9	
1092	0	Karajak	1	22	NB6	
6	0	Karakalpaks	39	16	RN2	
416	442	Karamojong	21	42	FK8	Aj30
1194	0	Karanga	23	71	FS5	
522	0	Karanguru	30	81	OI5	
383	0	Karankawa	6	5	NO7	Ne16
821	383	Karankawa	8	79	NO7	
0	0	Kare	18	139	FH16	
540	0	Karelian Izhars	1	120		
643	458	Karen	26	26	AP7	Ei7
133	0	Karen	32	163	OJ1	Ei7
112	0	Kariera	29	52	OI14	Id5
777	0	Karina	9	156	SS16	
759	0	Karipuna	11	49	SR9	
696	0	Karmali	25	53		
611	0	Karok	5	91	NS12	Nb34
648	0	Karranga	18	108		
522	0	Karunbura	30	98	OI5	
726	0	Kasai River Groups	20	107		Ac21
540	0	Kashkais	38	19	MA13	
0	0	Kashkuli Bozorg . . . see Qashqai	0	0	MM3	
720	510	Kaska	1	86	ND12	Na4
1092	0	Kaskinampo	7	9	NN11	
796	0	Kassonke	17	98	FA27	Ag23
649	0	Kasua	32	64	OJ4	
834	0	Kasuiana	10	27	SQ22	
745	0	Katab	17	74	FF38	Ah1
1092	819	Kataligamut	1	72	NA13	
71	0	Katang-Worimi	30	18	OI5	
451	0	Kate	32	215	OJ1	
74	0	Kathlamet	4	14	NR6	
133	0	Kati	32	130	OJ4	
396	0	Kato	5	69	NS23	
782	0	Katu	27	74	AM24	
514	0	Katukina	9	81	SQ7	
522	0	Kauri . . . see Guarna	0	0		
819	0	Kaviagmut	1	71	NA13	
819	0	Kaviagmut	1	63	NA13	
348	0	Kavirondo	21	57	FL4	
601	0	Kawahib	11	57	SP10	
834	0	Kawahiwa	10	38	SP10	
693	0	Kawahla	18	115	MQ10	
1237	611	Kawaiisu	5	31	NS13	Nc27
611	0	Kawaiisu	5	40	NS13	Nc27
1092	0	Kawchottine	1	54	ND9	
828	0	Kayabi	12	33	SP2	
647	0	Kayan	28	46	OC5	
247	370	Kayapo	10	37	SP13	
540	0	Kazakhs	38	59	RQ1	Eb1
540	0	Kazakhs	39	33	RQ1	Eb1
648	0	Kecherda	18	92	MS22	
291	0	Kede	22	89	FK12	
993	0	Kederu	21	20	FJ19	
647	0	Kei Islands	32	169	OH13	Ic8
369	0	Kel Adrar	17	96	MS25	
1144	369	Kel Ahaggar, Tuareg	17	93	MS25	Cc9
369	0	Kel Ahaggar, Tuareg	15	4	MS25	Cc9
369	0	Kel Ajjer	15	10	MS25	
1144	0	Kel Antessar	17	87	MS25	
628	0	Kel Tamajaq	17	79	MS25	
133	0	Kela	32	200	OJ1	Ae21
1164	0	Kele	20	22	FI14	
993	0	Keliko	21	28	FO26	
993	0	Keliko	18	143	FO26	
772	0	Kenai	1	82	NA13	
178	640	Kenoy	27	24	OA37	
228	293	Kensiu	26	21	AN7	
647	0	Kenyah	28	47	OC5	
57	0	Kepkiriwat	11	63	SP24	
309	649	Kerabi	32	41	OJ1	

Cite 1	Cite 2	Culture	Map	No.	HRAF	Murdock's Atlas
275	0	Keres	6	44	NT12	
416	0	Kerewe	21	105	FN10	Ad43
609	0	Kern	5	47	NS22	
640	0	Ketagalan	27	55	AD4	
561	1005	Kewa	32	50	OJ4	
487	0	Kgalagadi	24	8	FV4	
463	0	Kgatla	22	68	FV6	
6	0	Khakasi	39	11	RS1	
540	0	Khalka-Mongols	40	12	AH4	Eb3
540	0	Khan	39	46		
602	540	Khants	39	37	RU3	
973	0	Khara (!Khara)	22	73		
696	0	Kharia	25	49	AW36	
602	0	Khasi	25	48	AR7	Ei8
155	0	Khawlan Al-Akiya	19	52	MJ4	
463	0	Kheni	23	83		
316	0	Khitar	19	108		
540	0	Khiva Yomut	38	61	RM2	
1204	0	Khmer	26	58	AM4	Ej5
647	0	Khmu	26	53	AM26	
318	0	Khorsa Bedu	38	13	MH8	
675	0	Khumi	26	48	AR4	
0	523	Khutu . . . see Kutu	0	0		
463	0	Khuze	24	31	FX20	
133	0	Kibenel	32	48	OJ4	
0	523	Kibo . . . see Biron	0	0		
559	0	Kickapoo	3	8	NP7	Nf15
1092	0	Kieltai	6	10	NO5	
0	523	Kien . . . see Gien	0	0		
416	1100	Kiga	21	94	FK6	
1092	0	Kigiktagmiut	3	56	NI5	
1092	1034	Kikitarmiut	1	55	NA9	
630	1158	Kikuyu	21	177	FL10	Ad4
1092	0	Killinermiut	1	40	NA9	
1092	0	Killtinhunmiut	2	61	NI5	
1092	0	Kilusiktogmiut	1	41	ND8	
2	0	Kimbu	21	144	FN18	
0	523	Kimukon . . . see Suk	0	0		
729	0	Kinaraya	27	20	OA11	
1205	0	Kinda	19	76	MK1	
0	0	Kindiga . . . see Hadzapi	0	0	FN11	
1219	0	Kinga	21	147	FN12	
576	1092	Kingnaitmiut	1	38	ND5	
522	0	Kiniyen	30	56	OI5	
293	228	Kintag	26	20	AN7	
819	0	Kinugumint	1	62	NA13	
0	0	Kioko . . . see Chokwe	0	0		
1092	0	Kiowa	6	29	NQ15	Ne17
1092	0	Kiowa	4	44	NQ15	Ne17
133	0	Kiowiai	32	152	OJ1	
880	844	Kipsigis	21	108	FL13	Aj9
627	0	Kirdi	18	45	MQ5	
540	0	Kirghiz	39	34	RP2	
985	0	Kirm	17	144	FC8	
675	0	Kisar	28	1	OF10	
1219	0	Kisi	21	64	FN12	
166	985	Kissi	17	134	FA23	Af2
991	0	Kita	32	216	OJ1	
927	0	Kitanemuk	5	34	SN20	
216	0	Kitsua	9	36	SC9	
445	0	Klallam	4	78	NR15	Nb16
517	0	Klamantan	28	49	OC7	
1041	1041	Klamath	4	31	NR10	Nc8
1092	0	Klikitat	4	42	R18	Nd17
733	0	Kluane	1	87	ND10	
57	0	Koaratira	11	95	SP16	
1092	0	Koasati	7	16	NN11	
640	0	Kodi	28	20	OF17	ic13
1092	1052	Kogluktogmiut	1	47	ND8	
782	0	Koho	27	61	AM27	
344	0	Kohuana	5	12	NT15	
439	0	Koiari	32	227	OJ1	Ie24
439	0	Koita	32	226	OJ1	Ie20
833	0	Kokama	9	83	SE11	
302	416	Koki	21	92	FI10	
648	154	Kokorda	18	94		
1092	0	Koksoakmiut	2	58	NI5	
0	523	Kokwamba . . . see Konkomba	0	0		
434	0	Kol	25	43	AW37	Eg8
373	0	Kolam	25	28	AW46	

Cite 1	Cite 2	Culture	Map	No.	HRAF	Murdock's Atlas
13	0	Kole	18	37	FF41	
696	0	Koli	25	20	AW47	
495	0	Kom	18	26	FF39	Ae54
1153	0	Kom	20	48	FF39	Ae54
183	0	Koma	19	123	FJ15	Ai46
0	0	Kombaingheri	30	19	OI5	
201	0	Kombe	20	7	FF41	
522	0	Kombobura	30	52	OI5	
540	0	Komi	1	119	RG7	
540	0	Komi	39	36	RG7	
1150	0	Komolom	32	175	OJ1	
595	0	Konai	32	89	OJ1	
133	0	Konda	32	164	OJ1	
373	0	Konda Kapu	25	24	AW59	
373	0	Konda Reddis	25	23	AW59	
796	0	Konde	24	35	FT6	
522	0	Kongalu	30	96	OI5	
1164	1192	Kongo	20	70	FO20	Ac14
388	0	Koniagui	17	156	FA36	Ag8
1092	0	Konith-Lushuamiut	2	64	NI5	
416	0	Konjo	21	90	FO22	Ad44
696	0	Konkan	25	18		
0	523	Konko ... see Konkomba	0	0		
1095	0	Konkomba	17	49	FA24	Ag10
927	1184	Konkow	5	72	NS15	
522	0	Konkubura	30	91	OI5	
985	0	Kono	17	132	FC4	
450	0	Konso	21	192	MP17	Ca1
372	373	Konyak	25	58	AR13	
159	0	Koobe	32	243	OM8	
340	0	Kopar	32	106	OJ4	
649	0	Kora	32	90	OJ1	
487	0	Korana	24	16	FX13	
166	0	Koranko	17	143	FC5	Ag24
536	0	Koreans	35	8	AA1	Ed1
789	0	Koreans	40	13	AA1	Ed1
0	0	Korekore	23	68	FS5	
133	0	Koriki	32	34	OJ1	
814	0	Koro	17	73	FF34	Af31
444	0	Koro	18	53	FF34	Af31
0	0	Koromba	17	83	FA28	
696	0	Korwa	25	45	AW38	
540	0	Koryak	1	95	RY4	Ec5
524	0	Koryak	1	97	RY4	
540	0	Koryak	36	2	RY4	
0	523	Kosso ... see Mende	0	0		
696	0	Kota	25	8	AW55	
201	1164	Kota	20	21	FI17	Ae41
627	0	Koto	18	71	MS9	
0	523	Kotokori ... see Igbira	0	0		
1144	0	Kounta	17	94	MS29	Cc18
696	0	Koya	25	11	AW32	Eg11
163	162	Koyukon	1	70	NA8	
1092	0	Koyukon	1	69		
0	523	Kpala ... see Kreish	0	0		
0	523	Kpankpama ... see Konkomba	0	0		
0	523	Kpara ... see Kreish	0	0		
13	0	Kpe	18	32	FF43	Ae2
13	0	Kpe	20	1	FF43	Ae2
985	0	Kpelle	17	126	FD6	Af15
0	523	Kpese ... see Kpelle	0	0		
0	523	Kpunkpamba ... see Konkomba	0	0		
990	0	Kraho	12	13	SO8	
595	0	Kramo	32	67	OJ4	
985	0	Kran	17	124	FD7	
0	523	Krao ... see Kru	0	0		
154	0	Kreda	18	106	MS22	
990	0	Kreenakaroke	12	35		
124	0	Kreish	21	2	FJ16	
124	0	Kreish	18	119	FJ16	
990	0	Krene	10	63	SO8	
0	523	Krepo ... see Grebo	0	0		
990	0	Krikati	12	16	SO8	
357	985	Kru	17	120	FD7	Af48
0	523	Krumen ... see Kru	0	0		
0	523	Kuakuak ... see Kakwa	0	0		
1159	0	Kuba	20	64	FO23	Ac4
1202	0	Kuba	20	113	FV5	
595	0	Kubor	32	88	OJ4	

Cite 1	Cite 2	Culture	Map	No.	HRAF	Murdock's Atlas
946	0	Kueretu	9	82	SQ19	
725	0	Kuh-Giluye	19	92		
316	0	Kuhgalu	38	18		
134	0	Kuikuru	12	22	SP25	Si10
522	0	Kuinmurbura	30	103	OI5	
72	0	Kuke-Bura	30	93	OI5	
0	0	Kuki ... see Chin	0	0	AR8	Ei20
1092	0	Kukparungmiut	1	59	NA9	
775	0	Kuku	18	157	FJ5	Aj15
0	0	Kukukuku ... see Anga	0	0		
1109	0	Kukuruku	17	15	FF21	Af26
1109	0	Kukuruku	17	32	FF21	Af26
71	0	Kulin	30	11	OI5	
916	116	Kuma	32	56	OJ1	
771	0	Kumbu	17	103	FF48	
317	0	Kumyk	38	44	RH7	Ci3
193	0	Kunaguasaya	9	20	SS13	
650	1002	Kung (!Kung)	22	82	FX10	Aa1
889	0	Kunimaipa	32	219	OJ1	
133	0	Kunini	32	194	OJ1	
675	0	Kupangese	28	7	OF20	
745	0	Kurama	17	75	FF42	Ah21
0	523	Kuranke ... see Koranko	0	0		
19	0	Kurds	38	28	MA11	Ci11
416	0	Kuria	21	107	FL8	
71	0	Kurnai	30	3	OI16	
522	0	Kurnandaburi	30	71	OI5	
373	0	Kurumba	25	10		
834	0	Kuruya	10	39	SQ26	
860	859	Kutchin	1	56	ND10	Na20
1092	0	Kutenai	4	49	NF8	Nd7
62	0	Kutu	21	158	FO32	
640	152	Kuvalan	27	55	AD4	
291	0	Kuvale	22	109		
0	523	Kuwale ... see Kuvale	0	0		
522	0	Kuyani	30	37	OI5	
704	0	Kwahu	17	36	FE12	
91	90	Kwakiutl	4	100	NE10	Nb3
913	0	Kwalhiokwa	4	64	NR11	
291	0	Kwamatwi	22	92		
1138	0	Kwandi	22	44	FQ9	
291	0	Kwangali	22	88		
726	0	Kwangare	22	86	FP11	
726	0	Kwango River Groups	20	99		
1138	0	Kwangwa	22	27		
0	523	Kwanim-pas ... see Uduk	0	0		
231	0	Kwankhala	22	97		
726	0	Kwanyama	22	45	FX8	
0	523	Kwararofa ... see Jukun	0	0		
1225	649	Kware	32	63	OJ1	
973	0	Kwena	22	66	FV6	
973	0	Kwena	24	30	FV6	
291	0	Kwepe	22	111		
976	463	Kwera	22	64	FN27	
62	0	Kwere	21	161	FN27	Ad27
291	0	Kwisi	22	110	FP7	
1203	0	Kwoma	0	0	OJ13	Ie12
1226	0	Kyaka	32	75	DJ4	
0	0	Kyushu ... see Japanese	0	0		
0	523	Laga ... see Langa	0	0		
858	0	Lagunero	8	55	NH43	
807	0	Laheiwat (Safaiha)	19	3	MR11	
502	0	Lahiwapa	32	3	OJ1	
1178	663	Lahu	26	33	AP13	
749	747	Laiapo	32	80	OJ1	
317	0	Lak	38	45	RH8	
0	0	Lak ... see Nuer	0	0		
201	0	Laka	18	125	FI18	Ai13
133	0	Lakahis	32	148	OJ4	
1092	0	Lake Indians	4	57	NR19	
938	0	Lake St. John	2	33	NH6	
685	868	Lakher	26	49	AR8	Ei4
696	0	Lakher	25	61	AR8	
0	523	Lakkara ... see Lugbara	0	0		
74	0	Lakmiut	4	21	NR9	
926	0	Lala	23	56	FQ8	Ac33
926	0	Lala	22	14	FQ8	Ac33
234	926	Lamba	22	5	FQ8	Ac5
441	0	Lamba	17	51	FF64	
696	0	Lambadi	25	14		

Cite 1	Cite 2	Culture	Map	No.	HRAF	Murdock's Atlas
175	0	Lambya	23	38	FN21	
0	0	Lamisto	11	6	SE14	
202	0	Lamoot, Eastern	1	94	RU5	
524	0	Lamoot, Western	1	99	R45	
9	0	Lamotrek	34	7	OR21	If16
0	0	Lamut . . . see Lamoot	0	0		
796	0	Landuman	17	155	FB5	
412	0	Langamar	32	6	OJ4	
0	0	Lange . . . see Burun	0	0		
0	523	Langi . . . see Irangi	0	0		
416	248	Lango	21	49	FK9	Aj4
0	523	Langtumu . . . see Tikar	0	0		
529	0	Lano	21	16		
228	0	Lanoh	26	19	AN7	
647	0	Lao	26	29	AM8	
0	0	Lapps	1	118	EP4	Cg4
0	0	Lapps . . . see Saami	0	0		
539	0	Lapps, Skolt	37	39	EP4	Cg4
71	0	Laragia	29	14	OI5	
647	0	Larantuka	28	13	OF5	
71	0	Lardil	30	137	OI5	
316	0	Lashari Baluch	19	107	AT2	
283	0	Lassik	5	70	NS23	Nb37
540	0	Latvians	38	74	RB1	
133	0	Lavongai	32	252	OM9	
540	0	Laz	38	33	RI10	
377	0	Lebou	17	164	MS38	
761	0	Leco	11	83	SF14	
0	0	Lega . . . see Lendu	0	0		
0	0	Leik . . . see Nuer	0	0		
556	0	Lenca	8	19	SA14	Sa12
416	0	Lendu	21	79	FO25	Ai29
1151	0	Lendu	20	56	FO25	
0	523	Lengi . . . see Lenje	0	0		
224	0	Lengola	20	58	FO11	
767	0	Lengua	11	119	SK10	Sh9
63	0	Lengua	13	18	SK10	
547	0	Lenje	22	17	FQ6	
796	0	Lenje (Ila-Tonga)	23	57	FQ6	
0	0	Lepanto . . . see Igorot	0	0	OA20	
517	0	Lepu Mauts	28	52	OC7	
895	0	Lesu	0	0	OM10	Ig4
675	0	Leti	28	2	OF11	
547	0	Leya	22	55	FQ11	
317	0	Lezgian	38	41	RH8	
647	0	Li	27	56	AE2	Ed9
1092	0	Lillooet	4	92	NE12	Nd9
0	523	Lima . . . see Nyaturu	0	0		
166	0	Limba	17	150	FC9	
13	0	Limba	18	14	FH7	
13	0	Limba	20	4	FH7	
517	0	Limbang	28	55	DC10	
558	0	Limbu	39	52	AK1	
647	0	Lionese	28	15	OF9	
1092	0	Lipan Apache	6	7	NT27	Nh24
1063	0	Lipe	11	132	SE13	
269	663	Lisu	26	31	AE10	
540	0	Lithuanians	37	34	RB5	Ch9
540	0	Lithuanians	38	73	RB5	Ch9
0	0	Ljumu . . . see Yoruba	0	0		
0	523	Loango . . . see Vili	0	0		
606	463	Lobedu	23	85	FX14	Ab14
6	0	Lod	39	7		
421	0	Lodagaba	17	85	FE4	
920	0	Logauleng	32	199	OJ4	
1153	0	Logo	21	30	FO26	Ai31
1153	0	Logo	18	150	FO26	Ai31
416	0	Logoli	21	65	FL4	
578	0	Loinang	28	69	OG5	
166	0	Lokko	17	147	FC6	
726	0	Lomami	20	108		
0	523	Londoro . . . see Lokko	0	0		
74	0	Long Tom Creek	4	8	NR9	
71	0	Loridja	29	63	OI5	
0	0	Loritcha	30	117	OI5	
529	0	Lotuko	21	37	FJ13	Aj12
529	0	Lotuko	18	155	FJ13	Aj12
0	523	Lovedu . . . see Lobedu	0	0		
420	0	Lowiili	17	85	FE4	Ag36
146	0	Lowwe	23	23		
1138	408	Lozi	22	41	FQ9	Ab3
647	0	Lu	26	55	AO6	
1232	623	Lua	26	32	AO6	
0	0	Luaich . . . see Dinka	0	0		
925	0	Luano	22	15	FQ8	
199	0	Luapula	22	2	FQ5	Ac34
199	0	Luapula	20	112	FQ5	
174	726	Luba	22	11	FO27	Ae6
917	0	Luba	20	62	FO27	Ae6
1138	175	Lubale Lozi	22	36	FQ9	
0	523	Lubalo . . . see Luena	0	0		
222	0	Lucayans	7	63	SX5	
1138	0	Luchazi	22	29	FP8	Ac27
926	0	Luena	22	32	FP14	
914	0	Lufa	32	29	OJ4	
517	0	Lugats	28	64	OC7	
773	775	Lugbara	21	31	FK14	Ai32
0	523	Lugori . . . see Lugbara	0	0		
1092	0	Lugsiatsiak	1	3	NB4	
0	523	Luguru . . . see Guru	0	0		
640	0	Luilang	27	55	AD4	
726	0	Luimbe	22	49	FP9	Ac28
1201	609	Luiseno	5	17	NS14	Nc33
0	523	Luksage . . . see Luchazi	0	0		
1092	0	Lukshuamiut	2	59	NI5	
767	0	Lule	11	126	SI14	
1159	0	Lulua	20	101	FO27	Ae16
925	0	Lumbu	22	24	FO15	
0	523	Lumbwa . . . see Kipsigis	0	0	FL13	
1056	0	Lummi	4	88	NR15	Nb15
925	0	Lunda	22	8	FO27	
778	0	Lunda	20	95	FO27	
1139	0	Lunda-Ndembu	22	7	FP14	Ac6
71	72	Lungga	29	28	OI5	
1202	0	Lungu	23	49	FQ5	
1202	0	Lungu	21	134	FQ5	
1202	0	Lungu	20	120	FQ5	
199	0	Lungu	20	115	FQ5	
416	191	Luo	21	10	FL11	Aj6
0	0	Lur . . . see Alur	0	0		
522	0	Lurabunna	30	76	OI5	
0	523	Luri . . . see Alur	0	0		
540	0	Lurs	38	16	MA12	
0	643	Lushai Chin	26	46	AR8	
726	1138	Lushange	22	26	FQ10	
0	523	Luyana . . . see Lozi	0	0		
416	633	Luyia	21	60	FL4	
0	523	Lwena . . . see Luena	0	0		
7	0	Lwo . . . see Luo	0	0		
1202	0	Lyangalile	21	137		
161	0	Ma	32	120	DJ1	
807	0	Ma'aza	19	11	MR11	
807	0	Ma'aza	16	9	MR11	
647	0	Maanyan	28	45	OC9	
123	0	Mabinza	20	37	FO8	
767	0	Maca	11	123	SK9	
578	0	Macassarese	28	74	OG6	Ic1
553	554	Machiguenga	11	33	SE18	
946	0	Maco	9	138	SS15	
1092	0	Macorize	7	65	SX4	
514	413	Macu	9	99	SQ10	
444	0	Mada	18	50	FF45	
517	0	Madang	28	50	OC5	
155	0	Madhhij	19	53	MJ4	
993	0	Madi	21	35	FK10	Ai33
133	0	Madiri	32	192	OJ4	
578	604	Madurese	28	25	OE6	
750	749	Mae Enga . . . see Enga	0	0	OJ1	
496	373	Magar	39	59	AK1	Ee8
546	0	Magon	24	6	FX10	
1092	0	Maguan	7	68	SX5	
1092	0	Maguana	7	71	SV5	
444	0	Maguzawa	18	78	FF46	Cb1
0		Magyars . . . see Hungarians	0	0		
598	0	Mahafaly	23	15	FY13	
4	0	Mahi	17	28	FA18	
101	102	Mahican	2	24	NM10	
228	0	Mahmeri	26	7	AN6	
155	1104	Mahra	19	64	MJ4	
973	0	Mahura	22	59		

Cite 1	Cite 2	Culture	Map	No.	HRAF	Murdock's Atlas
463	0	Mekwa	22	70		
12	517	Melanau	28	62	OC7	
0	0	Menabe . . . see Tanala	0	0		
985	0	Mende	17	142	FC7	Af5
670	957	Mendi	32	52	OJ4	
228	0	Mendrio	26	17	AN7	
938	0	Menihek Lakes	2	52	NH6	
570	1045	Menomini	3	12	NP8	Nf9
647	604	Mentawei	28	40	OD9	Ib7
412	0	Menya	32	7	OJ4	
598	87	Merina	23	5	FY5	Eh2
581	776	Meru	21	186	FL5	Ad35
0	523	Metabi . . . see Ingassana	0	0		
101	0	Metoac	2	4	NM7	
1080	0	Mewu Fantzu	39	47	AE3	
1092	0	Mextitlaneca	8	40		
133	0	Meyach	32	161	OJ4	
1092	0	Miami	3	6	NP9	Nf4
696	0	Miana	39	61		
385	0	Miao	26	28	AE5	
540	0	Miao	40	3	AE5	Ed4
1092	0	Michigamea	6	16	NP6	
1092	0	Michigamea	7	11	NP6	
938	0	Michikamau	2	54	NH6	
92	1092	Micmac	2	28	NJ5	Na41
368	0	Midob	18	111	MQ13	Cb11
0	0	Midsi . . . see Tiv	0	0		
663	1232	Mien	26	34	AE6	
1112	0	Mikir	39	62	AR10	Ei17
133	0	Mikud	32	191	OJ1	
187	0	Millcayac	13	7	SI6	
522	0	Milpulko	30	41	OI5	
696	0	Mina	25	37	AW48	
578	647	Minahasa	28	68	OG4	
655	674	Minangkabau	28	33	OD10	Ib6
938	0	Mingan	2	46	NH6	
545	0	Mingendi	32	43	OJ4	
686	0	Mingrelian	38	50	RI11	
187	0	Minuane	13	23	SJ5	
71	0	Minung	29	99	OI5	
72	0	Miring	29	84	OI5	
72	0	Miriwong	29	27	OI5	
0	0	Miro . . . see Lango	0	0		
696	0	Mishmi	39	53	AR12	
556	0	Miskito	8	17	SA15	Sa9
993	0	Mittu	21	22	FJ18	
610	0	Miwok, Central	5	62	NS16	Nc5
610	0	Miwok, Coastal	5	65	NS16	
353	0	Mixe	8	28	NU23	Nj7
943	910	Mixtec	8	37	NU24	Nj12
696	0	Mizo	25	60	AR17	
696	0	Mizo	39	55	AR17	
177	782	Mnong	27	63	AM31	Ej2
1113	0	Moando	32	103	OJ1	
1091	0	Mobile	7	20	NN14	
1092	0	Mococo	7	58	NN18	
187	0	Mocovi	13	15	SI8	
317	0	Modeki	38	36		
1041	572	Modoc	5	92	NS17	Nc9
1041	0	Modoc	4	32	NS17	Nc9
726	0	Moer	20	114		
397	1072	Mohave	5	30	NT28	Nh21
311	1092	Mohawk	2	21	NM9	
938	0	Moisie	2	45	NH6	
508	0	Mojo	11	80	SF15	
647	0	Moken	26	23	AP8	
74	0	Molalla	4	24	NR18	
540	0	Moldavians	38	67	RE1	
769	0	Mompox	9	22	SC9	
647	0	Mon	26	27	AP9	
1044	1092	Monache	5	46	NS25	Nc23
0	523	Monbattu . . . see Mangbetu	0	0		
0	523	Monbuttu . . . see Mangbetu	0	0		
529	0	Mondari	21	18	FJ5	Aj16
529	0	Mondari	18	147	FJ5	Aj16
1091	0	Moneton	7	13	NN13	
487	0	Mongo	20	43	FO32	Ae24
789	603	Mongol	39	41	AH1	
789	603	Mongol	35	5	AH1	

Cite 1	Cite 2	Culture	Map	No.	HRAF	Murdock's Atlas
789	603	Mongol	40	11	AH1	
647	0	Mongondow	28	67	OG4	
647	0	Mongondow, Inland	28	68	OG4	
107	0	Moni	32	146	OJ4	
378	0	Mono	5	45	NR13	
782	0	Monom	27	70	AM30	
782	0	Monom	27	70	AM30	Nh6
701	938	Montagnais	2	29	NH6	
938	1028	Montagnais	2	31	NH6	Na32
1092	0	Montauk	2	4	NL6	
540	0	Montenegrins	37	8	EF5	
796	0	Moors	15	44	MY1	
1063	0	Moquegua	11	139	SE13	
133	0	Moraori	32	180	OJ4	
1091	0	Moratuc	7	31	NN15	
540	0	Mordvinians	38	64	RG6	
759	57	More	11	71	SP12	
578	0	Mori-Laki	28	73	OG7	
729	0	Moro	27	11	OA16	
647	0	Morotai	28	92	OH12	
993	0	Moru	21	21	FJ19	Ai34
761	0	Moseten	11	84	SF16	
1091	0	Mosopelea	7	12	NN13	
771	1010	Mossi	17	66	FA28	Ag47
439	0	Motu	32	225	OJ19	Ie10
154	648	Mourdia	18	96	MS5	
582	761	Movima	11	81	SF17	
463	527	Mpondomise	24	25	FX17	
201	0	Mpongwe	20	11	FI23	Ae46
696	0	Mru	25	59	AM17	
0	0	Muchic	11	2	SE21	
71	0	Mudbara	29	24	OI5	
147	296	Mugharbah	16	25	MT9	
0	523	Muila . . . see Mwila	0	0		
71	0	Mukjarawaint	30	10		
1092	0	Muklasa	7	22	NN11	
71	0	Mulluk Mulluk	29	20	OI5	
0	523	Mulochazi . . . see Luchazi	0	0		
74	0	Multnomah	4	19	NR6	
495	0	Mum	18	21	FF51	Ae50
647	0	Muna	28	80	OG7	
696	0	Munda	25	47	AW41	
0	523	Mundombe . . . see Ndombe	0	0		
993	0	Mundu	21	25	FO33	
133	0	Mundugumor	32	96	OJ1	
804	516	Mundurucu	10	29	SQ13	Sd1
802	829	Mundurucu	12	36	SQ13	Sd1
802	804	Mundurucu	11	56	SQ13	Sd1
829	516	Mundurucu	9	94	SQ13	Sd1
724	0	Mungo	18	13	FH7	
13	0	Mungo	18	31	FH7	
13	0	Mungo	20	2	FH72	
67	0	Mungoobra	30	126	OI5	
522	0	Munkibura	30	110	OI5	
0	523	Munshi . . . see Tiv	0	0		
522	0	Munyabora	30	54	OI5	
113	0	Mur	31	15		
829	0	Mura	10	26	SQ14	
829	834	Mura	9	93	SQ14	
0	0	Murd Guachey	15	46	M24	
113	0	Murilo	34	15	OR19	
71	0	Murinbata	29	23	OI5	Id7
522	0	Murubura	30	55	OI5	
956	0	Murut	28	54	OC7	
1092	0	Muskogee	7	18	NN11	
522	0	Mutabura	30	107	OI5	
77	0	Mutair	19	22	MJ4	Cj5
522	0	Muthi-Muthi	30	22	OI5	
791	0	Muyuw	33	6	OL6	
807	0	Muzeina	19	7	MR11	
0	523	Mvemba . . . see Bemba	0	0		
1138	0	Mwenyi	22	50	FQ9	
1098	0	Mwera	23	26	FN13	
0	523	Mweru . . . see Meru	0	0		
291	0	Mwila	22	108		
105	0	Mzab	15	17	MV7	Cc4
0	0	Naath . . . see Nuer	0	0		
40	0	Nabaloi	27	42	OA20	
217	0	Nabesna	4	140	NA5	Na1

Cite 1	Cite 2	Culture	Map	No.	HRAF	Murdock's Atlas
217	859	Nabesna	1	75	NA5	Na1
0	523	Nadh . . . see Nuer	0	0		
725	0	Nafar	19	96		
533	533	Naga	27	54		
373	0	Naga	39	54	AR13	
533	373	Naga	25	57	AR13	
309	0	Nagarwapuna	32	11	OJ1	
0	523	Nago . . . see Yoruba	0	0		
1052	1092	Nagyuktogmiut	1	43	ND8	
1092	0	Nahane	1	80	ND12	
1092	0	Nahane	4	126	ND12	
1106	155	Nahd	19	60	MJ4	
1092	0	Nahuatl	8	34	NU46	
696	0	Naikda	25	17	AW47	
0	0	Naitasiri . . . see Fiji	0	0		
45	0	Nakanai	32	246	OM16	
1182	0	Nakara	30	152	OI5	
0	0	Nalu	17	154	FB6	
487	0	Nama	24	3	FX13	Aa3
487	0	Nama	24	2	FX13	
112	0	Namal . . . see Nyamal	0	0		
973	0	Namaqua, Hottentot	24	12	FX13	
897	659	Nambicuara	11	96	SP17	Si4
659	898	Nambicuara	12	34	SP17	Si4
161	0	Namie	32	121	OJ1	
712	0	Namoluk	34	17	OR14	
0	0	Namonuito	34	11	OR19	
540	0	Nanaians	36	11	RX3	
540	0	Nanaians	35	10	RX3	
540	0	Nanaians	40	14	RX3	
1092	0	Nanaimo	4	96	NE13	
1151	0	Nande	20	53	FO22	
505	530	Nandi	21	68	FL13	Aj7
0	0	Nandronga . . . see Fiji	0	0		
1092	0	Nanoptaim	1	1	NB4	
1092	0	Nanticoke	2	3	NM11	
1092	0	Nanticoke	7	27	NM11	
1095	0	Nanumba	17	48	FE5	
416	0	Napore	21	38	FJ25	
309	0	Narak	32	76	OJ4	
487	0	Naron	24	5	FX10	Aa7
973	0	Naron	22	75	FX10	Aa7
1092	0	Narraganset	2	11	NL6	
71	0	Narrinyeri	30	27	OI18	
71	0	Narunga	30	31	OI5	
1092	0	Naskapi	2	47	NH6	Na5
938	0	Natashquan	2	48	NH6	
392	0	Natchez	6	8	NO8	Ng7
1092	392	Natchez	7	4	NO8	Ng7
0	0	Nath . . . see Nuer	0	0		
522	0	Naualko	30	43	OI5	
71	0	Nauo	30	35	OI5	
0	0	Nauru	34	23	OR13	If13
1092	0	Nauset	2	15	NL5	
565	0	Nauthars	39	60	AK1	
702	0	Nava	32	213	OJ1	
594	0	Navaho . . . see Navajo	0	0	FO12	Nh3
117	395	Navajo	6	39	NT13	Nh3
594	924	Navajo	5	26	NT13	Nh3
866	424	Nayar	25	6	AW11	Eg6
123	0	Nbombe	20	45		
1219	0	Ndali	23	36	FN21	
371	0	Ndau	23	75	FS5	Ab17
0	523	Ndaw . . . see Ndau	0	0		
463	0	Ndebele	24	42	FS4	Ab9
175	0	Ndebele	22	57	FS4	Ab9
463	0	Ndebele	23	81	FS4	Ab9
463	0	Ndeble	23	84	FS4	Ab9
1139	0	Ndembu . . . see Lunda	0	0	FP14	Ac6
1159	0	Ndenges	20	63	FO16	
201	0	Ndere	18	128		
61	0	Ndereko	21	160		
201	0	Ndibu	20	76		
0	523	Ndjeli . . . see Pande	0	0		
72	0	Ndjiband	29	66	OJ5	
291	0	Ndombe	22	114	FP15	
723	0	Ndongo	20	84	FP6	
495	0	Ndop	18	17	FF51	
775	0	Ndu Lendu	18	156	FO25	
107	0	Nduga	32	141	OJ1	
1138	0	Ndundulu (Lozi)	22	42	FQ9	
40	0	Negritos	27	36	OA31	
105	0	Nemadi	15	38	MS32	
144	0	Nemencha	15	8	MV8	
540	0	Nenets	1	113	RU24	
99	0	Nentsi	1	115	RU4	
540	0	Nentsy	39	38	RU4	
540	0	Nentz	1	116	RU4	
1092	0	Netcetumiut	2	67	NI5	
22	1052	Netsilik	1	36	ND13	Na43
1052	22	Netsilik	3	49	ND13	Na43
0	0	Netsilingmiut . . . see Netsilik	0	0		
647	0	Neua	26	54	AM8	
308	0	Neusiok	7	35	NN19	
1064	0	Neva	9	62	SE22	
133	0	New Britain	0	0	OM8	
241	113	New Caledonia	33	21	OP1	
1148	1119	New Hebrides	33	19	OO1	
133	0	New Ireland	32	241	OM10	
74	0	Nez Perce	4	40	NR12	Nd20
647	0	Ngada	28	17	0F9	
72	0	Ngadi	29	44	OI5	
647	0	Ngadju	28	44	OC9	
71	0	Ngadjuri	30	32	OI5	
72	0	Ngaiawongga	29	76	OI5	
72	0	Ngala	29	51	FO12	Ae28
753	0	Ngalakan	29	10	OI5	
72	0	Ngalia	29	60	OI5	
107	0	Ngalik	32	136	OJ11	
696	0	Ngalong	25	54		
112	72	Ngaluma	29	67	OI5	
1233	291	Ngambwe	22	107	FP18	
522	0	Ngameni	30	80	OI5	
237	0	Nganasans	1	110	RU4	
71	0	Nganda	29	75	OI5	
291	143	Ngangela	22	48	FP16	
201	0	Ngapou	18	126		
71	0	Ngarigo	30	2	OI5	
123	0	Ngbaka	20	47		
0	523	Ngbaka . . . see Bwaka	0	0		
123	0	Ngbandi	20	38	FO36	Ai26
0	523	Ngbanya . . . see Gonja	0	0		
985	0	Ngere	17	127	FA29	Af56
0	523	Ngie . . . see Jie	0	0		
0	0	Ngijiye . . . see Jie	0	0		
1098	0	Ngindo	23	27	FN13	
463	0	Ngoika	24	20	FX17	
0	0	Ngok . . . see Dinka	0	0		
809	0	Ngomane	24	38	FT6	
1219	0	Ngonde	23	37	FN17	Ad16
0	0	Ngoni . . . see Angoni	0	0	FR5	Ac9
71	0	Ngugan	29	74	OI5	
62	61	Ngulu	21	156	FN28	Ad51
925	0	Ngumbo	23	50	FQ5	
146	0	Nguni	23	63	FX17	
522	0	Ngurawola	30	79	OI5	
0	523	Nguru . . . see Ngulu	0	0		
0	523	Nguu . . . see Ngulu	0	0		
976	463	Ngwaketse	22	63	FV6	
0	523	Ngwana . . . see Dagomba	0	0		
0	523	Ngwana . . . see Swazi	0	0		
976	0	Ngwato	22	60	FV6	
463	0	Nhlangwini	24	29	FV6	
0	523	Ni-Turkana . . . see Turkana	0	0		
0	523	Nianga . . . see Nyanga	0	0		
1092	0	Niantic	2	10	NL6	
647	0	Niassans	28	39	OD11	
0	523	Nika . . . see Nyika	0	0		
0	523	Nilamba . . . see Iramba	0	0		
0	0	Nilotes . . . see Acholi	0	0		
0	0	Nilotes . . . see Alur	0	0		
0	0	Nilotes . . . see Dinka	0	0		
0	0	Nilotes . . . see Jur	0	0		
0	0	Nilotes . . . see Lango	0	0		
0	0	Nilotes . . . see Luo	0	0		
0	0	Nilotes . . . see Nuer	0	0		
72	0	Nimanburu	29	34	OI5	
522	0	Ningebul	30	101	OI5	
444	0	Ninzam	18	47	FF45	
1092	0	Nipmuc	2	14	NL5	
1092	0	Niquiran	8	9		

Cite 1	Cite 2	Culture	Map	No.	HRAF	Murdock's Atlas
51	0	Nisenan	5	68	NS15	Nc13
373	0	Nishis	25	55		
1092	0	Niska	4	112	NE15	
1018	0	Nisqually	4	80	NR15	
540	0	Nivkhi	36	7	RX2	
72	0	Njamal ... see Nyamal	0	0		
0	523	Njeli ... see Pande	0	0		
71	0	Njibali ... see Injibandi	0	0		
71	0	Njinin	29	39	OI5	
1215	0	Nkansi	21	136		
416	0	Nkole ... see Ankole	0	0		
201	0	Nkomi	20	14	FI23	
0	523	Nkonde ... see Nyakyusa	0	0		
0	523	Nkore ... see Ankole	0	0		
809	0	Nkosi	24	39	FT6	
1138	0	Nkoya (Lozi)	22	22	FQ10	
291	0	Nkumbi	22	100	FP17	
1159	0	Nkutu	20	65	FO16	
107	0	Nngalik	32	133	OJ1	
1052	1092	Noahonirmiut	1	48	ND8	
154	0	Noarma	18	103		
686	0	Nogai	38	56	RF6	
133	0	Nokon	32	247	OM10	
532	0	Nole	21	207	MP13	
414	0	Nomlaki	5	71	NS26	Nc1
0	0	Nongait	30	40	OI5	
677	0	Nongatl	5	84	NS23	
1092	0	Nontagnais	2	32	NH6	
250	966	Nootka	4	99	NE11	Nb11
1092	0	Nootsak	4	87	NR15	
1092	0	Noquet	3	13	NG6	
946	0	Norague	10	19	SR12	
938	0	Northwest River	2	51	NH6	
36	0	Norwegians	37	38	EP1	
926	0	Nsenga	22	19	FR4	
925	926	Nsenga	23	60	FR4	
495	0	Nso	18	18	FF51	
469	0	Nsula	15	26	MW5	
813	368	Nuba	18	121	FJ21	
577	0	Nubians	16	10	MR8	
577	0	Nubians	19	144	MR8	
295	0	Nuer	18	146	FJ22	Aj3
295	575	Nuer	21	4	FJ22	Aj3
1092	0	Nugsuak	1	28	NB5	
522	0	Nuku-Nukubura	30	59	OI5	
796	0	Nukulo	22	3		
133	0	Numfor	32	257	OJ22	
355	0	Numic	5	48	NT6	
1052	1049	Nunatagmiut	1	89	NA9	
1092	0	Nunenumiut	2	65	NI5	
1182	0	Nungabuya	30	145	OI5	
0	0	Nuong ... see Nuer	0	0		
812	25	Nupe	17	70	FF52	Af8
0	523	Nupechizi ... see Nupe	0	0		
0	523	Nupesizi ... see Nupe	0	0		
6	0	Nuristani	39	17	AU6	Ea5
133	0	Nusu	32	251	OM10	
1092	0	Nuvugmiut	3	53	NI5	
72	0	Nyaanyadjarra	29	62	OI5	
1116	0	Nyaginyagi	29	93	OI5	
1218	1219	Nyakyusa	23	35	FN17	Ad6
416	0	Nyala	21	61	FL4	
72	0	Nyamal	29	53	OI5	
206	0	Nyamb	21	98	FP16	
1215	206	Nyamwezi	21	128	FN18	Ad20
1151	0	Nyanga	20	54	FO22	
72	0	Nyangamada	29	48	OI5	
529	0	Nyangbara	18	149	FJ5	
774	0	Nyangbara	21	26	FJ5	
0	523	Nyankole ... see Ankole	0	0		
0	0	Nyarraweng ... see Dinka	0	0		
416	0	Nyaturu	22	13	FN19	
416	0	Nyaturu	21	120	FN19	
291	0	Nyemba	22	101	FP16	
1138	0	Nyengo (Lozi)	22	40	FQ9	
581	0	Nyeri	21	181		
72	0	Nyiabali	29	54	OI5	
72	0	Nyigena	29	46	OI5	
473	1215	Nyiha	21	140	FN21	
72	0	Nyining	29	25	OI5	
0	523	Nyiramba ... see Iramba	0	0		
45	0	Nyool-Nyool ... see Nyulnyul	0	0		
416	0	Nyore ... see Luyia	0	0		
416	54	Nyoro	21	77	FK11	Ad2
201	0	Nzakara	18	136	FI25	
0	523	Nzombo ... see Zombo	0	0		
1236	0	Oaycas	9	143	SQ18	
647	0	Obi	28	85	OH14	
1092	0	Ocale	7	55	NN18	
265	0	Occitanie	37	17		
844	0	Ogadein	21	184	MO4	
973	0	Ohekwe	22	62	FX10	
1159	0	Ohindo	20	60		
80	1136	Ojibwa	3	38	NG6	Nf1
77	0	Ojman	19	31	MJ4	
340	161	Ok	32	111	OJ4	
0	523	Okam ... see Yako	0	0		
169	1092	Okanogan	4	59	NR19	
416	0	Okebo	21	80		
0	523	Okiek ... see Dorobo	0	0		
708	0	Okinawans	35	9	AC7	Ed7
522	0	Olongbura	30	55	DI5	
0	523	Olugbo ... see Luluba	0	0		
1064	0	Omagua	9	78	SQ15	
0	0	Omaguaca	11	144	SI9	
327	0	Omaha	6	22	NQ12	Nf3
327	0	Omaha	3	22	NQ12	Nf3
327	0	Omaha	3	25	NQ12	Nf3
0	523	Ombe ... see Mbui	0	0		
0	523	Omundu ... see Mundu	0	0		
185	676	Ona	14	3	SH4	Sg3
595	0	Onabasulu	32	72	OJ1	
345	0	Ondo	17	21	FF62	
132	1092	Oneida	2	20	NM9	
904	0	Onge	26	24	AZ2	
291	0	Ongona	22	95	FI14	
85	1092	Onondaga	2	19	NM9	
998	49	Ontong Java	33	14	OT8	Ii5
494	493	Opata	8	77	NU25	Ni8
412	0	Opau	32	195	DJ1	
1109	0	Ora	17	18	FF21	
522	0	Orambul	30	89	DI5	
1008	228	Orang Laut	26	1	AN4	
228	0	Orangkanaq	26	2	AN4	
696	0	Oraon	25	46	AW39	Ef6
946	0	Oremano	9	109		
133	0	Oriwa	32	221	OJ1	
133	0	Ormut	32	124	OJ1	
1092	0	Ornoray	7	67	SX5	
540	0	Orochi	36	13	RX3	
540	0	Orochons	40	15	RU5	
133	0	Oroimo	32	193	DJ1	
1213	987	Orokaiva	32	220	OJ23	Ie9
412	0	Orokolo	32	33	OJ1	
540	0	Oroks	36	14	RX3	
0	523	Oromo ... see Galla	0	0		
556	0	Orotina	9	2	SA11	
556	0	Orotina	8	6	SA11	
656	0	Oru	17	5	FF21	
1092	0	Osage	6	17	NQ12	
133	0	Oser	32	171	OJ11	
1092	0	Osochi	7	48	NN11	
599	317	Osset	38	51	RH9	Ci6
647	0	Ot-Danom	28	43	OC9	
1092	0	Oto	3	20	NQ9	Nf11
1092	0	Oto	6	20	NQ9	Nf11
392	0	Otomac	9	128	SS14	
707	0	Otomi	8	42	NU26	Nj13
1092	0	Ottawa	3	4	NG6	Na40
759	0	Otuke	11	107	SF18	
0	523	Otuko ... see Lotuko	0	0		
144	0	Ouarsenis	15	18		
938	0	Ouchestigouek	2	41	NH6	
946	0	Ouiba	9	124		
1126	0	Oulad Djerir	15	21	MY4	
0	523	Oulof ... see Wolof	0	0		
938	0	Oumamiouek	2	39	NH6	
630	154	Ounie	18	95	MS5	
154	0	Ouria	18	88	MS22	
0	0	Ova Mbo ... see Ambo	0	0		

Cite 1	Cite 2	Culture	Map	No.	HRAF	Murdock's Atlas
0	523	Ovaherero . . . see Herero	0	0		
0	523	Ovakwangari . . . see Kwangare	0	0		
973	0	Ovambo	22	87	FX8	
0	523	Ovandonga . . . see Ndongo	0	0		
455	726	Ovimbundu	22	47	FP13	
723	0	Ovimbundu	20	83	FP13	
723	0	Ovimbundu	20	93	FP13	
125	0	Oyampi	10	20	SQ8	
820	0	Oyana	10	12	SR12	
309	0	Oybae	32	69	OJ4	
251	0	Ozette	4	76	NE11	
1064	0	Pacaas Novas	11	65	SP12	
0	0	Padang . . . see Dinka	0	0	FJ12	
985	0	Padebu	17	118	FD7	
416	0	Padhola	21	55		
576	1092	Padlimiut	1	31	ND6	
1092	0	Padouca	6	24	NO6	
216	0	Paez	9	32	SC15	Sf5
0	523	Pahouin . . . see Fang	0	0		
0	523	Pahuin . . . see Fang	0	0		
355	0	Pahvant	5	49	NT19	Nd57
355	0	Pahvant	6	38	NT19	Nd57
463	0	Pai	24	40	FT6	
761	0	Paikoneka	11	91	SF60	
354	572	Paiute, Northern	5	61	NR13	
1041	572	Paiute, Northern	4	33	NR13	
354	572	Paiute, Northern	5	50	NR13	
666	0	Paiute, Owens Valley	5	39	NR13	
573	416	Paiute, Southern	5	28	NT16	
640	0	Paiwan	27	54	AD13	Ia6
759	761	Pakaguara	11	72	SF19	
782	0	Pakoh Hoe	27	75	AM32	
736	29	Palau	34	1	OR15	If1
643	0	Palaung	26	41	AP10	Ei18
1183	605	Palawan	27	26	OA37	
231	0	Palenque	9	155	SS9	
426	953	Palestinian	38	8	MG1	
969	0	Palikur	10	16	SQ16	Sd3
696	0	Palivan	25	5		
15	0	Pallirmiut	3	40	ND6	
567	0	Pallisa	21	50		
1092	0	Palouse	4	54	NR18	
806	0	Palta	9	53	SD9	
0	523	Paluo . . . see Chopi	0	0		
416	0	Palwo . . . see Chopi	0	0		
201	0	Pambia	18	145	FJ20	
1092	0	Pame	8	45	NU27	
1092	0	Pamiagikuk	1	2	NB4	
0	523	Pan . . . see Sapo	0	0		
261	480	Panare	9	139	SS21	Sc13
769	0	Pancenu	9	12	SC9	
769	0	Panche	9	28	SC16	
201	0	Pande	18	7	FH21	
201	0	Pande	20	27	FH21	
228	0	Pangan	26	13	AN7	
1219	0	Pangwa	23	33	FN12	
0	523	Pangwe . . . see Fang	0	0		
769	0	Pantagoro	9	25	SC16	
806	0	Panzaleo	9	45	SD11	
540	0	Paoan	40	9		
493	341	Papago	6	53	NU28	Ni2
493	341	Papago	5	3	NU28	Ni2
1092	0	Paparo	9	7	SC12	
938	0	Papinachos	2	38	NH6	
1236	0	Paraitiry	9	105		
826	0	Parakana	10	52	SQ2	
416	0	Pare	21	167	FN4	Ad36
765	0	Paressi	11	100	SP19	Si7
522	0	Paringnoga	30	54	OI5	
829	0	Parintintin	11	62	SP10	
828	0	Pariri	10	53	SQ4	
522	0	Parnkalla	30	34	OI5	
522	0	Paruinji	30	44	OI5	
0	0	Pashai . . . see Tajiks	0	0		
857	0	Pasto	9	41	SC17	
946	0	Patamona	10	5	SR9	
946	0	Patamona	9	163	SR9	
834	0	Patasho	12	8	SN5	
696	0	Patelia	25	36		
6	5	Pathans	39	2	AU4	Ea2
616	0	Patwin	5	63	NS26	Nc22
946	0	Pauishana	9	104	SQ27	
0	0	Paumari	11	52	SQ17	
990	0	Pauserna	11	104	SF11	
156	0	Paushiana	9	106	SQ27	
416	412	Pawaia	32	35	OJ4	
1189	0	Pawnee	6	23	NQ18	Nf6
1189	0	Pawnee	3	23	NQ18	Nf6
556	0	Paya	8	18	SA16	
1064	0	Payanso	11	38	SE14	
647	0	Pear	26	61	AM7	
1092	0	Pecos	6	49	NT11	
1092	0	Pedee	7	37	NN13	
487	0	Pedi	24	41	FX16	Ab15
606	0	Pedi	23	87	FX14	
0	0	Pedi . . . see Pepi	0	0		
187	0	Pehuenche (Araucanian)	13	3	SG4	
187	0	Pehuenche (Araucanian)	14	14	SG4	
1092	0	Pend d'Oreilles	4	48	NR19	
0	523	Penin . . . see Banen	0	0		
1092	0	Pennacook	2	23	NL4	
1092	0	Penobscot	2	26	NL4	Ng4
1092	0	Pensacola	7	21	NN14	
133	0	Pepeha	32	37	OJ1	
1092	0	Pequot	2	70	NL6	
1092	0	Pericu	8	71	NU42	
318	0	Persians	38	20	MA1	
0	523	Pessi . . . see Kpelle	0	0		
574	0	Petamini	32	84	OJ1	
938	0	Petitsikapau	2	53	NH6	
0	523	Peul . . . see Fulbe	0	0		
691	665	Phoenix Islands	31	5	OW2	
1218	0	Phoka	23	43	FR6	
834	0	Pianokoto	10	22	SR12	
769	0	Piapoco	9	126	SC5	Sc17
566	0	Piaroa	9	141	SS15	Sc8
216	0	Pijao	9	31	SC15	
0	523	Pika . . . see Bolewa	0	0		
9	0	Pikelot	34	9	OR21	
767	0	Pilaga	11	125	SI12	
299	298	Pima	8	75	NU29	Ni6
299	869	Pima	6	51	NU29	Ni6
298	493	Pima	5	8	NU29	Ni6
264	0	Pima, Lower	5	2	NU29	
264	0	Pima, Lower	8	69	NU29	
726	1121	Pinde	20	96	FO46	
1092	0	Pingangnaktogmiut	1	46	ND8	
556	0	Pipil	8	23	NV8	
946	0	Piriou	10	23	SQ3	
275	1092	Piro	6	50	NT10	
1069	0	Piro	11	35	SE18	Sf8
133	0	Pisa	32	142	OJ4	
1092	0	Pisigsarfik	1	13	NB6	
71	0	Pita Pita	30	85	OI5	
23	0	Pitcairn	31	20	OW3	
985	0	Plawi	17	116	FD7	
0	0	Pmir . . . see Tajiks	0	0		
146	0	Podzo	23	19	FT5	
61	0	Pogoro	23	29	FN20	
416	61	Pogoro	21	149	FN20	
1092	0	Pohoy	7	59	NN18	
819	0	Point Barrow Eskimo . . . see Tareumiut	0	0		
529	0	Pojulu	18	153	FJ5	Aj13
529	0	Pojulu	21	19	FJ5	Aj13
416	0	Pokomo	21	176	FL15	Ad33
0	523	Pokot . . . see Suk	0	0		
309	0	Poles	32	47	EA1	
309	0	Poles	37	32	OJ1	
540	0	Poles	38	66	EA1	
31	396	Pomo	5	66	NS18	Nc17
201	0	Pomo	20	29	NS18	
308	0	Pomouik	7	33	NN15	
930	882	Ponape	34	18	OR16	If5
1092	0	Ponca	3	24	NQ12	Nf12
13	0	Pongo	18	30	FF36	
806	0	Popayanense	9	39	SC15	
0	523	Popo . . . see Hula	0	0		
512	353	Popoluca	8	35	NU30	Nj3

Cite 1	Cite 2	Culture	Map	No.	HRAF	Murdock's Atlas
1209	0	Portugese	37	21	EY1	Ce2
1092	0	Potano	7	50	NN18	
1092	0	Potawatomi	3	5	NP10	Na42
763	0	Potiguara	10	64	SO9	
1092	0	Poven	1	25	NB6	
1137	1136	Powhatan	7	29	NN15	
1092	0	Powhatan	2	2	NN15	
187	0	Poya	14	9	SH5	
945	0	Poyndu	30	158	OI19	Id8
769	0	Pozo	9	26	SC9	
133	0	Pranje	32	139	OJ1	
945	0	Premingana	30	154	OI19	Id8
74	0	Pudding River	4	20	NR9	
187	0	Puelche	13	2	SI10	
187	0	Puelche	14	16	SI10	
769	0	Puinave	9	122	SC18	
1052	1092	Puiplirmiut	1	44	ND8	
1092	0	Puisortok	1	6	NB4	
50	0	Pukapukans	31	9	OZ11	Ii3
9	0	Pulap	34	10	OR17	
9	0	Pulusuk	34	12	OR17	
6	0	Punjabi	39	20	AT2	Ea13
1092	0	Puntash	4	97		
1092	0	Puntlatsh	4	97	NE13	
1164	0	Punu	20	16		
945	0	Puraneters	30	157	OI19	Id8
834	0	Puri	12	38	SN6	
946	0	Purigoto	9	166	SQ22	
769	0	Puruha	9	46	SD4	
316	0	Pusht-I-Kuh	19	23		
1092	0	Puthlavamiut	2	68	NI5	
1018	1043	Puyallup	4	81	NR15	Nb17
627	0	Pygmy (Cameroon)	18	4	FH4	
15	0	Qaernermiut	3	47	ND6	
1092	0	Qahatika	5	4	NU29	
77	0	Qahtan	19	34	MJ4	
807	0	Qararsha	19	6	MR11	
56	725	Qashqai	19	89	MA13	Ea12
1092	0	Qaumauangmiut	3	52	ND5	
1092	0	Qaumauangmiut	2	62	ND5	
576	1092	Qinguamuit	1	39	ND5	
0	523	Quale ... see Kuvale	0	0		
1092	0	Quapaw	7	6	NQ12	
1092	0	Quapaw	6	12	NQ12	
1205	0	Quda'a	19	72	MK1	
344	0	Quechan	5	9	NT15	
20	0	Quechua	11	25	SE13	
849	0	Queets	4	73	NR17	
187	0	Querandi	13	25	SI10	
1092	0	Quero	8	4		
849	0	Quileute	4	75	NR16	Nb18
0	0	Quillaca	11	133	SF5	
857	0	Quillacinga	9	40	SC17	
216	0	Quimbaya	9	30	SC9	
850	849	Quinault	4	72	NR17	Nb25
769	0	Quindio	9	29	SC15	
796	0	Rabai	21	172	FL14	
782	0	Rade	27	66	AM35	
1182	0	Rainbarngo	30	150	OI5	
133	0	Raintana	32	172	OJ4	
316	0	Rais	19	106		
556	0	Rama	8	7	SA17	
71	0	Ramindjeri	30	29	OI5	
835	204	Ramko-Kamekra	10	65	SO8	Si4
12	0	Ranau Dusun	28	56	OC7	
0	0	Rangi ... see Irangi	0	0		
1104	0	Rashid	19	69	MJ4	
178	640	Ratagnon	27	29	OA18	
0	0	Rawalah ... see Ruwallah	0	0		
647	0	Red Tai	27	76	AL3	
647	674	Redjang	28	29	OD12	
0	523	Rega ... see Lega	0	0		
144	1144	Regeibat	15	47	MS29	Cc1
369	0	Rela	15	3	MS25	
1064	0	Remo	11	39	SE6	
416	968	Rendille	21	46	FL7	
488	0	Rennell Island	33	13	OT9	Ii10
103	0	Rewa ... see Fiji	0	0		
582	0	Reyesano	11	90	SF23	
0	0	Rhade ... see Rade	0	0		
180	0	Rif	15	32	MX3	Cd3
77	0	Rijal Al Ma	19	47	MJ1	
522	0	Ristebura	30	102	OI5	
1182	0	Ritarngo	30	149	OI17	
1205	0	Riyam	19	73	MK1	
368	0	Rizegat	18	120	MQ5	
308	0	Roanoke	7	32	NN15	
133	0	Roboda	32	238	OJ1	
782	0	Roglai	27	65	AM33	
463	0	Rolong	24	9	FV6	
463	0	Rolong	22	67	FV6	
938	0	Romaine	2	49	NH6	
0	0	Ror ... see Sangu	0	0		
991	0	Roro	32	206	OJ4	
540	0	Roshanis	39	25		
0	0	Rossel Island ... see Yela	0	0	OL5	Ig11
647	0	Roti	28	9	OF14	Ic4
0	0	Rualla ... see Ruwallah	0	0		
1063	0	Rucana	11	24	SE13	
416	0	Rufiji	21	159	FM2	
0	523	Ruguru ... see Guru	0	0		
640	0	Rukai	27	54	AD14	
540	0	Rumanians	38	68	ED1	Ch10
192	0	Rumanians	37	30	ED1	Ch10
522	0	Runbubura	30	101	OI5	
12	0	Rungus	28	60	OC7	
540	0	Russians	36	6	R1	Ch11
540	0	Russians	38	76	R1	Ch11
540	0	Russians	39	35	R1	Ch11
540	0	Russians	35	11	R1	Ch11
540	0	Russians	40	20	R1	Ch11
97	0	Russians	37	31	R1	Ch11
0	0	Rut Thoi ... see Dinka	0	0		
317	0	Rutul	38	43	RH8	
808	0	Ruwallah	19	14	MD4	Cj2
808	0	Ruwallah	38	4	MD4	Cj2
0	0	Rwala ... see Ruwallah	0	0		
206	0	Rwanda	21	99	FO51	Ae10
403	0	Ryukyu Islands	27	53	AC1	
1092	0	Saami	1	117	EP4	
1104	0	Saar	19	61	AL6	
1092	0	Sabaneque	7	66	SX5	
133	0	Saberi	32	129	OJ4	
578	0	Sadang	28	72	OG8	
316	0	Safari	19	99		
1215	0	Safwa	21	141	FN21	Ad17
0	0	Sag ... see Fipa	0	0		
1116	61	Sagara	21	152	FN22	
911	0	Sagdlirmiut	3	50	ND5	
144	0	Said Atba	15	13		
256	595	Sakalava	23	2	FY6	Eh8
416	0	Sakuye	21	189	FL7	
796	0	Sala	23	59	FQ6	
113	0	Sala y Gomez	31	23	SZ1	
647	0	Salajar	28	77	OG6	
133	0	Salakahadi	32	240	OJ1	
647	0	Salawati	32	166	OJ1	
608	0	Salinan	5	37	NS19	Nc26
432	0	Salineros-Cabezas	8	64		
250	0	Salish	4	93	NE12	
946	0	Saliva	9	136	SS15	
540	0	Salor	39	29		
640	0	Samal	27	1	OA16	
133	0	Samalek	32	159	OJ1	
729	0	Samar-Leyte	27	23	OA14	
416	61	Sambaa	21	166	FN24	
729	0	Sambal	27	39		
0	0	Sambas	28	42	OC1	
309	0	Sambia	32	8	OJ1	
828	0	Sambioa	10	48	SP9	
416	0	Samburu	21	180	FL12	Aj29
416	0	Samia, Gwe	21	59	FL4	
1092	0	Samish	4	86	NR15	
133	0	Samo	32	87	OJ1	
740	360	Samoa	31	4	OU8	Ii1
540	0	Samoyed	1	111	RU4	
1012	0	Sampits	6	37	NT19	
0	523	Sampur ... see Samburu	0	0		
647	0	Samre	26	51	AM7	

Cite 1	Cite 2	Culture	Map	No.	HRAF	Murdock's Atlas
356	0	San Cristobal	33	12	ON12	
767	0	Sanapana	11	120	SK10	
416	822	Sandawe	21	119	FN23	Aa6
0	0	Sande . . . see Azande	0	0		
1164	0	Sanga	20	25	FI27	
0	523	Sango . . . see Sangu	0	0		
1218	473	Sangu	21	145	FN9	Ad23
156	0	Sanhaja	15	28	MX3	
912	0	Sanpoil	4	60	MR19	Nd4
171	210	Santa Cruz	33	15	ON13	Ih9
373	696	Santal	25	51	AW42	Ef1
0	0	Santee . . . see Dakota Santee	0	0		
74	0	Santiam	4	25	NR15	
296	0	Sanusi	16	14	MT9	Cd20
796	0	Sanye	21	175	FL6	
647	0	Saoch	26	62	AM7	
133	0	Sapara	32	190	OJ1	
357	985	Sapo	17	121	FD7	Af49
201	0	Sara	18	68	FI28	Ai22
1007	0	Saranahua	0	0		
637	0	Sardinians	37	6	EZ8	
541	0	Sariq Turkomen	39	28	RM2	
859	0	Sarsi	4	102	NF9	Ne7
640	0	Sasaks	28	22	OF12	
1092	0	Satsup	4	70	NR15	
1092	0	Saturiwa	7	45	NN18	
649	0	Saui	32	46	OJ1	
834	0	Sauiana	10	31		
128	0	Sauk	3	11	NP11	
1054	0	Saulteaux	3	33	NG6	
576	1092	Saumingmiut	1	30	ND5	
647	0	Savunese	28	10	OF15	
647	0	Sawai	28	87	OH12	
133	0	Sawos	32	117	OJ4	
318	0	Sbaa	38	6	MJ4	
1236	0	Schamatairi	9	149	SQ18	
1236	0	Schiriana	9	150	SQ18	
0	0	Scho . . . see Chin	0	0		
874	919	Scottish	37	42	ES6	
0	0	Sea Dyak . . . see Iban	0	0		
415	0	Sebei	21	48	FK16	
729	0	Sebuano	27	18	OA14	
308	0	Secotan	7	34	NN15	
782	0	Sedang	27	71	AM36	
1092	0	Seechelt	4	91	NE13	
796	0	Segeju	21	163	FL14	
227	550	Sekani	4	115	NE14	Na28
213	0	Sekele	22	103		
239	540	Selkup	1	112	RU4	Ec11
540	0	Selkup	39	40	RU4	Ec11
533	0	Sema	0	0	AR13	Ei16
228	327	Semai	26	15	AN6	
907	1008	Semang	26	12	AN7	Ej3
133	0	Semariji	32	185	OJ1	
228	979	Semelai	26	4	AN4	
379	0	Seminole	7	62	NN16	Ng2
228	0	Semoq Beri	26	9	AN6	
146	0	Sena	23	20	FR4	Ac40
1	1092	Seneca	2	17	NM9	Ng10
925	0	Senga	23	52	FR4	
504	0	Senufo	17	129	FA31	Ag32
0	523	Sepei . . . see Sebei	0	0		
938	0	Sept-Iles	2	42	NH6	
133	0	Seramina	32	230	OJ1	
452	0	Serbians	37	10	EF6	Ch1
964	0	Sere	21	5	FJ20	
876	0	Serer	17	165	FA32	Ag22
493	98	Seri	8	74	NU31	Ni4
730	493	Seri	5	1	NU31	Ni4
854	1092	Serrano	5	20	NS20	Nc30
416	0	Sese	21	72		
700	0	Sewa	22	9	FQ8	
1062	0	Shacriaba	12	43	SP20	
317	0	Shaderli	38	31		
141	0	Shake	20	20	F129	
0	0	Shamkella	19	138	MR9	
77	318	Shammar	19	16	MJ4	
318	0	Shammar	38	3	MJ4	
10	77	Shamran	19	36	MJ4	
270	0	Shan	26	38	AE7	
270	0	Shan	40	2	AE7	
155	0	Shanafir	19	62	MJ4	
0	523	Shangala . . . see Berta	0	0		
146	0	Shangana	23	74	FT6	
0	523	Shangoma . . . see Baka	0	0		
0	523	Shangul . . . see Berta	0	0		
547	0	Shanjo	22	52	FQ9	
0	0	Shapra . . . see Candoshi	0	0		
0	523	Shara . . . see Chara	0	0		
77	0	Shararat	19	15	MG2	
531	0	Shashi	21	109	FN25	
232	0	Shasta	5	81	NS21	Nb32
232	0	Shasta	4	30	NS21	Nb32
0	0	Shatt . . . see Thuri	0	0		
718	0	Shavante	12	30	SP20	Sj11
718	0	Shavante, Opaye	12	49	SP20	Sj11
144	0	Shawiya	15	14	MV8	
129	1092	Shawnee	6	15	NN17	Nf13
129	1092	Shawnee	7	10	NN17	Nf13
277	0	Shawya	15	39	MW10	
789	0	She	27	81	AF17	
789	0	She	35	1	AF17	
938	0	Shelter Bay	2	43	NH6	
693	0	Shenabla	18	122	MQ10	
670	449	Sherbro	17	146	FC8	Af14
718	0	Sherente	12	14	SP20	Sj2
827	835	Sherente	10	50	SP20	Sj2
0	0	Shesh-Baluki . . . see Qashqai	0	0		
1064	0	Shetebo	11	10	SE10	
926	0	Shila	22	6	FQ5	Ac35
72	926	Shila	23	47	FQ5	Ac35
964	0	Shilluk	18	118	FJ23	Ai6
964	0	Shilluk	21	1	FJ23	Ai6
6	0	Shina	39	18	AV3	Ee5
0	523	Shioko . . . see Chokwe	0	0		
834	0	Shipaya	10	41	SQ26	
1064	0	Shipibo	11	37	SE10	
1126	0	Shluh	15	41	MW11	Cd5
120	0	Shona	23	67	FS5	Ab18
175	0	Shona	23	67	FS5	Ab18
0	523	Shosho . . . see Birom	0	0		
609	1061	Shoshoni	4	43	NT22	
803	0	Shoshoni	5	58	NT22	
1061	609	Shoshoni	5	35	NT22	
1000	0	Shoshoni, East	6	35	NQ19	
1108	0	Shoshoni, Western	5	59	NT22	
0	0	Shuar . . . see Jivaro	0	0	SD9	
0	0	Shuara . . . see Jivaro	0	0	SD9	
834	0	Shucuru	12	2	SO3	
1092	0	Shuma	6	28	NU20	
540	0	Shunghanis	39	24		
0	0	Shupaman . . . see Mum	0	0		
1092	0	Shuswap	4	101	NE12	Nd11
627	0	Shuwa	18	66	MS9	Cb16
228	0	Siamese	26	22	AO1	Ej9
961	116	Siane	32	62	OJ1	Ie17
77	0	Sibea	19	30	MJ4	
425	0	Sicilians	37	4	EI10	
532	0	Sidamo	21	201	MP23	Ca16
598	0	Sihanaka	23	6	FY12	
647	0	Sikanese	28	14	OF9	
357	985	Sikon	17	122	FD7	
1092	0	Siksika	4	50	NF6	
1138	0	Simaa (Lozi)	22	43	FQ9	
133	0	Simore	32	147	OJ1	
761	0	Sinabo	11	70	SF19	
857	0	Sindagua	9	38	SC17	
540	696	Sindhi	25	40	AT5	Ea1
540	0	Sindhi	39	1	AT5	Ea1
1228	644	Sinhalese	25	1	AX4	Eh6
169	0	Sinkaietk . . . see Okanogan	0	0	NR19	Nd15
677	0	Sinkyone	5	85	NS23	Nb39
677	0	Sinkyone	5	76		
1166	0	Siona-Secoya	9	64	SE12	
0	0	Sioux . . . see Dakota	0	0		
640	0	Siraya	27	54	AD4	
1051	508	Siriono	11	88	SF21	Se1
520	0	Sise	20	78		
217	0	Sitka	4	119	NA12	
103	0	Siuai . . . see Bougainville				

Cite 1	Cite 2	Culture	Map	No.	HRAF	Murdock's Atlas
		Islands	0	0	ON5	Ig1
74	0	Siuslaw	4	7	NR5	Nb29
228	1008	Siwang	26	11	AN6	
1092	0	Skagit	4	85	NR15	
74	0	Skilloot	4	18	NR6	
1092	0	Skokomish	4	84	NR15	
17	0	Slave	4	127	ND14	Na17
0	0	Slavey . . . see Slave	0	0		
74	0	Snake	4	34	NR14	
1092	0	Snohomish	4	83	NR15	
1092	0	Sobaipuri	6	52	NU29	
1109	0	Sobo	17	8	FF21	
958	847	Society Islands	31	10	OX7	
0	523	Sodi . . . see Soli	0	0		
416	0	Soga	21	54	FP6	Ad46
0	523	Sokile . . . see Nyakyusa	0	0		
547	0	Soli	22	20	KQ6	
1064	0	Soliman	9	92	SQ25	
846	356	Solomon Islands	33	10	ON1	
647	0	Solorese	28	12	OF5	
796	0	Somali	19	120	MO4	Ca2
796	0	Somali	21	188	MO4	Ca2
957	628	Songhai	17	67	MS20	Cb3
1092	0	Songish	4	94	NR15	
1121	0	Songo	20	88	FO30	Ac25
723	0	Songo	20	92	FP6	
133	0	Songu	32	39	OJ1	
876	0	Soninke	17	158	MS21	
0	523	Sorko . . . see Bozo	0	0		
0	523	Sorogo . . . see Bozo	0	0		
113	0	Sorol	34	4	OR20	
1022	0	Sorongo	20	81	FO21	
0	523	Soso . . . see Susu	0	0		
999	966	Sotho	24	18	FW2	Ab8
0	523	Soto . . . see Sotho	0	0		
647	0	Souei	26	57	AM9	
0	0	Souix . . . see Dakota	0	0		
648	0	Soungor	18	109		
876	0	Souninke	17	161	MS21	
0	523	Soussou . . . see Susu	0	0	FA33	
891	30	Spanish	37	20	EX1	Ce6
1092	0	Spokane	4	56	NR19	
1092	0	Squamish	4	90	NE13	Nb13
277	0	Sraghna	15	37	MW10	
302	0	Ssingo	21	76		
938	0	St. Augustin	2	50	NH6	
938	0	St. Marguerite	2	44	NH6	
1092	0	Stalo	4	89	NE13	Nb27
217	0	Stikine	4	115	NA12	
74	0	Stiletz	4	11	NR21	
133	0	Suau	32	236	OJ1	
358	0	Subanun	27	3	OA33	Ia4
206	0	Subi	21	102	FQ11	
547	0	Subya (Lozi)	22	53	FQ11	
133	0	Sufrai	32	25	OJ1	
77	0	Suhul	19	32	MJ4	
442	0	Suk, Hill	21	45	FL13	Aj26
133	0	Suka	32	182	OJ4	
0	523	Suka . . . see Chuka	0	0		
1092	0	Sukkertoppen	1	14	NB6	
416	0	Sukuma	21	110	FN18	Ad22
647	0	Sula	28	81	OH15	
1092	0	Suma	6	59	NU20	
1092	0	Suma	8	68	NU20	
640	0	Sumba	28	19	OF17	Ic9
2	262	Sumbwa	21	122	FN18	
556	0	Sumo	8	13	SA15	
647	578	Sundanese	28	26	OE7	
316	0	Susians	38	14		
1092	0	Susquehana	2	5	NM8	
166	0	Susu	17	151	FA33	Ag26
133	0	Sutrai	32	125	OJ1	
0	523	Sutu . . . see Sotho	0	0		
807	0	Suwarka	19	8		
990	0	Suya	12	15	SP21	
899	0	Swahili	23	21	FM2	
416	899	Swahili	21	33	FM2	
925	0	Swaka	22	12	FQ8	
624	714	Swazi	24	37	FU2	Ab2
170	0	Swedish	37	37	EN1	
1193	0	Swiss	37	16	EJ1	

Cite 1	Cite 2	Culture	Map	No.	HRAF	Murdock's Atlas
522	0	Ta-Tathi	30	24	OI5	
0	235	Tabi . . . see Ingassana	0	0		
925	0	Tabwa	23	46	FQ5	
925	0	Tabwa	21	133	FQ5	
761	0	Tacana	11	79	SF23	
769	0	Tacarigua	9	134	SS8	
1092	0	Tacatacura	7	44	NN18	
938	0	Tadoussac	2	35	NH6	
178	0	Tadyawan	27	33	OA15	
640	0	Tagabili	27	5	OA34	
729	0	Tagalog	27	38	OA38	
178	0	Tagbanua	27	25	OA37	Ia7
721	0	Tagish	4	136	NA12	
662	312	Tahitians	31	11	OX7	Ij8
692	856	Tahltan	4	123	ND12	Na27
6	0	Taimanis	39	12	AU5	
598	0	Taimoro	23	10	FY7	
6	0	Taimuri	39	5	AU1	
222	0	Taino	7	75	SV5	Sb8
769	0	Tairona	9	13	SC7	
1186	1187	Tairora	32	12	SC7	
598	0	Taisaka	23	13	OJ1	
0	523	Taita . . . see Teita	0	0		
540	0	Tajiks	39	21	RO2	
316	0	Tajiks	38	17	RO2	
965	1041	Takelma	4	29	NR20	Nb30
64	0	Takpo	39	50	AJ1	
217	0	Taku	4	121	NA12	
0	0	Talaing . . . see Mon	0	0		
1092	0	Tali	7	17	NN11	
0	523	Talis . . . see Tallensi	0	0		
0	0	Tallanes	11	1	SE21	
350	349	Tallensi	17	57	FE11	Ag4
317	0	Talysh	38	39	RK4	
648	0	Tama	18	104	FK7	
261	0	Tamanaco	9	135	SS21	
1092	0	Tamathli	7	41	NN11	
1092	0	Tamaulipeco	8	43	NU32	
133	0	Tamaya	32	132	OJ1	
598	0	Tambahoaka	23	11	FY15	
925	0	Tambo	23	42	FN21	
696	0	Tamil	25	3	AW16	Eg2
834	0	Tamoyo	12	40	SO9	
862	1123	Tanaina	1	76	NA11	Na26
598	669	Tanala	23	9	FY8	Eh3
733	734	Tanana	1	73	NA8	
598	0	Tandroy	23	16	FY13	
495	0	Tang	18	24	FF51	
13	0	Tanga	18	1	FF41	
13	0	Tanga	20	8	FF41	
664	0	Tanga Island	32	250	OM12	Ig2
71	0	Tangara	29	81	OI5	
133	0	Tanggum	32	104	OJ1	
1111	0	Tanikutti	30	133	OI5	
133	0	Tanimbar	32	168	OF19	Ic6
598	0	Tankarana	23	1	FY9	
275	0	Tano	6	45	NT18	
598	0	Tanosy	23	18	FY14	
1062	0	Tapajo	10	42	SQ28	
944	0	Taparito	9	140	SS11	
187	0	Tape	13	35	SM4	
767	0	Tapiete	11	112	SK13	
1173	0	Tapirape	12	19	SP22	Sd2
57	0	Tapoaja	11	64	SP12	
362	68	Tarahumara	8	52	NU33	Ni1
278	0	Tarahumara	8	63	NU33	
0	523	Taraka . . . see Tharaka	0	0		
52	1048	Tarascan	8	48	NU34	Nj8
1034	0	Tareumiut	1	88	NA9	Na2
946	0	Tariana	9	117	SQ27	
1063	0	Tarma	11	19	SS8	
749	406	Taro	32	93	OJ1	
207	0	Tarramiut	3	54	NI5	
540	0	Tartars	36	15		
522	0	Tarubura	30	100	OI5	
125	0	Taruma	10	10	SR13	
522	0	Tarumbul	30	90	OI5	
815	0	Tasaday	27	6	OA28	
0	0	Tashkent . . . see Uzbeks	0	0		
1092	0	Tasiusak	1	27	NB6	
0	0	Tasmanians . . . see Poyudu	0	0		

Cite 1	Cite 2	Culture	Map	No.	HRAF	Murdock's Atlas
471	0	Totonac	8	36	NU40	Nj4
0	523	Touaregs . . . see Tuareg	0	0		
154	0	Toubous	18	85	MS22	
945	0	Tralakumbina	30	155	OI19	Id8
0	523	Trepo . . . see Grebo	0	0		
698	699	Trobriand	32	242	OL16	Ig2
699	698	Trobriand	33	8	OL16	Ig2
639	0	Trukese	34	16	OR19	If2
801	0	Trumai	12	21	SP23	Si2
64	0	Tsang Tibetans	39	49	AJ1	
1092	0	Tsattine	4	107	NF5	
973	0	Tsaukwe	22	76	FX10	
908	0	Tsembaga . . . see Maring	0	0		
973	0	Tserekwe	22	61	FX10	
258	859	Tsetsaut	4	114	ND12	
0	0	Tshwosh . . . see Abelam	0	0	FY10	
598	0	Tsimihety	23	3	FY10	
380	0	Tsimshian	4	109	NE15	Nb7
463	0	Tsonga	23	86	FT6	
0	0	Tsotso . . . see Luyia	0	0		
371	0	Tswa	23	76	FT6	
1131	0	Tswa	20	46		
974	0	Tswana	22	65	FV6	Ab13
976	977	Tswana	24	7	FV6	Ab13
74	0	Tualatin	4	16	NR9	
1074	113	Tuamotu	31	12	OX9	
1144	369	Tuareg	15	2	MS25	
796	0	Tuareg	17	77	MS25	
1144	0	Tuareg, Ferouan	17	78	MS25	
856	0	Tubar	8	61	NU35	
1168	0	Tubatulabal	5	44	NS22	Nc2
1216	0	Tubuai	31	13	OX4	
0	0	Tucano . . . see Cubeo	0	0	SQ19	Se12
633	0	Tugen	21	69	FL13	
490	0	Tuirimnainai	9	142		
540	0	Tujen	40	10	AE9	
1121	0	Tukkongo	20	102	FO22	
1122	876	Tukylor	17	162	MS27	
806	0	Tumbez	9	52	SD10	
1218	473	Tumbuka	23	34	FR6	Ac36
0	523	Tumbuku . . . see Tumbuka	0	0		
1202	0	Tumbwe	20	109	FO18	
767	0	Tumereha	11	118	SK14	
647	0	Tung	27	79	AL3	
540	0	Tungus	36	8	RU5	
540	1001	Tungus	39	39	RU5	
524	540	Tungus	1	100	RU5	
1092	0	Tunica	6	13	NO4	
716	1092	Tununirmiut	1	33	ND5	
716	0	Tununirusirmiut	1	34	ND5	
57	0	Tupari	11	93	SP24	
138	0	Tupi	12	37	SN7	
834	0	Tupina	12	6	SN7	
834	0	Tupinakin	12	41	SO9	
763	0	Tupinamba	12	7	SO9	Sj8
763	0	Tupinamba	10	55	SO9	Sj8
985	0	Tura	17	131	FA29	Af53
0	0	Turahumara . . . see Tarahumara	0	0		
416	288	Turkana	21	40	FL17	Aj5
542	0	Turkomen	39	32	RM2	Eb5
316	0	Turkomen	38	27	RM2	Eb5
888	695	Turks	38	32	MB1	Ci5
71	0	Turrbal	30	53	OI5	
0	523	Turu . . . see Nyaturu	0	0	FN19	Ad26
1092	0	Tuskegee	7	15	NN11	
217	722	Tutchone	1	58	ND10	
217	0	Tutchone	1	81	ND10	
74	0	Tutchone	4	139	ND10	
1092	0	Tutelo	2	1	NN13	
1092	0	Tutelo	7	25	NN13	
74	0	Tututni	4	3	NR22	Nb31
540	0	Tuvinians	40	17	RS3	
761	1064	Tuyuneri	11	31	SE15	
1131	0	Twa	21	95	FQ4	
1131	0	Twa	20	51	FQ4	
291	0	Twa, Southern	22	96	FQ4	
1092	0	Twana	4	71	NR15	Nb2
0	0	Twi	0	0	FE12	
0	0	Twij . . . see Dinka	0	0		
291	0	Twilenge-Humbi	22	106		

Cite 1	Cite 2	Culture	Map	No.	HRAF	Murdock's Atlas
0	523	Tyap . . . see Katab	0	0		
149	291	Tyavikwa	22	93		
0	523	Tye . . . see Gien	0	0		
291	0	Tyilenge-Muso	22	115		
0	523	Tyo . . . see Teke	0	0		
291	0	Tyokwe	22	104		
900	0	Tyrolians	37	14	EK4	
942	0	Tzeltal	8	27	NV9	Sa2
1169	1092	Tzotzil	8	26	NV11	
1236	0	Uaka	9	147	SQ18	
540	0	Uakhanis	39	23	RO2	
1236	0	Uana	9	151	SQ18	
413	0	Uanan	9	118	SQ19	
0	0	Ubena . . . see Bena	0	0		
0	0	Uckiamute . . . see Lakmiut	0	0		
94	0	Udam	18	36		
94	0	Udam	17	11	FF57	
540	0	Udeghe	36	12	RX3	
540	0	Udmurts	38	63	RG7	
993	0	Uduk	19	126	FJ15	
72	0	Ugarung	29	35	OI5	
107	0	Uhunduni	32	143	OJ2	
1012	0	Uintah	5	55	NT19	Nd58
1012	0	Uintah	6	34	NT19	Nd58
2	0	Ukonongo	21	130		
540	0	Ukrainians	38	65	RD4	Ch7
469	0	Ulad Yihya	15	25	MW5	
657	0	Ulithi	34	3	OR20	If9
556	0	Ulua	8	8		
57	0	Ulva	8	22	SA15	
1092	0	Umanak	1	23	NB6	
74	0	Umatilla	4	38	NR18	Nd19
0	523	Umiro . . . see Lango	0	0		
842	0	Umotina	11	101	SP8	Si8
74	0	Umpqua	4	6	NR22	
819	0	Unaligmut	1	90	NA13	
1012	0	Uncompahgre	6	32	NT19	Nd62
199	0	Unga	20	117	FQ5	
72	0	Ungarinyin	29	33	OI5	
522	0	Unghi	30	68	OI5	
522	0	Ungorri	30	63	OI5	
0	523	Uolamo . . . see Wolamo	0	0		
0	523	Upe . . . see Suk	0	0		
1092	0	Upernavik	1	26	NB6	
1109	0	Upila	17	14	FF21	
0	0	Upolu . . . see Samoans	0	0	Ii14	
373	0	Urali	25	9	AW64	
133	0	Urama	32	36	OJ1	
0	523	Urapang . . . see Jukun	0	0		
929	0	Urapmin	32	112		
369	0	Uraren, Tuareg	15	7	MS25	
1063	0	Uru	11	135	SF24	Sf9
514	57	Urupa	11	61	SP12	
107	0	Usagek Goliath	32	135	OJ1	
0	0	Usandwe . . . see Sandawe	0	0		
925	0	Ushi	23	48	FQ5	
2	0	Usukuma	21	121	FN19	
77	0	Utaibah	19	24	MJ4	
127	0	Ute	6	33	NT19	
1012	127	Ute	6	31	NT19	
1012	127	Ute	5	53	NT19	
355	0	Ute, Weber	5	56	NT19	
609	0	Utechem	5	38		
1092	0	Utina	7	51	NN18	
1092	0	Utuado	7	72	SV5	
789	215	Uygur	39	45	AI4	
540	0	Uzbeks	39	27	RN5	Eh8
237	0	Vadeyev Nganasans	1	109	RU4	
357	0	Vai	17	141	FD9	Af58
316	0	Vaisi	19	90		
0	523	Valaf . . . see Wolof	0	0		
291	0	Vale	22	94		
796	0	Valunka	17	149	SO6	
645	0	Vanatinai	33	4	OL5	
696	0	Varli	25	31	AW44	
487	0	Vatwa	22	112		
0	523	Vay . . . see Vai	0	0		
992	111	Vedda	25	2	AX5	Eh4
0	523	Vehie . . . see Vai	0	0		

Cite 1	Cite 2	Culture	Map	No.	HRAF	Murdock's Atlas
0	523	Vei ... see Vai	0	0		
606	463	Venda	23	79	FX19	Ab6
62	242	Vidunda	21	43	FN22	
782	0	Vietnamese	26	64	AM11	
782	0	Vietnamese	27	58	AM11	
767	0	Vilela	11	130	SI14	
201	0	Vili	20	71	FI34	
206	0	Vinza	21	123	FO42	
729	0	Visayan	27	37	OA30	
1221	0	Vonoma	21	84		
556	0	Voto	9	1	SA17	
556	0	Voto	8	5	SA17	
0	523	Vu ... see Vai	0	0		
626	0	Vugusu	21	56	FL4	Ad41
705	0	Wa	17	59	FE4	
643	0	Wa	26	37	AP12	
1030	0	Waagai	30	122	OI5	
914	0	Wabaga	32	74	OJ1	
0	523	Wabena ... see Bena	0	0		
0	0	Wabende ... see Bende	0	0		
133	0	Wabo	32	131	OJ1	
1091	0	Waccamaw	7	38	NN13	
0	523	Wachangi ... see Irangi	0	0		
0	523	Wachokwe ... see Chokwe	0	0		
142	0	Wadai	18	105	MS15	
71	0	Wadaman	29	18	OI5	
1116	0	Wadandi	29	97	OI5	
71	0	Waderi	30	141	OI5	
72	71	Wadjari	29	71	OI5	
0	523	Wafipa ... see Fipa	0	0		
71	0	Wagamen	30	127	OI5	
224	0	Wagera	20	59		
522	0	Waggumbura	30	64	OI5	
0	523	Wagogo ... see Gogo	0	0		
0	0	Waha ... see Ha	0	0		
0	523	Wahehe ... see Hehe	0	0		
329	0	Wai-Wai	10	33	SQ22	
0	0	Waica ... see Yanomamo	0	0	SQ18	Sd4
1092	0	Waicuri	8	72	NU42	
133	0	Waigeo	32	167	OJ25	
133	0	Waiiemi	32	45	OJ1	
283	1092	Wailaki	5	67	NS23	
72	0	Wailbri	29	43	OI5	
110	0	Waimiri-Atroari	9	103	SQ22	
1064	0	Wairacu	9	80	SQ21	
1064	0	Wairacu	11	43	SQ21	
0	523	Wairamba ... see Iramba	0	0		
370	0	Waiyana	10	15	SR12	
125	0	Waiyarikule	10	14	SR12	
0	523	Wajiji ... see Jie	0	0		
0	523	Wajita ... see Jita	0	0		
749	406	Waka	32	82	DJ1	
0	523	Wakamba ... see Kamba	0	0		
71	0	Wakelbura	30	94	OI5	
0	523	Wakikuyu ... see Kikuyu	0	0		
0	523	Wakinga ... see Kinga	0	0		
0	523	Wakopomo ... see Pokomo	0	0		
490	489	Wakuenai	9	113		
796	0	Wala	17	44	FE13	
596	617	Walapai	5	29	NT32	Nd65
0	523	Walega ... see Lega	0	0		
0	523	Walendu ... see Lendu	0	0		
790	748	Walibiri	30	84	OI5	Id10
1092	0	Walla Walla	4	41	NR18	
1092	0	Wallirmiut	1	52	ND8	
1092	0	Wallirmiut	1	53	ND8	
543	0	Walloons	37	26	EV3	Cg5
72	0	Walmadje	29	45	OI5	
1030	0	Walpari	30	121	OI5	
0	523	Waluchazi ... see Luchazi	0	0		
0	523	Waluena ... see Luena	0	0		
0	523	Waluguru ... see Luguru	0	0		
125	0	Wama	10	13		
0	523	Wambuela ... see Mbwela	0	0		
1092	0	Wampanoag	2	12	NL5	
71	0	Wanamara	30	116	OI5	
1092	0	Wanapam	4	55	NR18	
416	0	Wanda	21	139		
71	0	Wandjira	29	40	OI5	
0	0	Wandorobo ... see Dorobo	0	0		
72	0	Waneiga	29	42	OI5	
416	567	Wanga	21	63	FL4	
981	0	Wangara	17	105	FA31	
0	0	Wanki	8	15		
889	0	Wantoat	32	10	OJ1	Ie2
0	523	Wanyakyusa ... see Nyakyusa	0	0		
0	523	Wanyamwezi ... see Nyamwezi	0	0		
0	523	Wanyaturu ... see Nyaturu	0	0		
0	523	Wanyika ... see Nyika	0	0		
1230	0	Waorami	9	63	SE22	
0	523	Wapare ... see Pare	0	0		
161	0	Wapei-Paei	32	122	OJ1	
125	0	Wapishana	10	8	SR13	Sc5
0	523	Wapogoro ... see Pogoro	0	0		
1092	0	Wappinger	2	9	NM10	
396	0	Wappo	5	64	NS24	Nc20
495	0	War	18	19	FF51	
522	0	Warabul	30	99	OI5	
1030	0	Waramunga	29	123	OI5	
522	0	Waranbura	30	101	OI5	
0	523	Warangi ... see Irangi	0	0		
590	946	Warao	10	2	SS18	Sc1
946	590	Warao	9	157	SS18	Sc1
0	0	Warao ... see Warrau	0	0		
522	0	Warbaa	30	57	OI5	
133	0	Ware	33	3	OL4	
71	0	Warei	29	13	OI5	
490	0	Wariperidakena	9	120	SQ27	
444	0	Warjawa	18	72	FF46	
0	0	Warmsprings ... see Tenino	0	0	NR18	
753	0	Warndarrang	30	143	OI5	
647	0	Waropen	32	145	OJ26	
1030	0	Warramunga	30	123	OI5	
0	0	Warrau ... see Warao	0	0		
74	0	Wasco	4	37	NR23	
242	680	Washo	5	54	NT20	Nd6
224	0	Wasongola	20	57	FO45	
0	523	Wasukuma ... see Sukuma	0	0		
0	523	Waswahili ... see Swahili	0	0		
0	523	Wateita ... see Teita	0	0		
71	0	Wathi-Wathi	30	13	OI5	
0	523	Watumbuka ... see Tumbuka	0	0		
47	0	Watyi	17	34	FA18	
219	0	Waura	12	25	SP18	
0	0	Waushi ... see Aushi	0	0		
0	523	Wayao ... see Yao	0	0		
1064	0	Wayoro	11	94	SP16	
118	0	Wayumara	9	107	SQ22	
0	523	Wazaramo ... see Zaramo	0	0		
224	0	Wazimba	20	61	FO41	
0	523	Wazimba ... see Zimba	0	0		
308	0	Weapemeoc	7	30	NN15	
412	0	Weli	32	202	OJ1	
585	0	Welsh	37	41	ES11	
0	523	Wemba ... see Bemba	0	0		
0	523	Wenangumba ... see Ngumbu	0	0		
1092	0	Wenatchee	4	61	NR19	Nd16
522	0	Wenrohronon	2	8	NG5	
277	0	Werigha	15	34		
647	0	Wetar	28	4	OF21	
1116	71	Whadjug	29	90	OI5	
476	0	Whilkut	5	88	NS11	
71	0	Wi-Thai-Ja	30	14	OI5	
1092	0	Wichita	6	18	NO10	
1116	72	Widi	29	78	OI5	
71	0	Wiimbaio	30	25	OI5	
71	0	Wikmunkan	30	131	OI22	Id6
522	0	Willara	30	75	OI5	
1116	71	Wilmen	29	92	OI26	
522	0	Wilya	30	39	OI5	
1111	0	Wimmarao	30	134	OI5	
906	0	Winnebago	3	9	NP12	Nf2
1073	0	Wintu	5	74	NS26	Nc14
522	0	Wiradjura	30	15	OI5	
133	0	Wiram	32	189	OJ1	
71	0	Wiranggu	29	83	OI5	
1079	649	Wiru	32	44	OJ1	

Cite 1	Cite 2	Culture	Map	No.	HRAF	Murdock's Atlas
0	523	Wisa ... see Bisa	0	0		
1039	0	Wishram	4	42	NR23	Nd18
973	0	Witboois	22	79	FX13	
795	896	Witoto	9	68	SC19	Se6
495	0	Wiya	18	20	FF51	
677	0	Wiyot	5	86	NS27	Nb36
107	0	Woda	32	149	OJ1	
71	0	Wogaidj	29	21	OI23	
0	0	Wogait ... see Wogaidu	0	0		
71	0	Wogeman	29	16	OI5	
501	133	Wogeo Island	32	254	OJ27	Ie4
1005	0	Wola	32	53	OJ1	
997	0	Wolamo	21	193	MP26	
522	0	Wolgal	30	5	OI5	
522	0	Wollaroi	30	48	OI5	
377	0	Wolof	17	163	MS30	Cb2
161	0	Wom	32	118	OJ1	
522	0	Wongaibon	30	21	OI5	Id9
1159	0	Wongo	20	105	FO24	
522	0	Wonkamala	30	83	OI5	
522	0	Wonkanguru	30	77	OI5	
522	0	Wonkatyeri	30	82	OI5	
71	0	Workia	30	124	OI5	
72	0	Worora	29	32	OI5	
71	0	Wotjobaluk	30	12	OI5	
647	0	Wowoni	28	79	OG7	
1116	71	Wudjari	29	94	OI5	
0	523	Wugusu ... see Gishu	0	0		
72	0	Wunambal	29	31	OI5	
71	0	Wuningag	29	9	OI5	
71	0	Wurugu	29	4	OI5	
71	0	Wurunjeri	30	7	OI5	
627	0	Wute	18	6	FH24	Ah8
849	0	Wynoochee	4	67	NR19	
487	0	Xam	24	11	FX10	Aa8
340	0	Xarirawi	32	107	OJ1	
110	0	Xaruma	9	164		
0	0	Xavante ... see Shavante	0	0		
487	0	Xhosa	24	21	FX17	Ab11
222	0	Xixime	8	57	NU6	
1150	0	Yab-Anim	32	176	OJ28	
981	0	Yadsi	17	86		
155	0	Yafi	19	59	NJ4	
310	0	Yagua	9	71	SE20	Se4
1092	0	Yaguabo	7	69		
676	186	Yahgan	14	2	SH6	Sg1
0	0	Yahi ... see Yana	0	0		
0	523	Yaka ... see Kaka	0	0	FO49	Ac20
1092	0	Yakima	4	62	NR18	
347	346	Yako (Ekoi)	18	40	FF60	Af4
201	0	Yakoma	18	133	FI8	
552	446	Yakut	1	103	RV2	Ec2
540	552	Yakut	36	10	RV2	Ec2
540	0	Yakut	40	19	RV2	Ec2
217	0	Yakutat	4	137	NA12	
217	0	Yakutat	1	84	NA12	
829	0	Yamadi	9	88	SQ23	
1066	0	Yamamadi	11	50	SQ23	SQ33
1092	0	Yamasee	7	43	NN11	
0	523	Yambi ... see Iramba	0	0		
0	0	Yameci ... see Yemici	0	0		
1064	0	Yameo	9	74	SE20	
74	0	Yamhill	4	17	NR9	
1184	620	Yana	5	77	NS28	Nc11
1182	0	Yandjinung	30	153	OI17	
643	0	Yang	26	40	AP7	
201	0	Yanghere	18	8	F16	
753	0	Yangman	29	17	OI5	
522	0	Yankibura	30	105	OI5	
150	673	Yanomamo	9	110	SQ18	Sd9
522	0	Yantruwunta	30	73	OI5	
1121	0	Yanzi	20	89	FO17	Ac26
789	0	Yao	27	78	AB6	
91	0	Yao	23	28	FT7	Ac7
789	0	Yao	40	5	AB6	
71	0	Yaora	29	37	OI5	
72	0	Yaoro	30	49	OI5	
668	982	Yap	34	2	OR22	If6
1037	1038	Yaqui	8	70	NU8	Ni7
74	0	Yaquina	4	10	NR5	
522	0	Yargo	30	60	OI5	
522	0	Yarmbura	30	66	OI5	
1062	0	Yaro	11	16	SJ5	
1062	0	Yaro	13	28	SJ5	
96	651	Yaruro	9	127	SS19	Sc2
13	0	Yasa	20	9	FI26	
1021	70	Yate	32	19	OJ2	
395	584	Yauapai	5	22	NT14	
801	0	Yaulapiti	12	26	SP18	
522	0	Yaurorka	30	78	OI5	
1063	0	Yauyo	11	22	SE13	
395	0	Yavapai	5	5	NT31	Nd66
522	0	Yawai	30	58	OI5	
1236	0	Yawani	9	146	SO18	
1150	0	Yei	32	179	DJ19	
199	0	Yeke	20	106	FO27	Ae19
16	791	Yela	33	5	OL5	
859	0	Yellowknife	4	129	ND14	
1150	133	Yelmek	32	173	OJ1	
522	0	Yelyuyendi	30	84	OI5	
133	0	Yemai	32	210	DJ1	
769	0	Yemici	9	23	SC9	
540	0	Yemreli	39	31		
696	0	Yenadis	25	12	AW61	
133	0	Yerakai	32	110	OJ1	
133	0	Yeraki	32	100	OJ1	
237	0	Yesey	1	104	RU4	
463	0	Yesibe	24	28	FX20	
444	0	Yeskwa	18	51		
133	0	Yeti	32	123	OJ1	
522	0	Yetti-Maralla	30	104	OI5	
1205	0	Yhamad	19	77	MK1	
540	0	Yi	40	4	AE4	
340	0	Yimas	32	101	OJ1	
0	523	Yimbe ... see Limba	0	0		
71	0	Yir-Yoront	30	128	OI25	Id12
0	523	Yira ... see Konjo	0	0		
524	540	Yokaghir	1	101	RV3	Fc6
1092	0	Yokuts	5	41	NS29	Nc3
1022	0	Yombe	20	73	FO50	Ac8
541	542	Yomut (Turkmen)	38	23	RM2	
74	0	Yoncalla	4	27	NR9	
1185	0	Yorok ... see Yurok	0	0		
41	4	Yoruba	17	27	FF62	
556	0	Yosko	8	11		
113	0	Ysabel	33	10	ON16	
465	287	Yuan	26	30	AO6	
1092	1025	Yuchi	7	14	NN20	Ng11
1116	0	Yued	29	88	OI5	
459	0	Yugoslavians	37	9	EF1	
753	0	Yugul	30	144	OI5	
71	522	Yuin	30	1	OI5	
1092	0	Yuit	1	64	RY5	
597	0	Yuki	5	73	NS30	Nc7
176	0	Yuko	9	18	SC10	
0	0	Yukon ... see Koyukon	0	0		
72	0	Yulbaridja	29	49	OI5	
0	0	Yulenox ... see Kwakiutl	0	0		
1067	0	Yuma	11	51	SQ24	
344	1042	Yuma	5	16	NT29	Nh22
806	0	Yumbo	9	44	SD14	
488	0	Yunnan	26	47	AF16	
761	0	Yuqui	11	89		
761	0	Yuracare	11	87	SF25	
202	0	Yuraks	1	114	RU4	Ec4
1068	0	Yuri	9	84	SQ11	
1185	0	Yurok	5	89	NS31	Nb4
834	0	Yuruna	10	40	SQ26	
1092	0	Yustaga	7	49	NN18	
6	0	Yusufzai	39	19	AU4	
0	0	Zaafaranlu ... see Kurds	0	0		
0	523	Zabarma ... see Djerma	0	0		
858	1092	Zacatec	8	51	NU43	
598	0	Zafisoro	23	12	FY7	
154	648	Zaghawa	18	102	MS5	
1100	0	Zambales	27	40	OA4	
1062	0	Zamuc	11	113	SK14	
0	523	Zande ... see Azande	0	0		
1064	0	Zaparo	9	66	SF22	

Cite 1	Cite 2	Culture	Map	No.	HRAF	Murdock's Atlas
569	157	Zapotec	8	32	NU44	Nj10
155	0	Zaraniq	19	51	MJ1	
0	523	Zarma . . . see Djerma	0	0		
277	0	Zayr	15	35	MW5	
277	0	Zemmur	15	33	MW5	
1144	0	Zentan	16	28	MT9	
796	0	Zezhru	23	69	FS5	
0	523	Ziba . . . see Haya	0	0		
62	0	Zigula	21	162	FN28	Ad28
133	0	Zimakani	32	183	OJ1	

Cite 1	Cite 2	Culture	Map	No.	HRAF	Murdock's Atlas
291	796	Zimba	22	99	FO41	
291	796	Zimba	23	64	FO41	
206	1100	Zinza	21	103	FN8	Ad49
1022	0	Zombo	20	86	FO21	
353	0	Zoque	8	30	NU23	
607	0	Zulu	24	33	FX20	Ab12
612	275	Zuni	6	47	NT23	Nh4
313	612	Zuni	5	25	FT23	Nh4
296	0	Zuwayah	16	20	MT9	

ABOUT THE AUTHOR

David H. Price is a Doctoral Candidate in the Department of Anthropology, University of Florida. He is a member of several academic associations, including the American Anthropological Association, the American Institute for Biological and Cultural Research, and the American Institute for Yemeni Studies. He is currently studying traditional irrigation systems in the Yemen Arab Republic under a grant provided by the National Science Foundation.